IN RECKLESS HANDS

IN
RECKLESS HANDS

Skinner v. Oklahoma and the
Near Triumph of American Eugenics

———◆———

Victoria F. Nourse

W. W. Norton & Company
New York *London*

For information about permission to reproduce selections from this book,
write to Permissions, W. W. Norton & Company, Inc.,
500 Fifth Avenue, New York, NY 10110

For information about special discounts for bulk purchases, please contact
W. W. Norton Special Sales at specialsales@wwnorton.com or 800-233-4830

Manufacturing by Courier Westford
Book design by Rhea Braunstein
Production manager: Julia Druskin

Library of Congress Cataloging-in-Publication Data

Nourse, Victoria F.
In reckless hands : Skinner v. Oklahoma and the near triumph of
American eugenics / Victoria F. Nourse. — 1st ed.
p. cm.
Includes bibliographical references and index.
ISBN 978-0-393-06529-9 (hardcover)
1. Skinner, Jack T., d.1977—Trials, litigation, etc. 2. Involuntary
sterilization—Law and legislation—Oklahoma. 3. Involuntary
sterilization—Law and legislation—United States.
4. Eugenics—United States—History. I. Title.
KF224.S486N68 2008
344.7304'8—dc22

2008013140

W. W. Norton & Company, Inc.
500 Fifth Avenue, New York, N.Y. 10110
www.wwnorton.com

W. W. Norton & Company Ltd.
Castle House, 75/76 Wells Street, London W1T 3QT

1 2 3 4 5 6 7 8 9 0

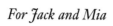

For Jack and Mia

Lawyers, with rare exceptions, have failed to lay bare that the law of the Supreme Court is enmeshed in the country's history; historians no less have seemed to miss the fact that the country's history is enmeshed in the law of the Supreme Court.

—Felix Frankfurter [1]

The study of United States legal history will come of age when its practitioners give as much effort to framing questions as to assembling answers.

—James Willard Hurst [2]

Contents

IN RECKLESS HANDS

Prologue: An Intellectual Seduction

[E]ugenics is a virile creed, full of hopefulness, and appealing to many of the noblest feelings of our nature.
—Sir Francis Galton, founder of eugenics, 1905[1]

It was an almost irresistible intellectual seduction: a promise that asylums and prisons would fade away and that the problems of the old and infirm and unemployed would "cease to trouble civilization."[2] The seduction was once named the science of eugenics. Law would confront this seduction and its science in a case called *Skinner v. Oklahoma.*

The unlikely tale begins during the Great Depression in an Oklahoma prison, a place recalled today only because it plays a minor role in John Steinbeck's *The Grapes of Wrath.* A "brain trust" of prisoners would fight a law decreeing that they should be sterilized. With the help of a frightened warden and a set of home-schooled lawyers, the prisoners' case would reach the Supreme Court. The men of McAlester would win their battle against eugenics—in part because some of them died and escaped, violence being their principal currency—but mostly because larger events foretold the victory. It was Hitler's threat from abroad, and a constitutional revolution at home, that would propel the prisoners' case toward success in America's highest court.

———◆———

Skinner v. Oklahoma was witness to some of the greatest failures and successes of governing in the twentieth century—a constitutional drama, a world war, and a dream that nature would resolve the public's most pressing problems. And yet *Skinner*'s history has never been told. Legal experts view the Supreme Court's opinion as difficult or dangerous, even incomprehensible. As the great historian of science Thomas Kuhn once admonished his students, it is precisely when the incomprehensible rears its head that time reveals what we have forgotten. Then, history becomes discovery: it offers up hidden and orthogonal assumptions, inviting questions that the present does not and cannot even think to ask because the consciousness of the past has been lost. This book not only tells a story of ordinary men involved in an extraordinary legal case, but also a story of ordinary concepts—of equality and race, liberty and right—that were once lived and thought so differently that a racial science could be seen as both banal and constitutional.

The real secret of *Skinner v. Oklahoma* is not, however, about constitutional law. The vast majority of this book concerns something different: the history of crime, inequality, and nature. Eugenics is only one of the many ways in which scientists and social scientists have attempted to find the "natural" secret to criminal tendencies, from theories that measured skulls to ones that posited "born criminals," to the present day's failed claims of chromosomes and genes and the evolutionary necessity of crimes like rape.* The failure of such arguments over decades and even centuries should remind us of what the great anthropologist Mary Douglas has warned against: society's tendency to ground its social order—ideas of who is high and who is low—in the idea of nature. The Supreme Court in *Skinner v. Oklahoma* rightly decided that "crime," defined by arcane legal rules, cannot be found inside the "bodies" of men, that to make the great common law of crimes into a "rule of genetics" is to commit a very basic category mistake. The history of *Skinner v. Oklahoma* is thus a natural history: a history of how an idea of nature is transformed into an idea of political order.

In a day and age in which genes are touted as the grand cause for everything from criminality to spirituality, it is important to

* Randy Thornhill & Craig T. Palmer, A Natural History of Rape (2000).

remember *Skinner*'s history. *Skinner* recognized the public paradox of science: that once science exits the lab it may absorb the very politics and culture it aims to conquer. There was nothing about the discovery of the gene in Thomas Hunt Morgan's laboratory that required the sterilization of the men of McAlester prison; for that the gene would have to exit the lab and become part of a solution to the public problems of crime and insanity. Institutions are selfish, and political institutions particularly so—they transform scientific questions quite readily into political questions. Once translated into the public sphere, there is no theory of nature that cannot become a grand political claim; this is a lesson that, in the day of the "God gene" and the "gay gene," more should remember.*

The title of this book is taken from a single line in the Supreme Court's opinion striking down Oklahoma's sterilization law, warning that, "in reckless hands," entire "races or types" might "wither and disappear." In June 1942, when that line was written, few Americans could have known that the Nazis would truly try to eradicate "the Jewish race" on the theory of its natural inferiority. What Americans did already know was that eugenics, a fifty-year-old science, was a "cloak for class snobbery, ancestor worship and race prejudice."[3] As Clarence Darrow so aptly put it, eugenics was a "gaudy little plan" to save civilization by imposing a "caste system."[4] There had been scientific critics of eugenics all along—those who knew that eradicating recessive genes was a fool's errand—but it would take politics to reveal the political pretensions of this science. By the late 1930s, the Nazis' insistent portrayals of America itself as unfit and full of weaker white "races" transformed the public's understanding of racism from a matter of science into one of politics and, with it, the public's understanding of eugenics. By then, even eugenicists sought to distance themselves from racial assumptions and rebrand their science as "democratic."

Today, this history has largely been forgotten because *Skin-*

---

* Dean H. Hamer, The God Gene (2004); Dean H. Hamer & Peter Copeland, The Science of Desire: The Search for the Gay Gene and the Biology of Behavior (1994).

ner's meaning for legal experts is embroiled in the controversies of today. Because its opening lines refer to procreation as a "civil right," *Skinner* is thought to lead to *Roe v. Wade*'s right to privacy, the most controversial of constitutional claims.* But, if this book is correct, *Skinner v. Oklahoma* has been embroiled, by left and right, in a debate that depends upon historical fallacy: *Skinner* was never argued or decided as a case primarily about rights. *Skinner v. Oklahoma* sits at the great fault line of constitutional law in the twentieth century. Before World War II, what we now consider basic civil rights were often weak, easily overcome by the needs of the common welfare, then called the "police power." In Hitler's shadow, and with the help of *Skinner*'s concept of "strict scrutiny," the very idea of rights and equality would change in the postwar world. As Justice Frankfurter, the true author of *Skinner*'s equality rationale and the great avatar of judicial restraint, once warned, rights are not timeless legal rules but containers of political experience, what I call "vessels of history." The Supreme Court's decision in *Skinner* would not end sterilization in America, but its terrible compromises should not obscure its proper meaning today. *Skinner*'s notions of right and equality reflect a long American history: the American Revolution and the Civil War were both fought to end forms of blood aristocracy, one known as monarchy, the other as slavery. Eugenics was simply known by a different name, the name of science.

———•———

The history of law and science has too often been told as a tale of powerful men and sacred texts, but *Skinner*'s history cannot be understood without the history of social meanings and human emotion. During the Great Depression, it would take men who had no stake in the intellectual seduction of eugenics, self-taught lawyers and lonely prisoners, to challenge the claims of men who ran for president and sat on the Supreme Court and vied for Nobel Prizes. The lives of the ordinary men would nearly be forgotten. This is what is left of their battle against a law and its science.

* *Skinner* is rarely taught in law school classrooms but, since 1990, has been referenced over 1500 times in the legal literature.

CHAPTER 1

The Justice, the Governor, and the Dictator

[E]ugenics is as large as man's capacity to hope and dream, as deep as his capacity to penetrate and control the laws of his own nature, and as wide as his capacity to organize his social efforts to ever more and more fruitful ends.
*   —Albert E. Wiggam, popular science writer, 1927[1]*

The year is 1932, the third year of the Depression, a hungry year, a year of labor violence and kidnappings and odd spontaneous eruptions of the never-employed. The place is the Vinita, Oklahoma, asylum for the insane and feebleminded. Pajama-clad bodies are huddling "in little knots" on the exercising porch, jittery and muttering, whispering to avoid the attendants' ears. Some, the more courageous ones, asked for copies of the law that frightened them. One trusted patient, a reporter who committed himself to Vinita to cure his alcoholism, held a copy of the statute close, worried that he would be mobbed. The patients were searching for a law decreeing that they should never have children—that all imbeciles, epileptics, insane or feebleminded persons were to be sterilized, in the name of eugenics.[2]

The doctors at the Vinita asylum told patients that it was for the best; they said that mothers could go back to their children and families would be reunited. It was cruel to keep people in a hospital for their entire lives when they could go home, safely. Sterilization, the doctors urged, was compassionate, not cruel. Some patients said they would do anything if they could go home. Some wanted to die: "If they do that to me, they might as well kill me . . . If they don't I'll kill myself anyhow . . . I won't give a damn what becomes of me." Others sought revenge: "I'll kill the man who orders it done if it takes the rest of my life." One patient bemoaned the fact that "[n]one of us can go into court and fight it. Most of us haven't a dime." Another added: "We can not use a telephone . . . [or] send out a telegram without special permission . . . We are hedged in; practically buried."[3]

The men and women inside the Vinita asylum never challenged the statute that frightened them. Men more dangerous and familiar with law, men in Oklahoma's McAlester prison, would battle the law and the science of eugenics, in a case that would become known as *Skinner v. Oklahoma*.

———

On December 22, 1933, an odd troika of men—a justice, a governor and a dictator—appeared in the largest-circulation paper in New York City, the tabloid *New York Daily News*. Oliver Wendell Holmes, Jr., the most famous justice of the United States Supreme Court, was painted in his library, looking distinguished and characteristically dapper, with a vested suit, handlebar mustache, pocket watch, and book in hand. Above him was a portrait of Alfalfa Bill Murray, the populist governor of Oklahoma, collar points askew but, with his spectacles, appearing seriously engaged. Beside them was the dictator who made it a tabloid affair. Their appearance together reflected a shared knowledge and approval of eugenics and sterilization.[4]

Although hardly a household name today, Alfalfa Bill Murray was one of the more famous governors in America at the time. He was a colorful character, a politician likened to the wild "genius" of the state he had helped to create. Murray was beloved for his straight talk, his hobo's look, his long wrinkled brow and tousled mop of hair. When local newspapers ridiculed Murray for wearing trousers that didn't cover his ankles, letting his underwear show, and living in a house with dirt floors and outdoor plumbing, Murray embraced the charges, knowing that many of his supporters, poor farmers, had more to worry about than the length of his rumpled linen suit.[5]

In 1933, the long night of the Depression had already fallen. Murray campaigned for the governorship by blasting Wall Street and big business, carrying along a pound of cheese and a box of crackers as a symbol of both his and the people's poverty. When he won, he pledged, "by the Eternal God," that he would protect the poor and unemployed, telling Oklahomans that as long as he could utter a breath, he would care for the "farmer without seeds to plant" and the "starving children" of the working man. Murray promised to be the governor not only of the "better element," but of "Oklahoma Indians, niggers, and po' white folks." By 1932, his righteous pioneer politics would land him on the cover of *Time* magazine, and launch his "bread, butter, bacon and beans" bid for the presidency.[6]

Once in the governor's office, Alfalfa Bill thrilled the national press with the image of the ornery self-made Westerner. They loved his campaign song, "Hoover Made A Soup Houn' Outa Me," his bewhiskered face, his appeal to down-and-out farmers, his story about being born in a "cotton patch," and his prairie jargon topped off with references to Aristotle. There were good reasons to admire him. Murray's definition of a politician was above reproach: a man "too honest to be bought; too wise to be deceived; too brave to be intimidated." And the times were right for his populist message; as the news magazines put it, Murray was the "political darling of really poor men everywhere." Murray was choked with emotion when, in 1931, he screamed at the state Senate for blocking his tax proposals: "With men and women under the very shadow of the capitol begging for clothing and food, you with big salaries in your fine hotels cannot understand the danger."[7]

Governor Murray was full of contradictions. He was an avid constitutionalist, a reader who clung to a library of five thousand volumes even in his leanest years. And yet he would become known less for his learning than for his militarism. Murray would declare martial law no less than thirty-four times during his tenure as governor, whether to regulate the price of oil, to enforce the color line in Oklahoma City, or to police the sale of football tickets at the University of Oklahoma. No wonder newspapers said, in the early days of the Depression, that, like Huey Long, Murray was becoming one of the nation's more notorious "strong men."[8]

In 1933, Governor Murray had been supporting Oklahoma's sterilization law for two years. The law he signed in 1931 sought to sterilize persons "afflicted with hereditary forms of insanity" as well as "idiocy, imbecility, feeblemindedness, or epilepsy," whether those persons were housed in asylums or in any institution supported by public funds, a term broad enough to cover the state's prisons. Murray hoped that the law would not only reduce the number of inmates in Oklahoma's asylums, but also frighten criminals out of the state. In this, Murray was no pioneer, nor was he uneducated. Many of America's most respected geneticists, biologists, zoologists, and social scientists held out the hope that crime, mental illness, and even poverty might be traced to genes. As Edwin Grant Conklin, a Princeton biologist, explained: "All modern geneticists approve the segregation or sterilization of persons who are known to have serious hereditary defects." By 1928, over 375 American universities and colleges taught courses in eugenics, as many as 20,000 students took these courses, and 70 percent of high school biology textbooks endorsed eugenics in some form. America was not alone; eugenics was a worldwide phenomenon, stretching from Canada to Denmark and Sweden and beyond.[9]

By 1933, sterilization laws spanned the nation from California to Vermont, some decades old; twenty-seven of the forty-eight states had sterilization laws. Not surprisingly, there were those in Oklahoma who feared that the state was behind the times. Although Murray's attempt to use the law against criminals appeared novel, habitual offenders had been the subject of the earliest sterilization laws, reaching back to the first decade of the century.[10] In Oklahoma, newspapers proudly announced that sterilization was a "terrific blow in the protection of society," and a "very advanced step, sanctioned by many of the leading medical authorities and criminologists of the country." Even the critics held out hope for progress, fearing the remedy drastic yet lauding Oklahoma's policy as a "pioneering movement in social science."[11]

Eugenics was controversial for some; sterilization laws were loudly opposed by the Catholic Church, for example. But there was also a long history, by 1933, of politicians on both the right and left who supported these laws. There were nativists like Madison Grant, whose bestselling book *The Passing of the Great Race* extolled the Nordic race and fretted about democracy's tendency to yield "lower types." There were also reformers like Margaret Sanger, who saw in eugenics the hope that law could provide release from suffering. The great progressive president Theodore Roosevelt preached the virtues of Anglo-Saxon blood and warned of the failure of the better classes to breed at the same rate as their inferiors, a phenomenon he said could lead to "race death." By the 1930s, eugenics attracted a large and diverse political following, from Junior Leagues and school principals and the Kiwanis to prohibitionists and birth control advocates and anti-miscegenationists.[12]

Like many progressives, Murray would defend eugenics as a measure to prevent suffering—as prevention of everything from crime to birth defects. "Sterilization is not a punishment but a protection," he explained. "By preventing reproduction, one of the basic causes [of weak minds] can be cured." Murray's favorite story about sterilization appealed neither to nature nor to genetics, but to the fears of every parent. "The most honorable lawyer I ever knew, able and upright, with whom I once practiced, has two sons, and they are both in the Institution at Enid, because he, at sixteen years of age, contracted syphilis. Infection was prevented but it did not purify the blood. I am sure [that] he had rather been sterilized."[13] In this, Murray echoed those who claimed that, far from being cruel, sterilization was compassionate: "If you loved your children, surely you would want to spare them the suffering . . . If you were blind, congenitally deaf, epileptic, or insane, would you conceivably want to have children badly enough to run the risk of passing on these defects to them?" Some went even further, invoking the language of rights. Harry Laughlin, a tireless promoter of sterilization laws, declared that the state had the "inherent right" to set up its own biological standards, as a matter of self-protection. The zoologist Michael Guyer went further, dubbing the right to a eugenic birth the "right of rights."[14]

Although such pronouncements may sound outrageous today, at the time eugenics was a good deal more banal than we imagine. Like all sciences, eugenics was proud and insistent, but its subject was close to home. "What's bred in the bone," "blood will tell," "chip off the old block"—these were the familiar sayings that people used to explain their lives and families. These were also the phrases that the apostles of eugenics used to popularize the creed that its founder, Francis Galton, claimed should become a scientific religion. When critics suggested that there might be something terribly dangerous about it all, supporters simply asked: Who could deny that "it was better to be healthy than sick, vigorous than weak, well fitted than ill fitted"?[15]

In the early 1930s, eugenics appeared frequently in the anodyne language of health. Good marriages were termed eugenic, there were eugenic babies, eugenic theories of child-raising, and even eugenic housing. Eugenicists urged mothers to fill out baby books (to trace the family pedigree) and divorce lawyers urged couples to separate based on eugenic reasoning (a fear that their progeny would be unfit). Housing was eugenic if children flourished, marriages were eugenic if their progeny were healthy, and child-raising was eugenic if it focused on health rather than on the superficial qualities of beauty or success. Eugenics inspired everything from baby contests to poetry to art.[16]

The Depression lent a new sense of urgency to questions of public health, as portraits of destitute and sick children began to appear on the front pages of the newspapers.[17] Eugenics had always thrived on a sense of doom, that the germ plasm (an early term for the gene) was degenerating, that the numbers of insane or impoverished people were increasing exponentially. By the 1930s, this seemed less theoretical, less a question of future population than of everyday life. Any day now, the tent-city rabble might march, the new governor might turn out to be a Red, the labor unions might beat the living daylights out of businessmen, the color line might be broken, marching farmers might occupy the statehouse.

To some, it seemed almost as if the world hung on the edge of a moral abyss. As one Oklahoma editorialist put it: "The old code that lifted men, in spite of their savage impulses, to honor, nobility and decency," was dead; "standing as we do between two worlds, one that is dying and another not yet born, a new code of behavior, a new ethic [has] not been put in its place."[18] By the 1930s, degeneration was no longer merely a theoretical preoccupation; it was a daily worry about whether democracy or life had spent itself, whether the world was spiraling into self-destruction. In a day of dust and drought and depression, the degeneration of the race might well have felt too palpable to be dismissed as the obsession of a few.

If there were doubts about sterilization, the Depression removed them. There wasn't any money left. On January 15, 1933, ten thousand farmers threatened to march on the Oklahoma capital to force relief. Meanwhile, the heads of Oklahoma's asylums and prisons had warned Governor Murray that they were bursting at the seams, with men lining the walls in cots, constantly threatening riot or escape. At the asylums, it was thought that sterilization would allow the release of borderline cases dangerous only because of their potential to propagate. As for the prisons, it was hoped that sterilization would frighten men so much that they would leave the territory. In a day when California deported its "indigent" poor on trains to their "native" states, and Governor Murray issued banishment paroles, Oklahoma hoped to prevent criminals from even entering the state.[19]

———◆———

If Oklahoma's sterilization law made Alfalfa Bill rather obvious pictorial fodder for the *New York Daily News*, there is still the puzzle of why, in late December 1933, his picture was situated above (of all places) that of Oliver Wendell Holmes, Jr., one of the most revered legal minds in the country. Lawyers are familiar with the answer: Governor Murray could not have hoped to do what he was doing without support from the Constitution. And there was no single

human being in the United States more important in making sterilization the constitutional law of the land than Holmes.

Before World War I, during the first burst of intellectual enthusiasm for eugenics, at least twelve states had passed laws calling for
sterilization. By 1924, over thirty bills had been passed. Outside
California, very few of these laws were implemented in any significant way. They were not implemented because of legal doubts; doctors feared that, in performing the operation, they could be found
to have committed a crime (the ancient crime of mayhem, defined as
the intentional destruction of body parts). The result was that very
few sterilizations were actually performed before the late 1920s. In
many states, the law was window-dressing, a "dead letter" (as the
eugenicists themselves put it).[20]

All that would change with Justice Holmes's opinion in the
Supreme Court's 1927 decision in *Buck v. Bell*.[21] Carrie Buck's case
would become one of the most infamous of the twentieth century.
The eighteen-year-old girl had been sent to a home for the feebleminded, the same one in which her mother, Emma, resided. Carrie had had a child out of wedlock and the state of Virginia sought
to sterilize her on the theory that her offspring, then only seven
months old, represented the third generation of degeneracy in the
family. Decades later, researchers would find evidence that Carrie
had been rather successful at classwork (she had been taken out of
school and put to work by her foster parents while only in the sixth
grade). They would also find that Carrie Buck's child was of normal intelligence and that Carrie, along with many others, had been
institutionalized largely based on the idea that she was immoral,
loose, given to improper affections. Only later would the travesty of
Carrie's case be discovered: Carrie Buck's daughter was the product
of rape and Carrie was institutionalized to avoid bringing shame to
her foster family.[22]

In the commitment papers, Carrie's foster family claimed that
she was feebleminded, epileptic, or both. At her trial, Carrie was
described as "incapable of self-support and restraint." Though she
was eighteen when tested, Carrie scored at the level of a nine-year-
old on the revised Stanford–Binet intelligence test.[23] The term "fee-

bleminded" was no vague epithet at the time but a quasi-medical term encompassing persons we might today call insane, others we might call mentally disabled, and many who were no different from you or me. In 1927, however, the world of the "subnormal"—of the "feebleminded"—was divided among three technical classes: idiots, imbeciles, and morons. Idiots had a mental age of one or two, imbeciles between three and seven, and morons between eight and twelve. These terms were widely used in the field of psychology and psychiatry, not to mention sociology and social work. To apply them required the emerging discipline of intelligence testing.[24]

The testing vogue began after World War I, when one million intelligence exams were administered to men in the Army. A standard early version asked questions like the following: "The *Knight* engine is used in the Packard, Lozier, Stearns, or Pierce Arrow? The Wyandotte is a kind of horse, fowl, cattle, or granite? *Isaac Pitman* was most famous in physics, shorthand, railroading, or electricity? *Bud Fisher* is famous as an actor, author, baseball player, or comic artist? *Salsify* is a kind of snake, fish, lizard, or vegetable? *Rosa Bonheur* is famous as a poet, painter, composer, or sculptor? *Cheviot* is the name of a fabric, drink, dance, or food?"*

Not surprisingly, America's fighting men turned out to be less intelligent than they, or anyone else, imagined. It was reported widely that the average intelligence of American army recruits was not much more than a moron, hovering around the fourteen-year-old level. And, if that were true, "nearly half of the white draft (47.3 percent)" was "feebleminded." Despite the obvious absurdity of this result, the survey inspired enormous respect, and a great deal of fear, for it fit with burgeoning worries about population decline—"degeneration," they often called it. This was not simply a matter of a few people in an asylum, a few Carrie Bucks, but the fate of the nation, a nation apparently slouching toward stupidity.[25]

---

* The answers are Knight Engine: Stearns; Wyandotte: fowl; Pitman: shorthand; Bud Fisher: comic artist; salsify: vegetable; Rosa Bonheur: painter; Cheviot: fabric. Paul at 66 (reprinting facsimile test). The test is taken from *Psychological Examining in the United States Army*, 15 Memoirs of the Nat'l Acad. of Sciences (Robert M. Yerkes ed., 1921) (examination Alpha, Test 8: Information, Forms 8 & 9).

To the public, the scientific glue holding these claims together was the idea of feeblemindedness as fixed and permanent, an inherited trait of great danger. The feebleminded immigrant was routinely blamed for the waves of crime reported after World War I. The feebleminded would even be blamed for flooding the labor market and causing the Depression. If, as the army tests had seemed to show, the average intelligence of Americans approached that of the feebleminded, was it any surprise that the poor were starving? How was a nation of morons to sustain a market economy, in this fast and sophisticated age of the machine gun and motorcar? As one of America's leading scientific eugenicists put it in 1932: "in this world . . . of the reign of terror of the criminal, of the tragedy of unemployment, eugenics ceases to be the cult of the few pioneers . . . it is forced on our attention." It was not so far from bodily contagion to the body politic.[26]

Curiously, even those who claimed to be the inventors of this science of intelligence testing recognized that what they were talking about was a moral and social order. The psychologist Henry Goddard, who did more than anyone in the early part of the century to promote the idea of feeblemindedness, explained that the feebleminded differed from the dull normal person because they could not tell right from wrong. Carl Brigham, the psychologist who helped design the army tests, explained that "the diagnosis is . . . in the last analysis, a social diagnosis." Even a person who passed the intelligence test might be determined to be feebleminded, if judged to be "incapable of performing [his or her] duties as a member of society." "[S]ocial inadequacy," sometimes termed "social inefficiency," made at least some of these people "weak-minded."[27]

Eugenics reveled in the appearance of the feebleminded. One of the most well-known "feebleminded" persons in the United States, Deborah Kallikak (whose life was made famous by Goddard), was astonishing to those who studied her because of her beauty, sweet demeanor, and her ability to do a variety of complex tasks despite her very low scores on intelligence tests. In the end, the judgment was that Kallikak had to be feebleminded because she was "socially inadequate." That judgment, in turn, was based in part on the fact that she had the "unmistakable look of the feeble-minded," that a "glance sufficed to establish" low mentality. As eugenics popularizer Leon Whitney would put it in his book on sterilization: "We can visit the institutions where some of them are segregated, and see for ourselves what they look like; decide whether they seem good social animals." Goddard was so convinced of the "look" that, as Stephen Jay Gould would ultimately unearth, he doctored the pictures in his books to make the "unfit" appear sinister.[28]

It was the "look" that would in the end spell the greatest difficulty in Carrie Buck's case. Experts insisted that Carrie was feebleminded. Part of the proof lay in Carrie's mother, who was also institutional-ized as feebleminded based on a "record during life of immorality, prostitution, and untruthfulness." The other evidence was Carrie's seven-month-old child, Vivian. A social worker, influenced by those who ran the asylum, concluded that "[t]here is a look about [the child] that is not quite normal, but just what it is, I can't tell." The baby was said not to be developing properly in her foster family—the same one that had thrown Carrie out. As one witness summed up the three generations: "These people belong to the shiftless, ignorant, and worthless class of anti-social whites of the South."[29]

Carrie Buck's case was pursued by Virginia officials with the Constitution in mind. In 1917, Dr. Priddy, the head of the hospital where Carrie was institutionalized, had a legal problem. He was an enthusiastic advocate of sterilization, so enthusiastic that he had gone ahead and sterilized the wife and child of a local working-man and was promptly sued. Although Priddy won the case, he was warned by the court not to engage in any more sterilization opera-tions without more precise legislative authority. By 1924, Priddy and others had convinced the Virginia legislature to pass a law provid-ing for the sterilization of inmates within the asylum. Even those who advocated the law had "grave doubt[s]" about whether it would withstand constitutional scrutiny.[30]

Carrie's best friend in this matter was less her lawyer (a friend of Dr. Priddy and a founding member of the institution that sought to sterilize her) than the law itself.[31] At the time, existing legal prec-edents were clearly in Carrie's favor. Before World War I, there had already been several constitutional challenges to sterilization laws in state courts; six of seven challenges had been successful.[32] There were difficulties, of course. There was a great deal of confusion among lawyers about why sterilization laws were unconstitutional. Some courts found that the laws violated equal protection; others focused on cruel and unusual punishment; still others on procedural due process or bill of attainder (a constitutional term for a legislative, as opposed to judicial, punishment). And yet high and low courts across the country, in New York and Nevada, Iowa and Oregon, New Jersey and Indiana, had struck down sterilization laws. Some of these courts would later reverse themselves,[33] but as Carrie Buck's case wound its way to the Supreme Court, no lawyer reviewing the legal precedents could have concluded but that the law favored her.

It was not the pain of the operation that was relevant, one federal court urged, but its legacy; sterilization was as degrading and humiliating as castration, it was "mental torture." It was a "brand of infamy," worn for life, like branding cheeks or cutting ears. Experts testified that sterilization would tend to "create a class of people by themselves who would feel that they were . . . different from normal humanity." It was "beyond . . . comprehension," said one judge, to believe the rosy predictions of the eugenicists that sterilization was an "awakening note to a new era." Legislatures were known, under the pressure of extraordinary crimes, to adopt "strange methods of repression." This, said one court, "belongs to the Dark Ages."[34]

Almost none of this skepticism was expressed in terms familiar today; none of the cases striking down sterilization laws in the pre-*Buck* era relied upon natural or fundamental rights—much less on what today's lawyers would call "the right to procreate"—as a prominent part of their rationale. Courts were far more likely to rely upon the unusual nature of the punishment or problems of "class legislation." Today, the term "class legislation" is largely unknown to lawyers, but at the time it was not only a popular expression that could be found in newspapers but also a particular form of constitutional equality argument.[35] For example, New Jersey's highest court wondered aloud whether the law might be used by majorities simply to pick on the poor, or other disfavored classes: "[T]he feeble-minded and epileptics are not the only persons in the community whose elimination as undesirable citizens would, or might in the judgment of the legislature, be a distinct benefit to society. . . . There are other things besides physical or mental diseases that may render persons undesirable citizens . . . in the opinion of a majority of a prevailing legislature." As if to make the case even clearer, the court imagined the possibility that sterilization might be based on "[r]acial differences," and this risk was greatest in communities (presumably the South) where the racial "question is unfortunately a permanent and paramount issue."[36]

By 1927, then, when Carrie Buck's case reached the United States Supreme Court, a lopsided majority of courts had found these laws unconstitutional as both dangerous and degrading. They might have even smelled the whiff of racism that clung to sterilization; even if the statutes did not point to particular ethnicities or races, as the New Jersey Supreme Court had said, there were many attributes that could render persons undesirable in the eyes of a legislative majority, and the most obvious, in a world agitated over immigration and lynching, was race. Even Carrie Buck's counsel mentioned that there was always the danger that, in the name of science, new "classes" and even "races" might be added to the scope of the statute.[37]

These arguments were ignored in Justice Holmes's peremptory five-paragraph opinion. Although Carrie's lawyer claimed she had a right of "bodily integrity," Holmes never used those terms, dismissing Carrie's claim of right as obviously untenable because too strong. It "seems to be contended that in no circumstances could such an order be justified," Holmes wrote, as if to resolve the claim by declaring it absurd. The great bulk of the brief decision extolled the community's interest in sterilization and the dangers of the unfit. There were references to war, patriotism and sacrifice: ". . . the public welfare may call upon the best citizens for their lives. It would be strange if it could not call upon those who already sap the strength of the State for these lesser sacrifices." There was talk of a society "swamped with incompetence." There was even a call to prevent starvation: "It is better for all the world, if instead of waiting to execute degenerate offspring for crime, or to let them starve for their imbecility, society can prevent those who are manifestly unfit from continuing their kind."[38]

In this, Holmes was evoking ideas deeply embedded in his and the nation's past. He had experienced the horror of the Civil War, and it haunted him for much of his life. Like many eugenicists, Holmes was disgusted at the waste of the war, yet perfectly willing to accept that nature might "starve" the imbecile. Although eugenicists detested man-made extermination, they were quite willing to accept the death handed out by nature. As Herbert Spencer, one of the eugenicists' favorite philosophers, had decreed, "If they are sufficiently complete to live, they *do* live, and it is well they should live. If they are not sufficiently complete to live, they die, and it is best they should die."[39] This was viewed not as cruelty, but compassion.

Justice Holmes later wrote that, in deciding *Buck* as he did, he was "getting near the first principle of real reform." The Court's opinion struck a resounding note in favor of the legislative will to sterilize. All the proper procedures had been accorded Carrie Buck, wrote Holmes: "There can be no doubt that so far as procedure is concerned the rights of the patient are most carefully considered"; the asylum had been "in scrupulous compliance with the statute and . . . there is no doubt that in that respect the plaintiff . . . has had due process of law." The state's power to vaccinate was "broad enough to cover cutting the Fallopian tubes."[40] Rejecting the most prevalent judicial argument against sterilization, Holmes declared equal protection irrelevant. He dismissed it as the "usual last resort" of constitutional arguments to point out "shortcomings of this sort" (because the claims were so common at the time and because they failed more often than they succeeded). It was for the legislature to decide to whom sterilization should apply; so long as the law indicated a public policy and sought to apply it to all similarly situated, the fact that the statute was underinclusive—that it did not include all diseased or feebleminded persons but only applied within the asylum—posed no constitutional inequality. "Three generations of imbeciles [were] enough." Only Justice Butler, the Court's sole Catholic member, expressed his dissent, and then without opinion.[41]

The *Buck* opinion would become one of Justice Holmes's most flagrant embarrassments. At the time, however, it was precisely because Holmes wrote the opinion in *Buck v. Bell* that it was thought likely to influence legal and popular opinion to embrace sterilization as a progressive cause. Holmes was known for the "realism, humanity and progress" of his opinions; as one commentator put it, "[p]ages would be needed even to list his civilizing, liberalizing decisions." Holmes was the Supreme Court's champion of judicial deference to popular majorities and state legislatures, in large part because of his stand affirming labor legislation. If deference to legislative will was the measure of progress and humanity, then the opinion in *Buck v. Bell* amounted to exactly that: it deferred to sterilization laws on the books across the nation. As the legal historian Lawrence Friedman has put it, "To Holmes, and so many of his contemporaries, the decision was progressive." Legal doubts, lingering for almost two decades, appeared finally to have been put to rest.[42]

The first wave of largely symbolic sterilization statutes was now followed by a second wave, more effective than the last. Two years after *Buck* was decided, twelve states had passed new sterilization legislation; within four years, twenty-two states had introduced new sterilization bills in their legislatures. In 1932, Jacob Landman, a student of eugenic legislation, would explain that "*Buck v. Bell* has now definitely committed the United States to a policy of human sterilization for good or for bad as a means of coping with the socially undesirable in our midst." In the years to follow, the "average number of operations performed under compulsory sterilization statutes in the United States jumped tenfold" (before 1920, the average number per year was approximately 200; during the 1930s, the average per year was over 2,000).[43] After *Buck*, there would be a series of constitutional challenges in the states,[44] challenges rebuffed or evaded—until a case called *Skinner v. Oklahoma*.

———◆———

The immediate cause for our troika's appearance in the *New York Daily News* in December 1933 was neither Governor Murray nor Justice Holmes. Today, it is the third portrait that catches the eye, the grandiose pose, the uniform, the mustache. The world's greatest experiment in eugenics was about to begin. The sheer scope of the proposal was stunning: 1,800 hereditary health courts were to be created and 400,000 people sterilized. This dwarfed the American experience; in the ten-year period from 1907 until 1917, there were only 1,422 sterilization operations performed in the United States. Even at its height, the average number of operations per year in America hovered between 2,000 and 3,000.[45]

When the German sterilization law was first proposed, the press emphasized the analogy to American laws. In 1933, the *New York Times*'s editorial page explained that the Nazi program, upon examination, turned out to be little different from those advocated in "every civilized country." Although noting that the Germans would be disappointed if they believed that sterilization was a cure-all, the editorial nevertheless continued: "Germany is by no means the first to enact laws to permit or compel sterilization of hereditary mental defectives. Some 15,000 unfortunates [since 1907] have thus far been harmlessly and humanely operated upon in the United States to prevent them from propagating their own kind."[46] It was precisely the analogy between German and American laws that revived the American sterilization debate. National news magazines like *Time* and *News-Week* and *Literary Digest* ran stories on sterilization, as did papers across the country, in Chicago and Los Angeles and New York. By 1934, *Scientific American* had issued a four-part series on sterilization and the German program. Hollywood types even made a movie about the dangers of sterilization, promoting it newsreel style: "News Flash! Germany! Hitler Decrees All Unfit to Be Sterilized! 27 States Put Sterilization Laws into Practice / The Topic that's on Everyone's Tongue!"[47]

It had only been a year since Hitler took power; in a brief six months, he had acquired complete dominance over the German government. America hoped to look the other way but, by the middle of 1933, few resisted the notion that Hitler was the greatest autocrat of the civilized world. From the beginning, there were claims that Hitler's invective was ludicrous and vain, that the Nazis' assaults on religion and voting and free speech and minorities—obvious even in 1933—would crumble his regime. Mainstream publications like *Time* ridiculed the new dictator and his followers as violent buffoons, fond of clownish pageantry. Yet some saw the situation in a different light: that the "strong man" was an inevitable need in a new, complex world; that democracy had spent itself and Hitler had proven it; or, at the very least, that it was time to "understand" the regime rather than to "scold it."[48]

In some ways, there were strong resemblances between Germany and America of the early 1930s: the crippling unemployment, the parade of political and private violence, the humiliations of national and personal failure. The fear of degeneracy and the inability of the people to govern themselves had soured many average Germans on parliamentary democracy. It had also soured thousands of Americans, who were beginning to turn to the strong men of the 1930s. This was the day of Huey Long and Alfalfa Bill, of the radio priest Father Coughlin and the Hitler-following Khaki Shirts, a day of leaders who were not afraid to go directly to the people, to issue incendiary warnings, or to call out the National Guard. Even those who favored Roosevelt's experiments thought that there might be something vaguely Fascist about the New Deal.[49]

Reports from Germany were often enthusiastic about the dictator's great successes. Visitors from Oklahoma reported the German people's enthusiasm for the godlike dictator who got things done. Pointed contrasts were made to America, where Dillingers and Barrows and other public enemies robbed and killed their way across the Midwest in 1933 and 1934. As one Oklahoma visitor exclaimed, "crime practically has been done away with under Hitler . . . for the first time since the war [I] felt safe." And the German people were not complaining, despite the closed elections, the attacks on Communists and Catholics, the Nazi dominance of the press. Exhausted by the endless parliamentary wrangling of the Weimar period, the German public embraced Hitler as the last chance for a bit of order.[50]

In a world where some still held out hope for the great German dictator, it is not surprising that there were those who praised the Nazi sterilization program for its ambition and resolve. Leading

American eugenicists gave their initial approval to the plan. Leon Whitney, former executive secretary of the American Eugenics Society, told the press, "This action of Hitler's certainly stamps him as one of the greatest statesmen and social planners in the world, because it requires real statesmanship to plan long-time social programs such as he has by this action." The German compulsory sterilization law shared much with its American predecessors. Like most American laws, the German law applied to those deemed insane, feebleminded, or epileptic. As in America, sex offenders were covered, but in Germany the penalty was harsher: castration. Unlike American laws, however, the German law required doctors to report for sterilization anyone they encountered who fell under the law, including not only the feebleminded but also those with severe physical deformities, hereditary deafness, blindness, and habitual alcoholism. In response to religious opposition to sterilization, the German law offered an exemption for those who chose to commit themselves to an asylum during their entire reproductive lives.[51]

Just months after the announcement of the Nazis' proposal, the shadow of race already darkened reports of the program. Hitlerian enthusiasm for the Nordic type was hardly a secret at the time (*Mein Kampf* had been published in 1925), even if the new German state's attacks on the Jewish "race" did not necessarily stand out from its harangues against Communists or Catholics.[52] The science page of the *New York Times* raised the question of Aryanism directly. Waldemar Kaempffert, the science editor, was so enthusiastic about eugenics, he thought it raised questions more important than "the machine" (referring to the automobile). But he was quite direct when it came to the Nazis: when one considers "how the Germans have twisted the meaning of the word Aryan, out of all semblance . . . the skeptical naturally wonder." Given "Germany's present reign of political terror, geneticists wonder whether a law which has much to commend it will be enforced with strict scientific impartiality." Presciently, Kaempffert asked, "What is to stop the governor of a concentration camp from recommending sterilization for a malformed Communist or member of the Catholic Centre?"[53]

Fears of abuse mounted as news of the extent of the program

began to find its way west. In January 1934, it was reported that
Germany's sterilization law would apply to children as young as ten.
Two weeks later, the Germans ordered a census of incurables and
demanded that the German criminal courts be scoured for "hereditary defectives" (despite the fact that the original Nazi statute did
not cover habitual criminals). Doctors who failed to report a defective individual were to be fined heavily. In February, it was reported
that eugenics authorities were insisting on the immediate sterilization of the "Negroid children in the Rhineland and the Ruhr," the
legacy of "invading French colonial troops" during World War I.[54]

If Hitler's program raised fears of racism, it was a racism different from today's. In 1934, race was a slippery term: it referred easily
to what we would today call a religion—as in "the Jewish race"—or
ethnicity, as in "the Italian race" or "the Irish race."[55] It was not
unusual for eugenicists to talk of the feebleminded races or of a race
of criminals, on the theory that these groups had a common heredity. For many eugenicists, race and genetics were synonymous; both
depended upon inheritance. The prominent zoologist S. J. Holmes
would boast that geneticists had the knowledge to "breed an albino
race, a deaf race, a feeble-minded race, an insane race, a race of
dwarfs, a race with hook-like extremities instead of hands, a race of
superior intellectual ability, or a race of high artistic talent."[56]

There was nothing particularly German about this idea of race;
the racism of eugenics, whether abroad or in America, was primarily directed against those we no longer see as races. When Madison
Grant, a well-known eugenics popularizer, wrote in a bestselling
book that inferior races were "moral perverts, mental defectives, and
hereditary cripples," he was referring to southern and eastern European immigrants who had flooded the country after World War
I. Grant insisted that, when the Nordic races bred with the lesser
immigrant races, it sapped the "native American aristocracy" of its
vigor and health, reducing it to a lower, more primitive type. This
same calculus led the eugenicist Lothrop Stoddard to write that the
"basic factor" in human affairs was "not politics, but race": as Grant
put it, race was "everything." Stoddard railed against miscegenation; America, he wrote, was a sitting duck for those who would

"pacific[ally] penetrat[e]" it—those who by immigration would fester within, tainting American blood. For both Stoddard and Grant, America was, quite literally, being raped by the feebleminded and "criminalistic" races (races we would today call immigrants). Grant's solution was artificial selection, that is, sterilization:

> A rigid system of selection through the elimination of those who are weak or unfit—in other words, social failures—would solve the whole question . . . [and] get rid of the undesirables who crowd our jails, hospitals and insane asylums. . . . [T]he state through sterilization must see to it that his line stops with him. . . . This is a practical, merciful and inevitable solution of the whole problem and can be applied to an ever widening circle of social discards, beginning always with the criminal, the diseased and the insane and extending gradually to types which may be called weaklings rather than defectives and perhaps ultimately to worthless race types."[57]

Grant's book was not only widely popular, it was reviewed favorably in scientific journals. After all, its claims were not terribly different from those of some scientists of the day. As one text of genetics lectures put it: "from one thousand Roumanians today in Boston, at the present rate of breeding, will come a hundred thousand two hundred years hence to govern the fifty descendants of Harvard's sons!"[58] As in most matters of American racism, African-Americans suffered the worst slurs. The zoologist Holmes would write, with apparent approval, that "Negros" were "becoming bleached," and that, if they were ever destined to be "absorbed" into white culture, they would "be considerably bleached before they [were] assimiliated." The logic of this position depended, as the eugenics popularizers Paul Popenoe and Roswell Johnson would insist, on the fact that the "Negro race must be placed very near zero on the scale" of racial value.[59]

It is not surprising, then, that, when criticized for their eugenics program, Nazi Party officials turned the tables: how could the German program be so terrible when it mirrored the laws of many

American states, laws that criminalized racial intermixing and sterilized the unfit? Statements defending the German program seemed to be written so that "the good example" set by the United States was always in the first few paragraphs. The articles used terms that would not have sounded strange to Governor Murray or Justice Holmes, or to a variety of eugenicists. Dr. Arthur Guett, counselor to the Reich Ministry of the Interior, talked of the "imminent" danger of race degeneration: the "unfit" had been kept alive by social "counter selection," allowing them to poison the bloodstream by outbreeding "the healthy and ambitious." When all was said and done, as in America, Nazi propagandists invoked the economy, claiming that hereditary defects, antisocial persons, and criminals cost Germany one billion marks a year.[60]

In the face of news of the German program, many American commentators remained agnostic, embracing eugenics while worrying about possible abuse. Others found in the German program an "outstanding accomplishment" and "a keynote in social welfare," a confirmation and encouragement for what they believed to be compassion. In January 1934, the *Oklahoma News* would compare Oklahoma's law with the new German program: "Coincident with a more far-reaching program in Germany, Oklahoma today began preparations for sterilizing several hundreds, or thousands of insane and habitual criminals." We are "deliberately and knowingly breeding menaces to future society," insisted the editorial. In such a world, "we can't see that it is wrong for the state to tell an inflicted [*sic*] man or woman that he or she may not produce a child which is likely to bring suffering to all, including the child itself."[61]

CHAPTER 2

The Brain Trust

The armies of defective and delinquent persons in every nation and race, the crowded hospitals, asylums, jails and penitentiaries in almost every country, the enormous cost of caring for this human wreckage and wastage, all testify to the fact that there is urgent need for improvement. Indeed it is merely a question of how long civilization can continue to carry this ever-increasing burden of bungled and botched, of paupers, feebleminded and insane, of bums, thugs and criminals.
— *Edwin Conklin, Princeton biologist, 1930*[1]

On April 18, 1934, the *Oklahoma News* reported that the call of "science for a better human" had been answered "by the surgeon's knife." In the office of Dr. Griffin, the Norman asylum's superintendent, six women "[s]tanding mute and without protest" appeared before the state Board of Affairs, the three-man state committee charged with administering the Oklahoma sterilization law. The papers said that the patients "showed little interest in the proceedings." After being introduced by Dr. Griffin, each "sat, staring vacantly, while she was identified." Dr. Griffin pronounced the patients "incurable."[2]

The *Daily Oklahoman* summarized each of the six cases, explaining that all the women had mental ages between five and eight, some were epileptics, others had insane or weak-minded relatives, and one had a "record of associating indiscriminately with men, and running away from home." Wanda Alvin, the first patient, wore a purple dress, chewed gum, and fingered her bracelets nervously. When asked if she had anything to say, she replied, "It's all right with me if I can go home to mother after it's all over." "You see," she said, "I was just a little kid when I came here and I want to see my mother." Doctor Griffin told the press that consent had been obtained in all cases.[3]

Richard Cloyd, a state senator and lawyer hired by the Board of Affairs as the women's guardian, "raised no objections as each case was decided." As the *Oklahoma News* editorialized, "Why would anyone protest the sterilization of an incurably insane person or a chronic criminal? We examine and license plumbers and steamfitters to make sure that they are competent. . . . Is it going too far then to say that the unqualified human be enjoined from creating life, and instilling in a baby a diseased or criminal mind?" Oklahoma's experts appeared to agree. As Wyatt Marrs, the University of Oklahoma professor of sociology, explained: "This law is a stepping stone to a more intelligent attitude toward the problems of the mentally deficient in society." Some in the national press seemed a bit more wary; the *Literary Digest* covered the Oklahoma law with significant skepticism in the "religion and social service" section of the magazine. But the *Los Angeles Times* reported that the Board's order "marks the beginning of a long and carefully planned official program for sterilization of mentally unfit persons and habitual criminals."[4]

It would take only twenty-four hours before controversy would stall the hearings. She was, as the *Oklahoma City Times* put it, a "pretty twenty year old woman inmate," "neat and attractively dressed." The *Norman Transcript* called her a "sad-eyed girl" from Carter County who said she "wanted to get married and have children." She "remained throughout the hearing . . . looking nervously at the floor, interrupting testimony with logical answers and objections, and correcting hospital medical" personnel, despite the fact that she had been admitted to the asylum several times. She claimed that her mental trouble was not, as Dr. Griffin said, dementia praecox, but "over-study in school." The

Board of Affairs listened to the objections and postponed the case, announcing to the press that the Board's funds were running low (the law put the expense of the hearings on the Board) and that it was now time to turn to the men of McAlester prison. The sad-eyed girl's objection did little to change minds about sterilization; the next day "[t]wo high state officials," including the state's health commissioner, pronounced sterilization "one of the greatest steps forward since statehood."[5]

In the spring of 1934, Oklahoma's eugenics enthusiasts were impatient. Some in the Oklahoma press had written that the sterilization law had become a "joke," mired in delay and "red tape." At the prison, Warden Brown had been twice ordered to begin preparation of a "list of some 300 'eligible' prisoners" and had refused, fearing riot and escape at the prison. But, after three years, Brown could no longer stall. The local papers in the nearby city of Muskogee warned that "[o]ne of the most comprehensive sterilization programs in American history" was about to be undertaken in Oklahoma. This was an exaggeration; California's program was far more extensive by this time. But whether inside or outside McAlester prison, those who read the Oklahoma papers that day believed that hundreds of habitual criminals were waiting for the knife.[6]

———◆———

On a Sunday in early May 1934, Claud Briggs headed toward McAlester prison. Briggs knew the road well; he had grown up not far from McAlester. His home, Wilburton, population 1,925, was in one of the poorest parts of Oklahoma, Latimer County, just across the border from Arkansas. It was green and hilly land, the remainder of a turn-of-the-century timber and coal boom gone bust. History said it was desperado country, home to the caves that housed the famed Oklahoma outlaws of yesteryear, Belle Starr, the Doolins, and even the Dalton gang—a refuge for the tainted, the alien, the criminal.[7]

Claud Briggs was a self-made lawyer. When he was fourteen, his father, a blacksmith and farmer, was injured and Briggs had to quit school and work to support the family. Before he was twenty, Briggs ran his own general store and printed his own newspaper, the *Howe Star*. Later, Briggs would say that his "earliest ambition was to be a lawyer." Briggs couldn't afford to go to law school; he took what was called a "home course," placing second in the state when he took his bar exam. From there, it was a quick ascent: from county attorney, to state representative, to a leadership position in the Oklahoma Senate. Always affable and grinning, overly talkative, Briggs prided himself on supporting the little guy, the injured worker, the miners and the farmers in Latimer County. He was "always a friend of the oppressed," and fought for the "masses against the classes."[8]

Claud Briggs might have wondered why Warden Brown had called him at all. The warden had said that a prisoners' committee wanted to meet with him about a legal challenge to the sterilization law. To an outsider, Briggs might not have seemed an obvious ally of the prisoners' cause. It was Briggs who had proposed the very amendment that allowed Governor Murray to claim that the new sterilization law would deter crime, an amendment that said the law would apply to any public institution (which in theory might include prisons). But that was 1931, when Briggs, like everyone else, was thrilled with Murray. Once, Briggs listened as Murray, in an emotion-choked voice, begged the Senate to pass his salary tax bill so that people could eat. By May 1934, things were different. In 1933, Briggs had opposed Murray's choice for Senate leader, and the governor turned on him, blasting him in his personal newspaper, the *Blue Valley Farmer*, and campaigning against him. By the time he took the road to McAlester prison, Claud Briggs was no longer the "administration man" he had once been.[9]

From the company he brought, it was clear that Briggs was taking the warden's invitation seriously. Briggs drove to McAlester with his new law partner, Fay Lester, former chief justice of the Oklahoma Supreme Court. The Lester family was part of a political powerhouse in "little Dixie" (southeastern Oklahoma), and Fay Lester was its aging dean. Lester was often described as a man of the people and a democrat "of the old school," who grounded his politics in "Christian Citizenship." As a judge, Fay Lester was a "stickler for compelling legislation to track the Constitution." Like Briggs, by

1934, Lester was no friend of Alfalfa Bill Murray's; Murray had lost him his seat on the Oklahoma Supreme Court by campaigning for him (the people feared that the semi-dictator Murray was in personal control of the justices he supported in the election).[10]

If neither Briggs nor Lester worried about offending the governor, they could not have been insensitive to the difficulties of the warden's proposal. By 1934, supreme courts all over the West—in Kansas and Utah and Nebraska and Idaho—had followed the precedent set by *Buck*.[11] Oklahoma's case law, the law that would control the prisoners' lawsuit, was no different. In 1932, Oklahoma arranged a suit to test the constitutionality of the 1931 sterilization law. The object of the test case was Samuel Main, a World War I veteran and patient at the Central Oklahoma State Hospital at Norman. Main was on public relief and had one child too many. The Board of Affairs appointed him a lawyer and guardian, Richard Cloyd, the same man who had represented the women at Norman. At his sterilization trial before the Board, the social service workers candidly admitted that Main had been originally sent to an asylum for abusing his wife and children, and that his symptoms coincided with these attacks (in modern parlance, Main was a batterer). Based on this evidence and despite doubts about the diagnosis, the Board of Affairs found that Main was "afflicted with a hereditary form of insanity," and, in February 1933, the Oklahoma Supreme Court affirmed the constitutionality of Main's sterilization. The *Main* opinion was a virtual carbon copy of *Buck*, concluding that the state had the police power to sterilize.[12]

The *Main* decision not only affirmed the constitutionality of sterilization in Oklahoma's asylums, but also inspired the legislature to amend the law. If there had been doubt about whether the law applied to Oklahoma's prisons, a new, improved, 1933 sterilization law specifically named McAlester prison and the state reformatory at Granite. The circumstances triggering sterilization were expanded. The 1931 law sought to sterilize persons "afflicted with hereditary forms of insanity" as well as "idiocy, imbecility, feeblemindedness, or epilepsy." The 1933 law added two more grounds for sterilization, but was unclear whether only one was required: if the "patient" himself or herself was "likely to be a public or partial public charge" or was a "habitual criminal," defined as "any person convicted of a felony three times."[13]

The 1933 law was the work of one of the most prominent doctors in the state, a newly-elected legislator and eugenics enthusiast, Dr. Louis Henry Ritzhaupt. Dr. Ritzhaupt was a rising political star, a Democratic senator who had broken one of the state's few Republican strongholds, in Logan County. Like Briggs, Ritzhaupt came from humble origins; his father was a German immigrant and baker. But, unlike the self-made Briggs, Ritzhaupt touted his educational pedigree and his eastern medical school degree. The balding Ritzhaupt (or "Ritzy," as he was known to his friends) was ambitious, telling newspapers, soon after his election to the state senate, that he planned to run for governor. He was positively enthusiastic about breeding; it was his hobby. In 1935, he would exhibit his prize-winning poultry, "Bearded Black Crested Black Polish Bantams," at Madison Square Garden.[14]

Ritzhaupt was a strong supporter of eugenic legislation; doctors were often the principal authors of sterilization laws. By the mid-1930s, the number of medical skeptics was growing, but there remained strong advocates of eugenic sterilization in a field whose journals once touted involuntary vasectomy as a "public right" to protect the race. Dr. Ritzhaupt believed that weak minds were dangerous because they would lead to radical political change; if the more educated did not "lead them," the rest of the citizenry would become "the prey of communism, anarchy, bolshevism and . . . red ruin." The doctor not only sponsored the 1933 Oklahoma sterilization law but also offered to wield the knife himself, telling reporters, "Our jails, penitentiaries and homes for [the] mentally deficient are growing larger and their maintenance adds yearly to the tax burden." The only way to "curtail this expense is to stop production of potential inmates."[15]

———

If Briggs and Lester knew that the prisoners' challenge posed an uphill legal battle, they also should have known that their potential clients posed an even greater challenge. In the spring of 1934, as Briggs and Lester traveled to McAlester, an army of police were searching six midwestern states for Dillinger, after his escape from the Little Bohemia resort in northern Wisconsin. Bonnie and Clyde were making their way through Oklahoma to meet their end in Louisiana. Just days before, six-year-old June Robles had been kidnapped in Arizona, only to be found buried in a box in the desert. From baby Lindbergh to the oilman Urschel in Tulsa to the banker Hamm in Minnesota, to mention only a few, the snatch racket had united the public in fascination and fear for their families. The country was fighting the very kind of men Briggs and Lester were to meet—the repeater, the habitual, the public enemy.[16]

Franklin Roosevelt inherited the problem in dramatic fashion. In February 1933, the president-elect found himself the intended target of an assassin's bullet. At a Miami rally, just weeks before Roosevelt was to take office, Giuseppe Zangara, a self-proclaimed anarchist, shot at him but missed, instead killing the mayor of Chicago and wounding several others. As he did in many other matters, Herbert Hoover had paved the way for Roosevelt's response. At the end of his term, Hoover had invited the states to "war" against crime, even as he insisted that it was the states' responsibility to do the work; Roosevelt had no qualms about federal involvement. And, so, although the New Deal is rarely remembered for its war on crime, President Roosevelt would wage one.[17]

By the fifth year of the Depression, law seemed to have capitulated to violence. The gangsters personified the sense of lawlessness; as one of the great historians of the period recounts, "While five thousand law officers pursued [Dillinger] he stopped for a haircut in a barber shop, bought cars, and had a home-cooked Sunday dinner with his family in his home town [and] [w]hen he needed more arms, he raided the police station." But it was not simply the celebrity gangster whom people feared; there were too many other cases, too many children dead and kidnapped, too many lawless mobs. In April 1934, two-and-a-half-year-old Dorette Zeitlow was "snatched" by a thirteen-year-old and left to die in an icehouse outside Chicago. Ten thousand mobbed her funeral. That same month, in Louisiana,

Fred Lockhart, a white man, was held for murder of a sixteen-year-old; officers had to fight off a mob with tear gas. Months before, two white kidnappers of a twenty-two-year-old were strung up on a tree in San Jose, California, the governor announcing to the nation that the crowd had done a "good job" and that this was "the best lesson California has ever given the country."[18]

Worried about a growing sense of lawlessness, President Roosevelt chided the public for its fascination with the public enemy, warning citizens that law could not survive in a world where the public "looked with tolerance" on or applauded efforts to "romanticize crime." The fight against crime was of "first importance," he said; it was a battle in which there would be no "relenting." It was a day, after all, in which popular authors linked the economic situation to crime, telling the public that "the annual crime bill in America [was] from ten to sixteen billions of dollars," a sum claimed to exceed the much-worried-about federal deficit. It was also a day in which foreign countries regularly ridiculed America for its gangster excesses; as Nazi papers editorialized in April 1934, Dillinger's exploits revealed America's "leniency for murderers and the congenitally inferior," a reminder that the United States should follow Germany's plan to sterilize the habitual criminal.[19]

By the spring of 1934, the president and Chief Justice Hughes called for war before the most respected legal audiences in the country. And war they did. There would be new armies of "government-men" with college degrees and new scientific technologies, like fingerprinting and lie detector tests, and newly empowered institutions, like the FBI. J. Edgar Hoover would emerge from anonymity and failure to construct a propaganda machine, creating popular heroes, the G-men, who stalked the low and the dangerous and found themselves in everything from prepared news features to comic strips. This war would not only use new technologies (Attorney General Cummings asked Congress for airplanes and armored cars) and fighting forces, it would realign political power—in this case, the power of nation versus state in the enforcement of the criminal law. And it would have as its paradigmatic image the public enemy, the habitual criminal, the repeater.[20]

As Jacob Landman, a student of eugenic legislation, wrote, it was the "acute current crime wave" which provided the political inspiration for the mass of sterilization legislation born out of *Buck v. Bell*: "Criminologists and eugeni[cists] alike saw in the constitutionality of the Virginia human sterilization statute one solution to our great social problem of crime." Landman's link between crime and sterilization was not without support in the expert thought of the day. The very idea of habitual criminality, although old, had received renewed intellectual respectability in the early 1930s, when Harvard law school's reigning criminologists, Sheldon and Eleanor Glueck, wrote book after bestselling book on *500 Career Criminals* and *1000 Juvenile Delinquents*, emphasizing that crime was a product of recidivism. By the 1930s, habitual criminality had found its way into the halls of legislatures, yielding a wave of what we today call "three-strikes" laws (then popularly called Baumes laws after their principal legislative sponsor).[21] It also inspired respect, by some experts, for the notion of sterilizing the habitual criminal.

Criminologists knew that crime itself could not be inherited, yet they believed that habitual criminality reflected mental deficiency, which could be inherited. Edwin Sutherland, one of the most important criminologists of his generation, would write: "In so far as it can be determined that criminality is connected with an inherited abnormal trait, it is clearly desirable to stop the reproduction of people who have that trait . . . Probably all such persons should be sterilized."[22] However qualified these pronouncements (and they were qualified), they were widely shared; in 1932, Harvard's Sheldon Glueck considered proposing a sterilization law for Massachusetts and would write, in 1936, that when more was known it would be the "task of society to reduce the reproduction" of the "criminalistic."[23] Some simply echoed the position of the eugenicists that "many criminals, especially those who offend against the person, are feeble-minded"; the University of Wisconsin's John Gillin wrote that until the "procreation of [the] feebleminded" was stemmed, "we shall have the problem of crime."[24]

As Briggs and Lester approached McAlester prison, the building emerged, an immense gray cement façade built in the classical
style, sitting awkwardly on a red dirt plain, rising high above the
trees at its gate. McAlester prison was a building meant to humble;
the outside walls were twenty feet high and eighteen inches thick,
with eleven towers manned constantly by well-armed guards. The
building matched the operation; McAlester was a farm and a ranch
and a broom and brick factory, surrounded by thousands of acres
of what had once been known as Indian territory. At times, during
the Depression, the prison was one of the few moneymaking operations in the state, providing brick for houses, trousers for workers,
and twine for farmers. The work helped in the humbling process.
The "boys," as they were called, broke rock when they first came
to McAlester, lifting axes in "the pits," a hole in the ground about
"fifty or sixty feet deep, and several acres wide." Breaking rock at
the brickyard was both initiation and punishment. If the convict
was lucky, he was lent out "trusty" to do the prison's less demand-
ing jobs, as a dairyman or cowboy. If not, he was sent back to the
brickyard.[25]

In the early 1930s, the local newspaper reported that McAlester's
townspeople carried pistols as they had in the pioneer days. Bank
presidents and insurance salesmen played at "shoot-outs," explaining
to reporters that they carried revolvers because of McAlester. The
prison was built for 1,800 men, but often housed almost 2,000 more
during the early 1930s. Governor Murray would warn of a "seething
mass of criminality" at McAlester, explaining that "the hallways are
filled with cots, and there is a constant danger of a break." He would
even threaten the legislature that he would "release 1,000 convicts"
if they did not support his plan for a new sub-prison to relieve the
overcrowding.[26]

For all the apparent danger, the public's image of the dangerous men of McAlester was something of an exaggeration. The
prison held the occasional celebrity, like the Kimes brothers, who
had roamed the Southwest robbing banks in the late 1920s, and
Ray Terrill, one of the most famous safecrackers in the nation. But
for the most part McAlester was packed with bootleggers and car

thieves and small-time confidence men. There were far more petty offenders than one might expect in Oklahoma's major prison, men like R. C. Lovette. Lovette had stolen two cows worth $80 and had been sentenced to two years. Forty percent of the prisoners, it was reported, did not stay there for more than seven months; they were sentenced for "violations such as chicken stealing or other small theft, drinking, the sale of whisky and the like." As Warden Brown himself told the papers, the Depression had turned "honest laborers to crime." Hunger had led them to steal for themselves and their families; they were not "big city criminals" or "sullen mixed blood aliens," as in the East Coast prisons.[27]

Warden Brown was known for his kindliness and meticulous wardrobe; his principal qualifications for the job were his business sense and his political connections. When Governor Murray's pick for the job was turned down by the legislature, Brown grabbed the job, even though his supporters acknowledged that he had not "an hour" of education on how to run a prison. Brown had served as the mayor of Elk City and sold lumber and hardware. When appointed, Brown confessed that he was "studying books on prison management" and that his principal hope was to bring more work, more education, and better movies to McAlester. Three years later, the warden had managed to turn a profit by cutting costs; he kept his job, despite his public opposition to sterilization.[28]

———◆———

The men that lawyers Briggs and Lester would meet that day in Warden Brown's office were described in the newspaper as a murderer, an embezzler, and a car thief, the kind of men one would expect to find in McAlester. In fact, these men were very different from the average McAlester prisoner. These men had families, were well educated, and had had jobs at one time. By contrast, the average McAlester inmate in the early 1930s was a drifter, a day laborer, or a sharecropper. One in twenty had never gone to school at all; one in eight had attended only the first three grades. All told, 2,000 men, or nearly half the male prison population at McAlester, had never reached the seventh grade. And, yet, in one important way, the men Briggs and Lester would encounter that day were like their brethren. These men were repeaters—men who couldn't seem to stay out of prison.[29]

No. 21466, Francis Hyde, was the youngest, younger-looking than his thirty-one years. He was a small, balding, gray-eyed, sensitive-looking man. Once upon a time, he had been an able attorney from a respectable family, but in 1929, the state of Oklahoma charged that Hyde had attempted to kill his mentor, the oil man and financier Samuel Collins,* by lacing a Dr. Pepper with cyanide. Hyde denied the crime, saying that "the jury may convict me, making a widow of my wife and orphans of my children, but I am not guilty." His family hired the best defense money could buy in Oklahoma. The lawyer Momen Pruitt was said never to have lost a case, even if he had to fabricate an alibi to do it. But neither Pruitt nor an insanity defense could save Hyde from the claims of a purported accomplice who testified that Hyde had asked him to kidnap and kill his boss, nor the damning fact that Hyde had been caught in a trap set by police outside of Collins's home. The county attorney asked the jury to "send this man to prison for life and then to hell and damnation on top of it."[30]

At his trial in 1930, Hyde was gaunt, recovering from what was called a nervous breakdown, and yet still proud that his family, his mother and wife and children, had stood by him. Released early in March 1932, only two years after he arrived at McAlester on a fifteen-year sentence, Hyde was back at McAlester before the month was out. He served five months for forgery and was released again. In 1933, he graduated to bank robbery; with Coda McHone, he held up the First State Bank at gunpoint for the sum of $350. At first, Hyde claimed that the "cause of his downfall," as the prison forms asked, was "bad company"; by the second conviction, it was "prejudice"; and finally, that third time, in 1933, it was the "destitution" of his family.[31]

No. 18051, Ralph Bainum (who later became known to local

* Collins was the brother-in-law of Ernest Marland, soon to be governor of Oklahoma.

newspaper readers as Bob King), was in for life, charged with murder. The casual observer could tell that Bainum was well educated; the *Tulsa Daily World* said that "Somewhere, sometime, King [had gone] to school. He must have gone to college. His very bearing indicates superiority of mind . . ." It was clear that, once upon a time, he had led a different existence. He had left a wife in Vicksburg, Mississippi, and a family in St. Louis. Bainum's jailer would dub his parents "aristocrats." The paper said that his father held a "very responsible position with the engineering department of the Missouri Pacific Railway company." It wasn't the first time that the father had been faced with his son's misdeeds. By the time he reached McAlester, Bainum had already served another sentence in Kansas's Lansing prison; the newspapers said that Bainum had a "criminal record," and had been brought to Oklahoma from Missouri, where he had been arrested on a bank-robbery charge.[32]

At his trial in 1927, he would claim that it was all a case of mistaken identity: that he had not been the shooter, that he had been somewhere else when C. E. Ryan, the guard at a warehouse in Okemah, died. Old man Burch, a bootlegger, had identified Bainum as a member of a gang with two more famous bandits, Chester Purdy and "Grandpa" Harrison (so-called because the twenty-two-year-old had the hardened face of a fifty-year-old). But Bainum would proclaim his innocence throughout the trial and on appeal: he had an alibi, he was in Tulsa having dinner when they said he was in Okemah. Bainum would insist that he had been railroaded by a prosecutor who convicted him after telling the jury that the guard had been "killed by the slick-haired, cane-sucking dudes from the city."[33]

Finally, there was No. 10072, J. J. Kelly, the oldest of the prisoners' committee. He was over fifty and had been in McAlester for close to a decade. Kelly was said to be a master thief, to have stolen two hundred cars all across the Midwest. He had first come to McAlester in 1919, at the age of thirty-nine, after having served sentences in Denver and Kansas City. By the time he was convicted in Oklahoma, Kelly had to tell his wife, Alma, that when he returned to Kansas City from McAlester he would be almost sixty years old. Kelly escaped from McAlester in 1923, only to be "returned" in

1929. Kelly was a Catholic, one of the few in McAlester, and he had spent sixteen years in school. He told prison authorities that, like Hyde, he had trained to be a lawyer.[34]

———•———

Hyde, Bainum, and Kelly knew that Warden Brown could no longer shield the prison from sterilization. Since the first law in 1931, Brown had repeatedly told the press that if Oklahoma tried to sterilize McAlester inmates, there would be violence at the prison, riots or worse. But by the spring of 1934, as fear of crime reached fever pitch, Governor Murray and his board had announced their firm intention to proceed with sterilization at the prison. Under pressure from the Board of Affairs, Warden Brown named George Winkler as a test case under Oklahoma's 1933 sterilization law. A guardian was appointed for Winkler, a local lawyer named Hulsey. But this arrangement was unlikely to satisfy the men of McAlester. After all, the court-appointed guardian in the *Main* case, Cloyd, had failed in the Oklahoma Supreme Court (he had filed a five-page brief, citing no cases, what would amount to legal malpractice today), and the newspapers had reported that Cloyd had registered no objections for the first women sterilized at the Norman asylum. If Warden Brown wanted to avoid violence, one thing he could do was to help the prisoners hire a lawyer who would fight the law.[35]

There is no official record of what happened that day in May, when the lawyers Briggs and Lester first met the prisoners Hyde, Bainum, and Kelly in Warden Brown's office. We will never know what Brown said about the threatened violence, or whether Briggs and Lester were impressed by the ex-lawyer Hyde or the apparently educated Bainum and Kelly (the three would soon be dubbed by the newspapers the "brain trust," a reference to Roosevelt's brainy New Deal advisors). Briggs would later tell a court that, at that first meeting, he warned the prisoners' committee that they had one major problem. This was not a criminal case, where the prisoners might have petitioned to have the state pay the court costs; the sterilization law had been dubbed a civil matter by the legislature. Even if Briggs and Lester volunteered to waive their own fees, there were still court costs and expenses, not to mention the costs of experts. Briggs told the prisoners that, to fight the law, they needed the "sinews of war"—money. The papers said the prisoners had saved "nickels, dimes and pennies," but it amounted to no more than a "few hundred dollars." At the end of the meeting, Briggs and Lester agreed to represent Winkler and the prisoners' committee in the administrative proceeding before the Board of Affairs, just a few months away in August. Left open was the question of how the prisoners would obtain the "sinews of war" for a full-scale legal attack.[36]

CHAPTER 3

Thoroughbreds

Let us but extend our vision from immediate suffering to the prospective suffering of the countless unborn descendants of our present unfit and ask ourselves the question, why should they be born? Havelock Ellis well says, "The superficially sympathetic man flings a coin to the beggar; the more deeply sympathetic man builds an almshouse for him so that he need no longer beg; but perhaps the most sympathetic of all is the man who arranges that the beggar shall not be born."

—*Michael Guyer, zoologist, 1927*[1]

Drought and dust topped the news on Friday, May 11, 1934. The *Tulsa Daily World* reported that "thousands of tons of top soil, pulverized by the intense heat" had been carried away in gales blowing eastward. Dense powder "clouded the skies like fog" in Tulsa, obscuring the sun and grounding an airliner. It was estimated that 12 million pounds of dust had been deposited on "loop desks and residential rugs" in Chicago—"four pounds each for every man, woman and child in the city." By the 12th, the dust was a thousand miles east, settling on New York and Boston and Washington.[2]

Preoccupation with dust and Dillinger might have distracted the press from the proceedings at McAlester prison on Friday, May 11, 1934. Yet the sight was unusual: a group of blue-jeaned prisoners were carrying signs saying "Save Your Manhood" and "Contribute here to the Sterilization Campaign." The next day, the picture in the *Oklahoma News* revealed some convicts seated, tired by the May sun, others standing, looking fierce but weary. The prisoners had improvised a cashier's cage under the sign "Keep Your Manhood," where a clerk-prisoner made out receipts for contributions. The men of McAlester were trying to raise money to fund a lawsuit against the sterilization law.[3]

Next to the canteen, Warden Brown posted a telegram from Clarence Darrow. At the time, Darrow was the most famous lawyer in the country, thanks not only to the Scopes Monkey Trial and his defense of evolution against the Bible-thumping William Jennings Bryan, but also to the murder trial of Leopold and Loeb, brilliant and wealthy Chicago teenagers who had kidnapped and killed a young boy, Bobbie Franks, apparently just for fun. To the prisoners of McAlester, however, Darrow was more: he was the most famous non-Catholic opponent of sterilization in America. In articles in *American Mercury* in the mid-1920s, Darrow had written that eugenics was "senseless and impudent," a "gaudy little plan for saving civilization" by imposing a "caste system."[4]

In his telegram to McAlester prison, Darrow politely declined to represent the prisoners, pleading the press of other business (he was busy in Washington investigating Roosevelt's pet project, the National Recovery Act). But he cabled his "full sympathy" with the prisoners' cause. The *Oklahoma News* reporter attending the protest wanted to know what the men thought of the reply; he asked the most famous inmate in the prison, the handsome boy-desperado bank robber Matt Kimes. Kimes reportedly said: "It does a man a world of good to know there is still somebody in this country who measures up to the size of a man from every possible angle, doesn't it?" Darrow was "a thoroughbred from the middle, both ways."[5]

Consciously or unconsciously, the prisoners were playing with their opponents' analogies: eugenicists were particularly fond of the comparison of man to horse. By the 1930s, the metaphor was almost a cliché. Margaret Sanger dedicated her *Birth Control Review* to "a race of thoroughbreds," and Charles Davenport hoped that "human matings could be placed upon the same high plane as that of horse breeding." One college sociology text opened its discussion of eugenics with the racing form: "Man-of-War was one of the greatest race horses of all time . . . and his son, War Admiral, was [an] outstanding racer . . . Artificial selection and breeding can produce amazing results." Harry Laughlin, a tireless promoter of model sterilization laws, spent his spare time publishing articles in scientific journals claiming to have found the secrets of the thoroughbred racehorse. It was, after all, a simple premise: if one could breed a more docile horse or cow, why not a gentler person? As Alfalfa Bill colorfully put it: "Any breeder of stock will agree that if he have a herd of fine, pure blooded white-face or shorthorn or Galloway, or any other breed of stock whether it be bovine or sheep or horses; if he continue to let into that herd scrub stock, very soon there will be no pure bloods at all. Just so with peoples and nations."[6]

The breeding metaphor had a lofty pedigree. Charles Darwin had written that "hardly any one is so ignorant as to allow his worst animals to breed." Herbert Spencer put it with characteristic starkness: "The first requirement for being a great nation is to be a nation of good animals." Francis Galton, the founder of eugenics, insisted, after Darwin, that man was no longer a fallen angel but a recently-risen ape. Some, like Darwin's son Leonard, a dedicated eugenicist, saw hope in this idea, urging that evolution showed the ape's "upward march" toward humanity. Others feared the potential for regression. Regression meant atavism, animal origins, a fall from grace and progress, a reversion to the hell of uncivilized and primitive society: the ape man.[7]

It was the logic of breeding to which the apostles of eugenics turned in the 1920s to spread the ideals of eugenics. In rural America, there was no better place to do that than at the state fair. There were "Fitter Family Contests," from Massachusetts to Michigan, listing humans between the pets and the milk goats. Right across the border from Oklahoma, the Kansas Free Fair erected a permanent Eugenics Pavilion. Families were judged by a team of "[m]edical, psychological, and biological" experts. Winners received medals and were paraded before the grandstands in cars. Enthusiasts like Albert Wiggam told readers of national magazines how the entire family, including "the boys and girls," was delighted and excited by these contests:

> They enter with the utmost seriousness into the entire program of being measured and weighed and tested mentally and physically in order to find out if they cannot win one of the Fitter Families medals. The teeth and tonsils, the digestion, lungs, kidneys, heart, circulation, bodily structure and mental traits, as well as the family Bible and all the records of the family, are examined with equal interest in order to discover just what the family has amounted to in the past and also what is the present mental and physical status of every member and how fit the younger members are to hand on the family heritage.[8]

If the winners inspired pride, the losers inspired fear and contempt. Displays reminded fairgoers of the cost of the feebleminded, the defective, the insane, and the criminal. In one exhibit, lights flashed every 7.5 minutes for the birth of a "high grade" person, but every 15 seconds for a person of bad heredity who cost the nation $100. Even more sensational was the sign reporting, "This light flashes every second. Every second, crime costs America $100,000." One woman reported how "wonderful" it was to "learn how these traits of feeblemindedness, epilepsy, and the like, came into my family." She had thought her brother's child was epileptic because he had bumped his head, and that her daughter had a "feeble-minded child" because of an accident before the child was born; now she was relieved to learn that it was a matter of heredity. She told the attendant at the exhibit that she wanted to "bring all of [her] family in for an examination." The attendant replied that a family with "so many defects" could not compete.[9]

If Warden Brown knew as much as the average reader of the *Tulsa Daily World* knew about McAlester prison, he knew that more than having children was at stake in sterilization. It was the meaning of sterilization: the men were being told that their blood was so impure that, as eugenicists would put it, "they [should] never [have] been born."[10] As their protest signs explained, the prisoners feared for their manhood. Would sterilization relegate them to the humiliating status of the "punks"—the prisoners they called "girls"? Not everyone was to be sterilized, after all; only the "habituals"—the ones who had been there more often—the ones more likely than not to be on the top, rather than the bottom, of the status heap.

Inside McAlester, it was sex and force and humiliation that determined status. The veterans, the strong, would sniff out the newcomers for weakness when they first came to McAlester: "The old timers," wrote an inmate, would "spot the[ ] young kids the minute they hit the Rotunda," bidding on them to serve as "girl friends." Forced sex meant not only the indignity of rape but permanent lesser status as "punks" and "sissies." There were rigid rules in the prison for the "girlfriends": separate water barrels, separate tables. A "girl" convict who forgot his place could find himself beaten or even killed, simply for drinking out of the "boys'" water barrel.[11]

As if to make the picture appear as hellish as possible, Walter Biscup, an eager young reporter for the *Tulsa Daily World*, wrote openly about sex slavery and violent death at McAlester. In a grisly tabloid portrait, he offered a shocking portrayal of "savagery":

> The new and the young inmates are known as "fish." Because of overcrowded conditions they are quartered in cells with six or seven other convicts who are considered old-timers. The "fish" is considered fair prey for them. One man in the cell, by reason of his leadership, acquires the "fish" who then becomes known in prison parlance as a "punk." As the consort of his so-called protector the "punk" finds himself a slave in every sense of the word.

It was this kind of perversion, Biscup explained, that was responsible for much violence in the prison. Coveting another's "punk" was a source of "[c]ountless fights and stabbings."[12]

These relationships were horrifying not because they involved, in many cases, coerced sex, but because same-sex sexuality was considered monstrous and bestial. In a day and age when many citizens, robbed of their jobs and angry at life, came to identify with the notorious bandits of the day—the Dillingers and Baby Face Nelsons—there grew up not only a standard romance of the public enemy but also a routine public condemnation of criminals. When journalists sought to unmake the gangster, to deprive him of his tough-guy image, they made him effeminate, given to caring about fine clothing and jewelry and inclined to like men more than women. When they wanted to explain inexplicable rage, they posited sexual humiliation. Clyde Barrow was characterized as a sissy, a little man who had been "punked" in prison and was venting his rage for this humiliation in a shooting spree across the western United States. At the time, "[e]ffeminacy was a kind of treason, for it meant that a man had betrayed his true nature, an act as contemptible and dangerous as that of a citizen who betrayed his country." No wonder the guards at the Oklahoma reformatory punished inmates by forcing them to display themselves wearing pink panties and dresses.[13]

Sterilization laws had always been written not only with heredity but also with sex in mind. More than a few laws imposed sterilization for rape and "perversion."[14] In some cases, this was a reference to pedophilia. But it also had a different meaning: homosexuality. In the 1929 case of Esau Walton, which reached the Utah Supreme Court, the claim for sterilization was based on the argument that Walton had committed sodomy and "acted lovingly towards other boys."[15] In Walton's case, there was clearly no procreation going on. But eugenics was never only about procreation.

Sex drew the line between races, and excessive sexual appetite was one of the great myths of racism. Historically, the sexual appetites of African-Americans, the Irish, the Chinese, and Italians have been used to mark the line between the savage and the civilized and thus to brand lesser races. E. A. Ross, the nativist sociologist and eugenicist, wrote in 1914 of the Jew's penchant for cross-racial "perversion," where perversion meant lust for Gentiles. Sterilization was sometimes dubbed "legal lynching"—not because its victims were primarily black, but because lynching and sterilization shared a focus on sexual danger. The lynched were often castrated, an injury-in-kind aimed at the source of the victim's alleged sexual power, just as sterilization was aimed at the sexual dangers of the feebleminded and unfit. As one lawyer explained at the time, "the general public knows of only one method of sterilizing males, castration, and knows of it primarily as a bestial preliminary to lynching."[16]

Eugenics preoccupied itself with sex, sliding between the sex that makes babies (procreation), the sex that makes populations (race), and the sex that brands one a cultural degenerate and social inferior. It was the latter which marked many for sterilization.[17] Almost three-quarters of the women sterilized in the California program, the country's largest by far, were labeled sexual deviates or prostitutes. The diagnosis was invariably "feeblemindedness." Even in 1936, one could find genetics texts confidently declaring that "the feeble-minded girl is characteristically prone to loose sexual relationships."[18] It was a circular, self-reinforcing mindset: apparent sexual immorality brought people like Carrie Buck and Esau Walton to the authorities' attention; that behavior was then, quite literally, ascribed to their blood, and then once there, circled back to confirm the diagnosis of weak mind. To realize that, however, is to raise the disturbing possibility that eugenics was capable of transforming rape into the genetic failures of its victims, not only for Carrie Buck but, no doubt, for young men in McAlester prison as well.

Clearly, sex had its social side: when the men of McAlester raised their placards asking to save their manhood, they were referring both to their status inside the prison and to marriage and family outside the prison. Sterile men were men whose marriages could be annulled by religion and terminated by law; sterilization meant that a man could lose his family. Would the prisoners' wives and girlfriends remain faithful if they would never have children? Could the prisoners ever be considered "normal" if they never had a son or daughter? As one prisoner's mother put it, sterilization could "ruin" a man for life. She meant that her son would no longer be a man, socially if not physically. As the great student of slavery Orlando Patterson has explained, it is not property that divides slaves from free men, but social death, and one of the great agents of social death is "natal alienation"—the deliberate taking away of the possibility of being a parent or having a child of one's own, the forced imposition of genealogical and familial isolation.[19]

———◆———

At first blush, the protest yielded hope of a strong ally. On May 13, 1934, Mrs. Lucille Milner, secretary of the American Civil Liberties Union in New York, read in the *New York Telegram* that McAlester prisoner George Winkler, whom the paper dubbed a "law student" and printer, had volunteered to test Oklahoma's sterilization law. Mrs. Milner wrote to Winkler, explaining that the ACLU was interested in "following the case" and asking whether Winkler was represented by a lawyer. A week later, Winkler replied that the law firm of Lester and Briggs had offered to "defend [his] rights" all the way to the United States Supreme Court, if necessary; that the prisoners had raised approximately $150 but the case would cost approximately $1,500 to pursue all appeals. Briggs had told the prisoners' committee that "he would not hold these monetary requirements positively obligatory," but Winkler explained that any financial help from the ACLU would be more than welcome, closing with "hearty and sincere thanks" for the Union's interest in the case.[20]

Elsewhere, the protest was not nearly so successful. In Oklahoma, some papers refused even to report the demonstration. There had always been the aroma of obscenity about sterilization talk; it was something editors tried to avoid, lest readers be offended.[21] Edith Johnson, one of Oklahoma's most influential columnists (the one who opined that Alfalfa Bill's pants were too short), thought the prisoners' protest a "disgrace to this commonwealth." There was no need to air the state's dirty laundry. A prison is "no place," she wrote, for organizing a movement to defeat the "laws of the state." Why a strong man governor would permit such a thing, she insisted, was beyond her. Johnson went on to praise Mrs. Roosevelt for refusing to support the prisoners: one McAlester prisoner had had his mother write, mother to mother, to the First Lady, imploring her to stop the state from sterilizing her son, and Mrs. Roosevelt was said to have replied, on the advice of legal authorities, that there was nothing that the federal government could do about Oklahoma's law. Goading Murray the Roosevelt-hater to follow suit, Johnson expressed outrage: "Why a mother whose son, a repeater in prison, would be eager for him to have issue with the possibility of the criminal strain reappearing is a mystery." After Johnson's column, there would be no more protest at McAlester prison. One prisoner penned a poem that would be referred to the Attorney General's office as evidence of a threat: "Page Edith," it began, and ended with a promise to take a scalpel to all those who would take from him his manhood.[22]

CHAPTER 4

Heat and Love

Oh, you who wish to confiscate
*   My powers of reproduction—*
And wish to trifle with my fate
*   Without the least compunction:*
I'd like to tell you, here and now
*   To where I'd relegate you,*

Why I denounce you filthy quacks;
*   Is not for my elation,*
But just a third time loser's hope
*   Lived in imagination—*
I'd like to think that some near date
*   Will satisfy my craving*
To get my hands upon you fiends
*   Who started all this raving*
                    —Anon. prisoner, McAlester prison, approx. 1934[1]

It was hot—very hot—the day that Claud Briggs and Fay Lester returned to McAlester for the sterilization trial of George Winkler. It was the kind of heat that parched the throat and made one weak from effort. By the end of the summer, drought had seared twenty-four states and 26 million people. In the summer of 1934, Oklahoma had, literally, never been hotter. As July dipped into August, complete strangers gathered to pray for rain. Letters to the editor fantasized about crazy recovery schemes, imagining the army hoisting giant hoses up into airplanes to sprinkle water on the dried earth and insisting that, in Texas, they were planning to bomb the clouds. Some blamed everything from God to the government. The newspapermen feared that they had used up their best phrases to describe the heat of "fiery furnace[s]" and "blazing rainless[ness]," and "hadean" days.[2]

On the day of Winkler's hearing, July 30, 1934, the temperature in Beaver, Oklahoma, hit 110 degrees; in Oklahoma City, it was a bit cooler, a mere 106. The Board of Affairs arrived early in the morning at McAlester prison. With awkward melodrama, reporters warned that the prison "grapevine" was throbbing with the "stealthy news" of the hearing, and that the "big house" was "fretful." The newspapers reported that Winkler's hearing "was the chief topic of conversation in the prison yards, factories and out on the expansive farms," and that the convicts had prepared to wage battle "[f]or months." They also said that the warden was apprehensive that hundreds of "repeaters" were waiting "grim[ly]" for the news, the picture of a "surgeon hovering over the prison with a scalpel . . . stamped . . . indelibly on the[ir] minds."[3]

There were twenty people packed into the warden's office to hear the case of George Winkler. Despite the heat, Winkler sat calmly in "civilian garb," nonchalantly dragging on his cigarette. Winkler was balding but still handsome, with a quiet, almost bookish, appearance. Across from Winkler was the Board of Affairs, led by its chairman, W. C. Hughes, a dignified man with steel-gray temples and the solid air of the lawyer and businessman. (Hughes's principal qualification for this job, the press reported, was that he had served at the Oklahoma constitutional convention with Governor Murray.) Next to Hughes was another friend of the governor's, Hugh Askew, slightly younger, dark-haired, but equally solid, businesslike. And, then there was the Republican member of the Board, Cash Cade, a silver-mustachioed man who looked the part of the western rancher. Warden Brown sat at his desk, waiting. Across from the Board of Affairs were the prisoners' lawyers, the lanky, wavy-haired, forty-something Briggs and his older, more distinguished-looking partner, Lester, along with W. J. Hulsey, the prisoners' official guardian (as required by the sterilization law), all of whom, for the price of the travel to McAlester and little more, had agreed to appear on behalf of Winkler. Seated next to them at the counsel table was the "brain trust": prisoners Hyde, Bainum, and Kelly. Across from them was the state's attorney, Jesse Ballard.[4]

If the "brain trust" expected legal pyrotechnics from Briggs and Lester, they were soon disappointed. One might have thought that Lester, a former supreme court justice, would have taken the lead in the case because of his greater prestige, but it was Briggs who stood to open Winkler's case. He made no lengthy speeches; he simply made a motion to dismiss the case. Asked by the Board whether he wanted to argue the matter, Briggs declined, preferring simply to list the claims. There were no jurors to convince, only the men of the Board of Affairs, who were not lawyers. Briggs knew that a list was sufficient for now, before the real show, the appeal to the district court that would in all likelihood follow the Board's hearing. It was, after all, very hot.

Winkler smoked calmly as Briggs read the reasons why the case should not proceed. Reporters scribbled the legal phrases quickly: cruel and unusual punishment, double jeopardy, ex post facto. As he listed them, however, Briggs had to suspect that all these claims were not enough. Before the decision in *Buck*, some courts had ruled that sterilization was "cruel and unusual" punishment. And Governor Murray had spoken as if the new law would deter crime; it would keep "foreign" criminals out of Oklahoma by frightening them. Yet the most important court, the court whose holdings would control this case, the Oklahoma Supreme Court, had just held, in the *Main* case, that sterilization was not a punishment. Sterilization was a eugenic remedy, one aimed at the health of the community. And yet, all the constitutional claims that Briggs had listed depended upon the idea that sterilization was what the law called "punishment."[5]

At the end of his list, Briggs shifted tack, making a final objection: he called the sterilization law "class legislation," a term then associated with constitutional equality claims.[6] To say that Oklahoma's sterilization law was class legislation was to say that the prisoners were being picked as easy targets, singled out for a special burden. There was common sense to this claim: the prisoners would persistently ask why the law did not apply beyond the guard towers or the asylum walls, to the purported millions who carried the genes of the defective and degenerate. If the eugenicists were right that there were millions who suffered from weak minds, why not sterilize them all?

Briggs left that argument to last for good reason. In *Buck v. Bell*, Justice Holmes had mocked the inequality argument. There were good reasons for Holmes's disdain; his theory was that courts should generally defer to legislatures on matters of health and safety and economy. Holmes and his Supreme Court brethren, from the turn of the century, had heard hundreds of cases in which railroads and mines and restaurants had argued that taxes and regulations violated the due process and equal protection clauses of the Constitution.[7] Like his colleagues Brandeis and Cardozo, Holmes believed that businesses were simply trying to avoid regulation and the will of the majority. From this perspective, *Buck v. Bell* was a progressive decision, in line with a variety of others in which Holmes and Brandeis would lead the charge by urging deference to popular majorities. This boded ill for the prisoners' case; it made their equality argument an exceedingly uphill battle, for it meant they would have to battle those, like Holmes, who might have, under other circumstances, been their allies: the liberals, the labor-men.

Briggs did not even mention liberty or the right to have children—the terms lawyers might use today. Not a single state Supreme Court case, before or after *Buck v. Bell*, had relied upon an unadorned claim that citizens had the liberty or the right to have children. As the Kansas Supreme Court explained in 1929: "Procreation of defective and feeble-minded children with criminal tendencies does not advantage, but patently disadvantages the race. . . . The race may insure its own perpetuation and such progeny may be prevented in the interest of the higher general welfare." The situation in Oklahoma was no different. Main's lawyer, Cloyd, in his exceedingly short brief, had tried such an argument in the Oklahoma Supreme Court—and he had failed, miserably. Today, we think of individual rights as trumping the needs of the common welfare, but then the law was different. As Chief Justice Fletcher Riley, a moderate Republican leading the Oklahoma Supreme Court, had put it in the *Main* case: "[A]ssuming that the right to beget children is a natural and constitutional right . . . this right cannot be extended beyond the common welfare."[8]

If the meaning of "right" was far different from what it is today, so too was the meaning of "liberty." When Briggs stood in the warden's office at McAlester in 1934, liberty did not mean, as it does for many constitutional lawyers today, a general claim of autonomy and human freedom. In legal circles of the day, liberty had a far different set of political and social connotations; it carried the smell of Hoover and the railroads and the wealthy, anti-labor crowd. When courts invoked liberty, they were more likely to be talking about the liberty to contract and the right to property, not the liberty of the dispossessed or the rights of the criminal. After all, it was a day in which the term "liberty" was invoked to argue in favor of child labor, on the theory that prohibiting it would interfere with an employer's liberty. The Liberty League opposed Roosevelt's New Deal on the theory that it suppressed the individual liberty of employers, and the American Bar Association was full of Liberty Leaguers whose livelihood depended upon representing corporations' liberty. Liberty had been invoked in other causes, for example, when in 1932 the Supreme Court had given a "respite from death" to seven black boys in the then infamous Scottsboro, Alabama, rape trials. But that was the exception that proved the rule.[9]

The legal arguments were over almost as soon as Briggs finished his list. "Overruled," said W. C. Hughes, chairman of the Board of Affairs. Briggs sat down. When one has no defense at law, one's only choice is to put the other party to its proof. And that is what Briggs did. He and the "brain trust" left it to the state of Oklahoma to prove its sterilization case against twenty-nine-year-old George Winkler.

———◆———

Jesse Ballard, the state's attorney, called his first witness, the prison's Bertillon man. A lost art today, the Bertillon method had been the rage at the end of the nineteenth century. Alphonse Bertillon, a sickly and pale young Frenchman, had become obsessed, in the 1880s, with the precise identification of criminals, and had developed a system for very exact physical measurements, in the belief that precise physical characteristics might hold the secret to the causes of criminality. The Bertillon method spread to the United States, but, over time, lost its focus on physical attributes and became instead a device to maintain records, to identify repeaters.[10]

Oddly enough, the Bertillon man would become the key to the state of Oklahoma's case—although the prisoners did not yet know it. To the "brain trust," and to the reporters, it may have seemed as if the lawyers were making much ado about nothing. After all, Winkler *was* a repeater. He had served time in McAlester twice before— once for eight months for an unarmed burglary committed in 1923, and again for twenty-six months for a $100 fraud. And, as the Bertillon man testified, Winkler was at the time of the hearing serving a sentence of two and a half years for burglary. Along with two rings, only one of any value, Winkler had stolen "canned goods, one pair of man's socks, one pair of ladies gloves, [and] two razors."[11]

Ballard would finish his case before lunch. He quickly called three expert witnesses, all doctors, all of whom explained that the vasectomy would not harm Winkler. On cross-examination, Briggs and Lester poked holes in the doctors' testimony: Dr. Griffin, head of the Norman asylum, had never performed a vasectomy operation; Dr. Steen had only performed two and admitted that he was not an expert in the field; Dr. Munn, the prison physician, had never performed the operation and confessed that his knowledge of the effects on prisoners extended to a single McAlester prisoner who turned out to be an epileptic (a condition that, for many, made him a far more credible candidate for sterilization than the general prison population). During cross-examination, the prisoners themselves asked Briggs to inquire specifically about compulsory sterilization. At the end of his questioning of Dr. Griffin, Briggs inquired, "One of the members of the [prisoners'] committee asked me to ask you if, in your research, you know of any psychological reaction from the operation." Griffin denied that the operation would have any ill effect; Briggs pressed him, asking how this could be true if the operation were compelled. Griffin again denied that there would be any permanent ill effect.[12]

Then, something unexpected happened. After the three doctors had been examined and cross-examined, the state rested its case, which meant that it intended to call no further witnesses. For a moment, the prisoners' lawyers may have thought that the state had blundered. Ballard had presented evidence about the safety of the operation and Winkler's criminal history—that was it. There was no testimony that Winkler was likely to pass on his "criminalistic" genes to his children; there was no testimony, as the law also appeared to require, that Winkler himself would become a "public charge." As Lester objected, "the mere fact he has been formerly convicted, in my judgment, doesn't touch side, head or bottom that he might become a public charge." Pressing the point, Lester continued, "If this man here was partially paralyzed, was blind or had deficiencies which might exist in some prisoners, then that might be . . . some evidence that he would become a public charge when he was released, but, if Your Honor please, I think clearly in this case there ought to be evidence of the fact . . . that when he is released he would become a public charge, and there is an entire absence here."[13]

The Board of Affairs was unperturbed, the chairman ruling that "the facts show, in the judgment of the Board, enough to justify a finding that this respondent is likely to become a partially public charge." Briggs objected, then Lester, then the official guardian, Hulsey, each in his own way, arguing that the Bertillon man's testimony could not possibly be enough to show that Winkler would become a public charge. Briggs and his team were stymied. If the Board accepted this proof, it would be quite easy to sterilize a vast number of prisoners, not simply the ones who were sick or epileptic or insane. If all that was required was the testimony of a doctor and the prisoner's record, the process could be perfunctory and bureaucratic, over for dozens of prisoners in a single day.[14]

Ballard would not budge from his assertion that the evidence was sufficient to sterilize, and began to raise technical objections to the legal motions Briggs was making to keep his clients' case alive. Reduced to sarcasm, the older and more experienced lawyer, Briggs, interrupted the young state's attorney: "I am getting a little law education here. I have been practicing so long, and I don't know very much, and I am learning something. . . . I didn't know we would have a technical barrage here." Finally, Briggs asked that the Board allow the prisoners time to put on an expert on the question of whether Winkler would become a public charge. Ballard just as strenuously insisted that the question was one of law, not fact, and only required proof of three prior convictions; from that, one could infer that Winkler was feebleminded or inherently "criminalistic" and thus would land back in jail or an asylum again. The Board of Affairs refused Briggs's request for delay to put on more evidence. The hearing was over. In the early afternoon, the Board ordered George Winkler sterilized. At Briggs's request, the order was stayed pending appeal to the district court. Now all the prisoners could do was wait.[15]

———————

The next day, the major headlines in Muskogee and Tulsa were not of Winkler's hearing. What did appear in two-inch type was a different, if seemingly familiar, tale. The *Muskogee Daily Phoenix* read, "Officer and Convict Near Death After Bloody Gun Fight in City." A police officer had died at the hands of a criminal; the convict and another officer lay wounded in the hospital. Charles Martin, a convicted Tulsa con man, had been allowed to leave McAlester prison Friday afternoon to visit his lawyer, Pres Lester, Judge Lester's brother and a close friend of Governor Murray's. Before he left the prison, the warden gave Martin permission to withdraw $125 from his prison account. Martin was accompanied out of the prison and into town by the prison's executioner, Rich Owen. There was nothing terribly unusual about this; prisoners were often accorded short day privileges for special reasons, deaths in the family and the like. Owen waited outside as Martin talked to Lester, which did not take long.[16]

As Owen and Martin turned the corner from Lester's office, they ran into an attractive dark-haired woman whom Martin introduced as his wife; she said she was ill, about to faint. It was very hot. Owen and Martin helped the woman to a drugstore, where she ordered a drink. Prisoner Martin asked to use the restroom and slipped out the back, called a taxi, and, jamming a piece of iron pipe into the driver's ribs, demanded to be driven out of town. In Muskogee, two officers on the beat pulled the taxi over in a residential neighborhood. Officer Billy Guy guarded Martin while officer Hensley moved the police car to allow another vehicle to pass in the narrow street. Martin attacked Guy and grabbed his gun; Hensley came running. Martin opened fire and Hensley returned it. All three fell; only Guy would survive.[17]

The eastern half of Oklahoma was incensed. The Tulsa county attorney threatened to indict the guard Owen and Warden Brown as accessories to murder. Local editorialists expressed outrage: "How many murders, how many bank robberies, how many slain policemen," must be tolerated? The people were practicing a "deadly leniency" with crime; they were too ready to believe that all the criminals were like Baby Face Nelson and Dillinger, celebrities and heroes and bandits, robbing the rich to pay the poor. A funeral procession for Officer Hensley wound its way through downtown Muskogee, 1500 people long.[18]

Two days after the shooting, another explanation surfaced. An eyewitness reported that, as Martin lay dying, the "outlaw" gave him his wife's telephone number in Tulsa and asked the stranger to tell her that he "did it for her. I love her." The last paragraph of a lengthy story in the *Muskogee Daily Phoenix* on August 1 revealed that "[p]rison officials said" that Martin "was worried about the eugenics program at the penitentiary and escaped at the hour that the first sterilization was ordered." Martin had gone to see his lawyer to try to buy a pardon for his third offense, so that he would not be sterilized as a habitual offender.[19]

Within the week, Briggs began preparing for an appeal to the district court; he wrote to the American Civil Liberties Union in New York, asking whether they would be willing to arrange to take depositions (out-of-court testimony given under oath) of expert witnesses to "break down" the state's theory of criminal inheritance. Neither Briggs nor the prisoners' committee had heard from the

ACLU since May. A legal opinion prepared by the New York lawyer
Herbert Jacobi at the behest of the ACLU's secretary, Lucille Milner, had voiced doubts about the prisoners' claims, refusing to reach
a constitutional conclusion, and suggesting that *Buck v. Bell* would
likely carry the day. Some within the ACLU who sympathized with
the prisoners' cause worried about the punitive intent of the law.
Later, ACLU memoranda would argue that sterilization could be
used as a means of "class or racial control," using the Nazi program
as a reminder of how far such laws might go, including non-Aryan
racial discrimination.[20]

In the summer of 1934, however, others disagreed. Arthur Garfield Hays, a powerful force on the ACLU's board, was known for
his legal acumen and his relentless style, not to mention his fame
for defending the dispossessed—from death row immigrants like
Sacco and Vanzetti, to the teacher in the Scopes evolution battle,
to an African-American doctor accused of murder (Dr. Sweet had
moved into a white Detroit neighborhood in the mid-1920s and was
greeted by what Hays's co-counsel Clarence Darrow would call a
"Nordic" mob.) In July, Hays had expressed significant doubts about
the prisoners' case: he was skeptical of the "punishment" argument
and rejected the claim that crime was different from mental inability, stating that "some people" think criminality is "inheritable."
Hays concluded that the ACLU would be "making a mistake to get
into what might be regarded by a great many as an alien field."[21]

On August 14, 1934, the ACLU officially declined to provide
financial aid or to participate as counsel in Winkler's case. The letter to Briggs explained that a majority of the board had concluded
that cases involving "freedom of speech and assemblage" were more
pressing. Ultimately, those within the ACLU who opposed sterilization would write a pamphlet declaring sterilization "cruel and
unusual punishment" and lobby against Oklahoma's sterilization
laws, but it was clear by the end of August 1934 that Briggs and
the prisoners would have to seek the "sinews of war" for their legal
battle elsewhere.[22]

CHAPTER 5

White Trash

The sentiment of caste or aristocracy in some form is well-nigh universal in mankind. . . . Among criminals the professional house-breaker feels himself to be of higher caste than the snake-thief, and in turn is surpassed by the bank burglar. Even in the insane asylum the feeling is rampant. With such a wide-spread tendency for a foundation the creation of a sentiment of eugenic aristocracy is by no means a visionary undertaking.
—Michael Guyer, zoologist, 1927[1]

In the fall of 1934, the prisoners returned to the press. But this time, unlike the angry May protest, they wore the calm mantle of the expert. On September 23, 1934, the feature page of the *Tulsa Daily World* announced in bold terms, "A 'Life Termer' Denounces Sterilization," by "Convict No. 18051." The author began: never "in the history of a penal law, has there been as much interest taken by prisoners in an act of the legislature." The men of McAlester had saved every paper or book they could find on sterilization from "textbooks on physiology, psychology and glandular therapy." They had studied and passed them around until the books were "little more than limp, raglike ghosts." The convicts themselves had read "opinions of the true geneticists, the genuine scientists," and done their own research on the "merits, and demerits, of sterilization from a physiological and psychological standpoint."[2]

To dramatize the point, the author made a surprising open-

ing concession: yes, it was true, some people should be sterilized—
the "feeble-minded, epileptic, insane [and] idiotic." But not every
prisoner inside McAlester, Convict No. 18051 insisted, was feebleminded. The author pleaded for readers to untangle the idea of
the criminal from men of weak mind. "Two months ago the writer
of this article examined the 'chaplain's sheets,'" a written record
"made upon the prisoner's entry into confinement." And he had
found that, of all the third-termers—423 men, according to the
article—only one of their 252 children had been institutionalized.
"Would the advocates of sterilization," he asked, have eliminated
the lives of 251 boys and girls for the sake of preventing the birth
of "one defective child?"[3]

Convict No. 18051 pushed harder. How could the law be about
health, he asked, if it required no physical or psychiatric examination? Without such an examination, sterilization was simply a matter of politics, a matter of picking on a "class of men" rather than
addressing the individuals who really did inherit mental and physical
deficiencies. The Board of Affairs was "not familiar with the laws of
heredity, eugenics, medicine, or psychiatry," he wrote. They were
patronage hires, political men who would do what the governor told
them. In naming the Board of Affairs to administer the law, it was as
if the state had passed a law governing the "teaching of the arts and
sciences in the state universities, and then turned the prosecution of
the law over to the members of the street sweepers' union."[4]

The author went on: "There is a wide difference between the
third-termer, a man who has actually served three prison sentences," and the man who has three convictions; "it is possible
for a youth of 16 or more years to go out at night and steal three
chickens. When the boy is caught and brought into court he either
pleads guilty or is convicted on three separate counts of chicken
theft." The judge then sentences him to three concurrent sentences for a felony. Such "a boy or man is legally thrice convicted
of a felony and is just as much a subject for sterilization as the man
who has served 10 sentences in as many different prisons." A man
can "become a 'habitual criminal' in a crime career that may not
have lasted more than 15 minutes." Why, then, was the "number

of times a man had been convicted" a measure of "value in judging the man fit to become a father"?[5]

The article ended with the concession with which it began: "sterilization is entitled to a place in the social and governmental order . . . if it is limited to bringing about the sterilization of only those persons whom a scientific examination can prove unfit for reproduction." With this, Convict No. 18051 challenged the law's drafters and, in particular, its principal proponent, the state senator and doctor Louis Henry Ritzhaupt, to explain why the prisoners of McAlester should not believe this law "unscientific, uneugenic, unnatural, [and] un-American"? He asked that Dr. Ritzhaupt offer a "thorough, intelligent and scientific denial" to the prisoners' charges.[6]

In a special note, the editors explained that Convict No. 18051 was "Robert King." King was the alias used by Ralph Bainum, a member of the prisoners' "brain trust" and a man with a history of affecting disguises. At his murder trial in 1927, he grew a mustache, hoping to escape identification; when the state objected, the marshal, with the aid of five deputies, had it shaved off right in the courtroom on the claim that the "brush," as they called it, was an obstruction to justice. Throughout the sterilization controversy, Bainum would adopt a variety of identities: some reporters called him a psychologist; on prison forms, he called himself a salesman. The editors of the *Tulsa Daily World* noted for the reader that, even according to the doctors at Winkler's hearing, King was "probably as well versed on the science of sterilization as any person in the state."[7]

Readers might have wondered whether Bainum was really the author of this mini-treatise. The prose had a lawyerly air to it; there were unmistakable references to legal arguments ("cruel and additional punishment" and "class legislation"). There was a good deal in the article that would never appear in the legal papers filed in the case, a good deal that was angry and proud (calling the law "un-American," for example), and aimed at the average reader. There were moments in which the florid style of reporter Biscup's hand seemed evident, in the exaggerated metaphors ("raglike ghosts") and comparisons (the street-sweepers' union). There was also evidence, however—particularly the study of inheritance inside McAlester—that with no "sinews of war" the prisoners had, in effect, become their own experts.[8]

———◆———

Convict No. 18051's public appeal produced a temporary ally. Her name was Mrs. Mabel Bassett, and she was chairman of the Oklahoma Board of Charities and Corrections. When she wasn't tending to her three children or to her grandchildren or to the orphans she brought home, Mrs. Bassett was tending to charity. In July 1934, she won her primary with a wider margin than in any other race in Oklahoma. And that was no fluke; as the *New York Times* reported, "Twice in her previous three elections she led the State in total votes received." Largely sidelined by the Murray administration, Mrs. Bassett was about to come back to political life.[9]

Mrs. Bassett believed that the citizens of Oklahoma wouldn't brook cruelty, that they would "insist upon proper treatment of persons in jails and State institutions." Mrs. Bassett believed in this as fervently as had her better-known predecessor, the great Oklahoma progressive Kate Barnard. Barnard was a tough act to follow; she had rescued Oklahoma convicts from death and torture in the Kansas mines. Like Barnard, Mrs. Bassett was elected to take the side of the outcast, the lonely prisoner or mental patient. Governor Murray had no stomach for a busybody woman telling him what to do and so he refused to fund her department. At the end of 1934, Mrs. Bassett had great expectations that her friend Ernest Marland, philanthropist and candidate for governor in the upcoming election, would put Oklahoma on a new path.[10]

Three days after Bainum's feature appeared in the *Tulsa Daily World*, Mrs. Bassett told the press that, if there was to be sterilization in Oklahoma, it had to be done right—it should be regulated by a board of psychiatrists and experts, rather than by the Board of Affairs. The Board of Affairs was made up "entirely of political appointees, without medical knowledge." That is "obviously wrong," Mrs. Bassett told the press. Within two days, the chairman of the Board of Affairs, W. C. Hughes, announced that advocates would go back to the drawing board, that a new eugenics law would be drafted at the request of "several legislators and doctors at state institutions." Sterilization would continue in Oklahoma asylums, but the Board, at least for now, was willing to tread lightly when it came to McAlester, to leave the issue to the new governor and his men to sort out.[11]

———◆———

By the end of 1934, the people of Oklahoma had tired of their semi-dictator, Alfalfa Bill Murray. Fatigue and contempt spilled over to Murray's chosen successor for governor. Enraged that his hand-picked man lost the Democratic primary, Murray turned coat; his newspaper, the *Blue Valley Farmer*, praised the Republican nominee and railed against the Democratic candidate, Ernest Marland. This move gained more publicity than votes. On election day, Marland won easily—on the strength of his promise to bring the New Deal to Oklahoma. On inauguration day, Marland would doff his Rooseveltian high silk hat at the crowds that thronged the parade route—a symbol that Murray, with his bare ankles and rumpled suit, had been banished as unworthy of a New Deal Oklahoma.[12]

On January 8, 1935, the fifteenth Oklahoma legislature was about to convene. The chamber was full of reporters waiting for one last quotable quote, one last "Murrayism." As Murray gave his farewell speech, Claud Briggs sat on the dais behind the soon-to-be-former governor as the new president pro tempore of the Oklahoma Senate, his reward for supporting Marland. Briggs listened as Murray gave the press what they wanted; it was reported as far as New York that Alfalfa Bill was bashing Roosevelt's New Deal brain trusters as "brain busters" who were destroying the government. He heard, also, that Governor Murray was not done, yet, with the men of McAlester. By the end of the speech, it was clear that the prisoners' temporary victory was just that—temporary.[13]

Four years earlier, Murray had emphasized the importance of sterilization to stem the tide of criminality. But by the end of his tenure, Murray—the putative strong man—was at risk of leaving a legacy of weakness on crime. Just before the election, *Tulsa Daily World* reporter Biscup revealed that Murray had issued a massive number of pardons, approximately two thousand in all. One hundred felons "went free" every day of 1934, the headlines read. The front page of the *Tulsa Daily World* showed Murray, in cartoon caricature, opening the jailhouse door.[14]

In his farewell, Murray used sterilization to repair the damage to his political reputation. He explained, "Some seven months ago, an escaped convict went to Georgia; committed a crime, and plead guilty, stating to the Court that he wanted the highest penalty possible to avoid being carried back to Oklahoma where he would be sterilized." (This story was true.) Oklahoma's law had "caused the 'repeating' convict, the habitual criminal," to avoid Oklahoma. Sterilization, Murray urged, had not only frightened criminals out of the state, it promised to "give to society a citizenship of pure blood and strong, law-abiding minds." The army intelligence tests had shown that 25 to 50 percent of the population were "drones on society," people that "eat up the substance of the other citizens," making the difference "between living in ease and squalid poverty." Murray insisted that the new legislature pass another sterilization law. If this plan to prevent poverty and depression and crime was controversial, so be it; "let the ignorant rave at me," Murray dared.[15]

It was the past, rather than the future, that propelled Murray's argument. He punctuated his talk of sterilization with references to the decades-old stories of the Jukes and the Kallikaks (or the "Jutes and Killikuks," as he put it).[16] By the 1930s, the tale had acquired almost parable form, linking genetics to traditional Christian morality. During the American Revolution, young Martin Kallikak, who came from a good family, had "dallied with a feebleminded girl he met in a tavern." The result was an illegitimate son, Martin Kallikak, Jr. (dubbed "Old Horror" in the tale). Martin Sr. later married a respectable woman, and from this union came a "multitude of descendants who were valuable citizens." From the original illegitimate union, however, there was an appalling line of drunkenness, poverty, and sexual immorality—a harvest of feeblemindedness, crime, and disease. "What a pity," Murray exclaimed, "sterilization had not been in vogue at that first birth."[17]

The form of the family study could be traced back to Richard Dugdale's 1877 report to the New York legislature, "The Jukes: A Study in Crime, Pauperism, Disease, and Heredity." In the course of his research, Dugdale found a line of criminality that could be traced for generations; Jukes family members had been convicted of everything from cruelty to animals, to rape, to murder. Dugdale himself believed that environmental means could retard this tendency, but when his study was redone in 1915 all the emphasis shifted to the hereditary nature of the problem. The Jukes and Kallikak studies inspired a vast array of similar efforts in the first decades of the twentieth century, family studies whose message was largely the same tale of inherited feeblemindedness and licentiousness and criminality. There were studies of the Smoky Pilgrims, the Hill Folk, the Nam Family, the Pineys of New Jersey, the Family of Sam Sixty, the Dack Family, the Tribe of Ishmael, the Dwellers in the Vale of Siddem, Mongrel Virginians, and the Bunglers. As the eugenics scholar Diane Paul writes, *The Kallikak Family* was so popular it "went through twelve editions" and nearly became a Broadway play; "references to the Kallikaks [were] everywhere" in the 1920s and 1930s.[18]

The family studies repeated, in each incarnation, the same set of "sticky" traits that emanated from Dugdale's report more than fifty years earlier: the excessive sexuality, the criminality, and the animality that were signs of what the eugenicist Charles Davenport called a "race of degenerates." The traits were "sticky" in the literal sense—they clung to their objects. The feeblemindedness and criminality and excessive sexuality were overly possessive, internalized in blood. The Piney was "[l]azy, lustful and cunning, he is a degenerate creature." The Hill family children were "shiftless and deficient in a general way." The Zeros "stole milk from the cows . . . [and] vegetables from the gardens, poultry and dogs from the barnyards." Sam Sixty and his family were "notorious law-breakers" who had committed every crime from incest to thievery to rape to riot. The Bunglers, well, they bungled—law, order and everything else.[19]

When Ralph Bainum and the "brain trust" took to the papers—when they paraded themselves as experts, studied records, and read scholarly journals—they were not only trying to undo the sticky traits of the family studies, to uncouple the criminal from the weak-minded and poor; they were *performing* their claim. It was as if they were saying, we know that you are calling us "white trash" and "human rubbish." In the very act of telling the story as they did, they were trying to demonstrate the possibility, of strong, not weak, minds; of industry, not laziness; of civility and civilization. So too, perhaps, was their lawyer, Briggs.

———◆———

As he listened to Murray's butchered references to the "Jutes and Killikuks," Briggs had just attained the highest political office he had ever held. His picture had made it to the front page of the Oklahoma City papers. As the *Times* put it, being third in line from the governor's chair wasn't bad for a blacksmith's son who had taught himself the law. Briggs knew the sticky traits of the family studies; he had spent most of his life trying to overcome them.[20]

The problem was not the existence of poor and immoral persons; by 1935, a majority of Oklahomans were poor. Murray was not talking about economics; he was talking about pauperism as disease and contagion, poverty as inherited tendency, permanent and ineradicable. Eugenicists equated the "unfit" with "white trash" for a reason: all cultures have ideas of dirt—that which must be separated if the culture is to survive. Eugenicists had no trouble branding men and women like the Jukes and the Kallikaks as "sweepings," "human residuum," "social wastage," "surplus," "wreckage," because they saw them as polluted, carrying the origins of "dirt" in their blood. From such a viewpoint, it made perfect sense to insist that such persons simply disappear; as the zoologist S. J. Holmes proclaimed, some means "must be instituted for encouraging [their] race suicide."[21]

As a self-described student of eugenics, Briggs cannot have been insensible to the fact that the sticky traits signaled a larger political philosophy—one that Briggs had rejected from an early age. Briggs prided himself on representing the injured man, the little guy, the poor, precisely those the eugenicists feared were marked by the invisible sign of the feeble mind. It was not only the openly racist Aryan-lovers who wrote of the "iron law of inequality" and touted racist aristocracy. Eugenic pioneers such as Charles Davenport had written that all men were "*bound* by their protoplasmic makeup and *unequal* in their powers and responsibilities." Geneticists like Harvard's Edward M. East wrote that equality was a fraud: the "cult of *égalité* . . . is a pose." Henry Fairfield Osborn, the president of the American Museum of Natural History, publicly derided the claim that all men were created equal as "political sophistry." The eugenics popularizer Albert Wiggam insisted that men were "irremediably and ineradicably *unequal*." The zoologist S. J. Holmes summed it all up: "If there is any one thing which has been thrown absolutely out of court by the advances of biology and psychology, it is the dogma of the natural equality of man."[22]

Briggs need not have been much of an expert in eugenics to know of its political pretensions. During the 1920s, eugenics enthusiasts like Albert Wiggam and French Strother had written article after article in magazines like *Pictorial Review* and *World's Work* deriding democracy and political equality. The "conception of the equality of man" was "too grotesque to need extended discussion," wrote Wiggam. It was a fiction of the "old liberal," that the "masses" would "rule themselves with sanity and intelligence. Without . . . a new reverence for superiority, a new application of the technical methods of science to their social and political affairs, they will not, because they cannot, rule themselves wisely and well."[23] Eugenicists differed greatly in their professed political beliefs; there were Communists and socialists and egalitarians among them.[24] But for every left-leaning enthusiast, there were many more eugenicists who declared democracy dangerous and who dreamed of an America which would approach "more nearly to the ideal aristocracy of talent which Plato dreamed than any previous civilization has."[25]

For Briggs to fight the aristocratic pretensions of eugenics was not, however, to explain his willingness to take a case that smelled

vaguely obscene and paid little if anything. Nor did those pretensions prove the law unconstitutional. Justice Holmes had said that
equality was not at issue in *Buck v. Bell*. If Briggs stood up in court
and announced that equality mattered, he would also have to explain
why Justice Holmes, the most revered legal mind of his generation,
was wrong. Who was going to believe a home-schooled lawyer from
the eastern hills of Oklahoma, the home of the "unfit" and "white
trash," when pitted against one of the greatest legal minds of the
twentieth century? For that matter, who would believe the prisoners of Big Mac, brain trust or not?

———◆———

By January 1935, as Murray exited the political stage and Briggs
took office as Marland's leader in the Oklahoma Senate, the men
of McAlester may well have hoped that Murray's plan for another
sterilization law would die a quick legislative death. But the senator who had offered to wield the scalpel himself, Dr. Louis Henry
Ritzhaupt, had other ideas. Shortly before the inauguration, Ritzhaupt traveled to Governor Marland's Ponca City mansion. There,
he announced to the press that, because of his stand on sterilization,
his life had been threatened (although he did not explain how and
by whom). Ritzhaupt vowed not to be intimidated and warned that
he was carrying a gun. There would be another sterilization law, he
said, if it was the last thing he did.[26]

At the very start of the Senate's session, Dr. Ritzhaupt proposed
Senate Bill 14, the third sterilization law in five years. This time,
the law—the Oklahoma Habitual Criminal Sterilization Act—
spoke only to criminality. The attorney general, prompted by local
county attorneys, would be in charge of petitioning for sterilization, which would require a jury trial and could be immediately
appealed to the state supreme court, bypassing intermediate courts.
Gone were references to public charges and social inadequacy: if
the jury found that the defendant was a habitual criminal and that
sterilization would not harm his health, then the district court was
required to issue a sterilization order. The law could be applied by
the attorney general to any person having the "status of an habitual

criminal," now defined as two prior convictions, not three as in the 1933 law.[27]

On January 30, 1935, Dr. Ritzhaupt's bill was reported favorably out of committee to the floor of the Senate and, the next day, Ritzhaupt urged that the bill be passed. Briggs, joined by Senator Commons, offered a blocking amendment declaring that the law imposed an "additional punishment." When the amendment was adopted, Ritzhaupt was forced to defer consideration on the bill, which now spelled its own constitutional death (even eugenics enthusiasts agreed that sterilization-as-punishment raised serious constitutional questions). It was clear that Briggs was not going to make it easy for Ritzhaupt; the doctor would take to the floor twice more at the beginning of February but would be forced to defer consideration of the bill each time.[28]

On February 18, 1935, the early editions of the newspapers reported that at Oklahoma's reformatory, in Granite, there had been a break of thirty-one young prisoners. In the wake of that news, to embrace the cause of the criminal must have seemed political suicide. That day, Ritzhaupt once again moved to debate the bill and to reconsider Briggs's punishment amendment. The amendment was tabled, killing it. There was no place to go other than to soften the bill by amendment. Briggs offered a number of changes, but only one was successful: sterilization was to be confined to those who had committed felonies involving "moral turpitude." Had Briggs simply wanted to limit the law to serious crimes, he might have left the bill as it was, referring to felonies. He didn't, for a reason: the term "moral turpitude" was both evocative of the kind of degeneracy eugenicists feared and at the same time vastly ambiguous (neither then nor now is there a clear legal definition). Any lawyer looking for an issue that would make it harder to sterilize, that could make a ground for appeal, is likely to have found felony of "moral turpitude" a phrase quite to his liking.[29]

There was an added advantage to Briggs's choice of words: crimes of "moral turpitude" carried the scent of racism. It was fairly well known by lawyers at the time that the term was one of the great legal agents of racism in the South. It had a history going back to the late nineteenth century, when Southern states amended their constitutions to evade the dictates of the Fourteenth Amendment: if blacks could not be barred from juries or the voting booth because of race, they could be barred because they had committed a "crime of moral turpitude." The term was so vague that it could be used to reject those deemed to be of "bad character." As one Southern jury commissioner admitted in testimony repeated by the Supreme Court of the United States in 1935, he had never met a "negro" who had not committed a crime of moral turpitude.[30]

The rest of the debate held few surprises. Senator Wright offered an amendment to require proof that the habitual criminal would transmit "criminal tendencies," and Senator Whitaker proposed that the law require proof of "a probability" of "moral degeneracy," both of which were tabled. In retrospect, these appear to be strategic losses, amendments offered by the law's supporters so that any court looking at the history of the law would see that the Senate had considered and rejected a rule requiring anything more than proof of prior felonies. Finally, Senator Commons moved to exempt "offenses arising out of violations of prohibitory laws, revenue acts, embezzlement or political offenses." This amendment was passed by unanimous consent. Who among the legislators wanted to face sterilization themselves? At the end of the debate, the third Oklahoma sterilization law passed the Senate handily, twenty-eight to three.[31]

Two months later, in April 1935, Briggs received an unexpected letter from the ACLU's secretary, Lucille Milner, inquiring about the Oklahoma sterilization case. On May 3, Briggs replied that a new sterilization bill had passed the Oklahoma House of Representatives "just a few minutes before final adjournment" for the session. Four days later, the ACLU telegraphed Governor Marland strongly urging that he veto the bill, writing that it was "difficult to justify" the law's constitutionality and that a law devoted only to criminals was an "additional penal provision" rather than a "scientific eugenic" law.[32] Marland may have been a New Dealer, but, like many politicians of the day, he had vowed to "war on crime." A week later, on May 15, 1935, Governor Marland signed the Ritzhaupt bill into law, calling the law one of "enormous social importance," adding that "twice-convicted criminals" would now "begin dodging Oklahoma." The attorney general's office told Dr. Ritzhaupt that there was nothing legally standing in the way of sterilization at McAlester prison. As the attorney general's assistant, Jesse Ballard, had put it: "A lot of criminals will be kept out, or run out of Oklahoma."[33]

CHAPTER 6

Skinner's Trial

I would be out and alone and could not marry and rear a family and would not have any inspiration, I would be by myself without inspiration.

—*Jack Skinner, October 1936*[1]

On May 13, 1936, the day after the attorney general filed the first petition under the new sterilization law, the men of McAlester finally broke. Newspapers reported that the "lowest class [of] convicts"—twenty-four men, all told—instigated a riot at the brickyard pit where the most dangerous prisoners were at hard labor. Drawing home-made knives, the ringleaders seized C. D. Powell, the brickyard foreman, and two guards, and shoved them all in a guard's new Ford. Over a dozen prisoners clung to the car as it raced from the brickyard toward the prison gate. Ten men were wounded inside McAlester's walls, tower guards firing as the car approached. Using Powell as a shield, the convicts demanded that the guards at the gate throw down their rifles. Once armed, the men fled in the Ford, taking the foreman and two guards with them as hostages. A mile away, in downtown McAlester, the foreman's dead body was jettisoned somewhere between Harrison and Tyler avenues.[2]

Posses flew out of neighboring towns; one paper estimated that, within the day, two hundred men were scouring the nearby Kiamichi mountains. Governor Marland ordered the National Guard to stand by, and the Oklahoma crime bureau issued orders to shoot to kill. Two days later, McAlester's warden set off to track the ringleaders with a fresh pack of bloodhounds. Near Antlers, where a group of escapees had stopped to eat with a poor family on Rattlesnake Mountain, there was a standoff. The two McAlester guards and a new hostage, a farmer, were all released as the convicts fled on foot.[3] News of the escape, with all its alluring detail of bodies thrown out of windows, cowboy hostages, and baying bloodhounds, traveled the nation. Paramount and Metro filmed a reenacted version of the brickyard riot for national newsreel distribution. The wire services filed a week-long flurry of on-the-scene bulletins in a style that seemed to borrow from an Edward G. Robinson movie, as posses searched first for one group of prisoners, then the next, until only one man, the ringleader Claud Beavers, was left. Before the week was out, Beavers would be returned to McAlester by deputy warden Jess Dunn.[4]

Two weeks earlier, on May 1, 1936, it was front-page news in the *McAlester News–Capital* that the state had chosen a five-timer named Hubert Moore to be the first test case under the new, improved 1935 sterilization law. On Tuesday, May 12, Oklahoma's attorney general, Mac Q. Williamson, filed the first petition for sterilization in the district court, the first legal step required under the 1935 law. The next day, the brickyard convicts broke free. The McAlester papers reported the two stories, sterilization and break, side by side, noting no connection between the two events. It was a big city paper, the *Oklahoma News*, that explained that "unrest existed in the prison because of the sterilization test case," that the chairman of the Board of Affairs said that the "new sterilization law" was "one of [the] factors in causes for the break." The paper reported that the leader of the break, Claud Beavers, was a habitual criminal serving his third term, making him eligible for sterilization.[5]

McAlester's new warden, Wash Kenny, denied reports that sterilization caused the great break of 1936. Kenny had recently succeeded General W. S. Key, Governor Marland's first choice to replace Sam Brown. Like Key, Kenny was a former military man, an army major in World War I. When Key was named to handle the state's more urgent economic relief effort, he handed over McAlester prison to his deputy, Kenny, a former track coach at Texas A & M.

Kenny may have denied that sterilization had anything to do with the great break of 1936, but six days after the break, on May 19, 1936, a substantial sum of money, $1,000, was released from the prisoners' canteen account (the money they raised by selling inmates small luxuries such as magazines and cigarettes and fried potatoes). The money was given to Claud Briggs, who promptly announced to the press that he would test the constitutionality of the sterilization law. The prisoners finally had the "sinews of war."[6]

If there was any doubt about whether sterilization could inspire attempts to escape, it was soon quite clear to all the lawyers involved. Briggs had been hired to defend Hubert Moore. Shortly after the petition against Moore was filed in May, Warden Kenny called the attorney general and reported that Moore had agreed to "submit to the operation." This was a strategy of delay, not submission. A little over a month later, Moore took what his lawyer, Briggs, called "French leave," escaping from McAlester. The attorney general lost no time in finding a new case. The day after Moore's escape, on June 12, 1936, the state of Oklahoma filed a petition against Jack Skinner.[7]

Incarcerated first as Jasper Ingram, he began life as a Skinner. His father had died when he was just a toddler; his mother remarried and the boy was given the name of Jasper Ingram. Skinner would take the pseudonym Joe Smith before his second trial, returning finally to Jack Skinner when he arrived at McAlester in 1934. It may have been coincidence, but "skinner" was prison slang at McAlester for the new convict, the uninitiated, the naïve, the easy target. At 5 feet 6 inches and 143 pounds, Skinner looked much younger than his twenty-seven years. The newspapers would eventually refer to him as "a cripple"—Skinner had lost his foot six inches above the ankle as a teenager growing up in the town of Shawnee, Oklahoma.[8]

In 1931, when the first sterilization law was passed, Jack Skinner was twenty-four years old and serving his second term at Oklahoma's Granite Reformatory; the first had been for eleven months, for chicken stealing, the second for armed robbery.* Granite was origi-

---

* The charges in the first case against Skinner alleged that he and a confederate named Fox had stolen "by stealth" twenty-three chickens. Records of the charges in the second case have been lost.

nally intended for juveniles and first offenders, but was far from a picnic; because of overcrowding at McAlester, it was stocked full of men who could hardly be called boys, but Skinner managed to survive. He saved money doing extra work for a manufacturer of pillowcases and was writing to his childhood sweetheart, whom he would marry when he got out, only to lose her when he returned to prison for his third offense, also armed robbery (he held up a gas station for $17). Skinner would later testify that he had signed a "waiver" allowing his wife to file for divorce, but did not know whether she had actually gone ahead with it.[9]

The newspapers suggested that the attorney general's office and the "brain trust" had agreed upon Skinner as the first test case under the third sterilization law. There were reasons both sides might have been satisfied with the choice. Convict No. 18051—Ralph Bainum— had warned that the three-time-loser law might cover the most minor of crimes, and Skinner's first offense was the proverbial minor crime, stealing chickens. The attorney general, on the other hand, may have seen Skinner as one who wore his deficiencies for all to see, a "cripple." The newspapers claimed that Skinner had volunteered; Skinner testified that he just wanted to get his wife back.[10]

———•———

Six months after the great break of 1936, on October 19, Skinner sat next to his lawyers, Claud Briggs and John Morrison, at the counsel table at the front of the Pittsburg County courthouse in McAlester. The aging Fay Lester had ceded the more strenuous trial work to the younger Morrison.

After a decade in Oklahoma's criminal justice system, this would be Skinner's first trial; in each of his prior criminal cases, he had pled guilty. Skinner was not the only prisoner in the courtroom. After the May break, Warden Kenny could not afford any more violence. A letter from Briggs about his strategy was "posted on a bulletin board in the prison yard," and elaborate precautions were taken inside McAlester and at the subprison at Stringtown, down the road. Kenny even dispatched two prisoners to the courthouse, a trusty (a prisoner who was trusted to live outside the walls in one of the road or cowboy camps) and one from inside the walls, to witness the proceedings first-hand, to avoid any miscommunication about the trial or its results.[11]

The attorney general's assistants were impatient. Owen Watts, who had taken over from Jesse Ballard, had already announced that he was ready for battle, telling the press, "This is one case where I want those on the other side to fight me."[12] It had been five years since the first sterilization law was passed. Aggravations had mounted: there were legal hurdles, poorly drafted legislation, and the escape of Hubert Moore. Sterilization was proceeding at Oklahoma asylums, but not at the prison. Briggs had repeatedly stalled, seeking extensions of time to file legal papers over and over again.

On October 20, Judge Robert Higgins, the aging district court judge in Pittsburg County and former Oklahoma Supreme Court justice, called the trial to order: "Gentlemen of the Jury," the court "wants to explain a little something about this case to you." Higgins warned that the case was "clear out of the ordinary": whether the law "is a good law or a bad one is not for you gentlemen to say, that is for the court to unravel." Higgins explained that sterilization "means an operation by which the inmate . . . can never again be the father of children." He promptly turned to the lawyers and asked, "What is the name of this operation?" "Vasectomy," the state's attorney responded.[13]

The state's attorney was blunt in his opening statement. The trial would be no spectacle. The case wasn't about whether Skinner would pass on his "bad" genes. "[T]he proof . . . is very simple, concise and brief," he said. All the jury had to decide was whether Skinner was a habitual criminal, and whether the operation of vasectomy would be harmful to his health. "We shall bring three or four physicians who will testify here briefly that they have made a general physical examination of this defendant in this case" and "according to their best judgment . . . being qualified, licensed, regular practicing physicians, that this operation of vasectomy . . . will not impair or be a detriment or injury or endanger in any way the general health of this defendant." Then, said Watts, "we will expect you to go into your jury room and . . . return a verdict . . .

saying that the man is an habitual criminal and under the laws of the State of Oklahoma should be made sexually sterile." Watts sat down to wait for Briggs's statement, but Briggs declined, asking that he reserve his time until the state had rested its case. Judge Higgins adjourned for lunch.[14]

———◆———

At 1:30, T. M. Fields took the stand. Fields was McAlester's record clerk; his task was to establish that Skinner was the man they thought he was, that he was the man who had committed two prior crimes and served two terms at Granite. What should have been a formality turned out to be rather more difficult than the young state's attorney, Watts, had hoped. All testimony in court must, according to evidentiary rules, be based on first-hand knowledge (what one has seen, for example). Fields had relied upon the fingerprint bureau in Washington to identify Skinner as the man who had served two terms at Granite. Briggs was on his feet in a second, objecting that the witness had no first-hand knowledge that Skinner was in fact Joe Smith and Jasper Ingram; Fields's testimony was hearsay. The objection was sustained.[15]

The state had no option other than to call Skinner himself to the stand. Briggs immediately objected: Skinner cannot convict himself; that violates his rights against self-incrimination. "You may be right," replied Judge Higgins, "but the objection will be overruled for the present." Skinner took the stand and answered the questions politely, responding "Yes, sir," "I did," "Yes sir," but along the way admitting without hesitation that he was the Jasper Ingram who had been sentenced to eleven months in the Granite reformatory in 1926 for stealing chickens and the Joe Smith who had been sentenced to ten years in Granite for armed robbery in 1929.[16]

Watts called the first expert witness, none other than the law's author, the Oklahoma state senator Dr. Louis Henry Ritzhaupt. Typically, legislators have very little to do with trials; at least in theory, however, Dr. Ritzhaupt was testifying as an expert on sterilization. Ritzhaupt rattled off his qualifications. He had earned his medical degree at George Washington University, he was the former superintendent and chief surgeon at the Oklahoma Methodist Hospital, and he had been on the surgical staff of two other Oklahoma City hospitals.

Watts moved on: "Will you explain, Doctor, to the court and jury just how this operation of vasectomy is performed?"

Ritzhaupt replied at length, explaining the nature of the incision, that the operation required only local anesthetic, and that it took less than half an hour. He testified there had been 21,000 of these operations in the United States, with "[n]o mishaps and no deaths due to the surgery."

"Do you know the defendant, Jack T. Skinner?" asked Watts.

"I met the gentleman . . . this morning."

"Did you have occasion to give him a physical examination?"

A "very brief one," replied Ritzhaupt.

Watts continued, "[W]ould you say under oath" that "to the best of your judgment as a physician and surgeon . . . the operation of vasectomy would not impair, endanger, injure or be detrimental to the general health of the defendant?"

"Yes, sir, I would."[17]

Briggs began his cross-examination slowly. "Dr. Ritzhaupt, when did you perform your first operation of vasectomy?"

"1917," he replied.

Briggs continued, "How many such operations have you performed since that time?"

"Probably three hundred in both sexes," said Ritzhaupt.

"Have you ever performed or had occasion to perform such operation upon one that was required to submit to it against his or her will?"

"No, I have not," replied Ritzhaupt.

Briggs pressed the point: "Have you had any opportunity to observe the results that might develop following such operation, if imposed upon one against their will?"

"Yes," said Ritzhaupt, "in my internship, and I have in the last year and a half in the institutions for the feeble minded of the State."

Briggs interjected: "I am talking about sane normal people now,

I am not talking about the feeble minded. Have you . . . observe[d] the results of such operation upon a normal person" forced to be sterilized? Ritzhaupt had to agree that he had not.[18]

Briggs moved on. "You were the principal author of this bill . . . that is, it was written by the Attorney General's office at your . . . request?"

"Yes sir," replied the witness.

"[W]as the intention . . . of this act to use it as a crime deterrent or to influence the repeater . . . to refrain from committing crimes?"

Briggs's question was risky: legislative intention was irrelevant to the trial; that was a legal question, not one for the jury to decide. But Watts did not object, yet. Ritzhaupt answered the question, replying that the purpose of the bill was to reduce the number of criminals, to get "to the source of production." He added that the "average individual who commits crimes would not desire . . . sterilization [and] would naturally be retarded from committing a third crime."

Briggs pressed on. "Then, Doctor, you did have in mind that this was to be used and applied . . . as a crime deterrent and . . . held up as additional punishment to induce the man to refrain from the commission of crime?"

Ritzhaupt, sensing that Briggs was trying to make him concede something important, replied in the language of prevention, not punishment. The principal aim of the law, he now said, was "to stop the production of hereditary criminals."[19]

Briggs shifted tack. "[Y]ou are of the opinion . . . that criminal tendencies are inherited?"

"Yes sir."

"Doctor, have you . . . made any inquiry or investigation in the Oklahoma State Penitentiary from the records out there?"

Ritzhaupt evaded the question, claiming he had studied "the facts . . . on the question of heredity," and "as to the facts which I have at my command, the study of different groups . . . not only the Oklahoma penitentiary but of New York and New Jersey—"

Briggs interrupted. "What [studies] are you referring to now?"

"Well, the recent regime [sic] of Professor Gluech [sic], professor

Demonstration, 1915. Advocates of eugenics hold signs with slogans such as "Would prisons and asylums be filled if my kind had no children?" *Courtesy of the Wisconsin Historical Society*

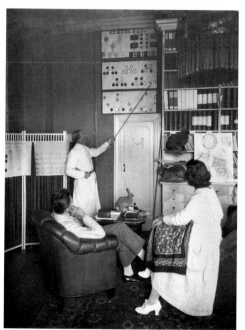

Eugenicist lecturing on Mendelian inheritance, c. 1920s. *Courtesy of the American Philosophical Society*

Contestants for the "Governor's Trophy" for fittest family. *Courtesy of the American Philosophical Society*

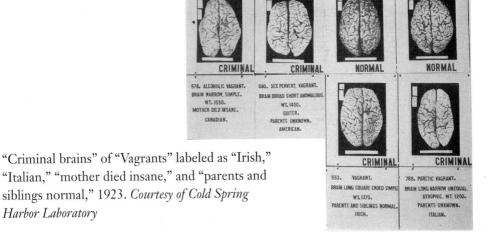

"Criminal brains" of "Vagrants" labeled as "Irish," "Italian," "mother died insane," and "parents and siblings normal," 1923. *Courtesy of Cold Spring Harbor Laboratory*

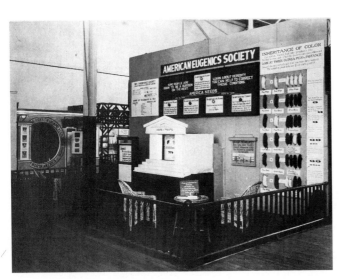

"Teaching Heredity," American Eugenics Society exhibition, 1926. *Courtesy of the American Philosophical Society*

HOVEL TYPE OF SOURCE OF DEFECTIVES.

Genetic pedigree typing for criminalistic traits: "Hovel Type" family. *Courtesy of Cold Spring Harbor Laboratory Archives*

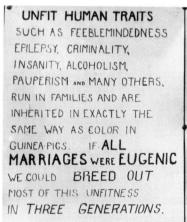

Flashing lights emphasize the cost of bad heredity: "Every 16 seconds $100 of your money goes to the care of persons with bad heredity such as the insane feebleminded criminals & other defectives." State fair display, 1926. *Courtesy of the American Philosophical Society*

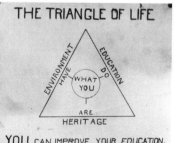

Eugenic educational display, c. 1929. *Courtesy of the American Philosophical Society*

The intellectual roots of eugenics, display, Third International Eugenics Conference, 1932. *Courtesy of Wellcome*

An unlikely troika of men who supported sterilization: Governor Alfalfa Bill Murray, Justice Oliver Wendell Holmes, and Hitler, pictured in the *New York Daily News*, December 22, 1933. *Courtesy of NYDN*

Skinner's lawyer, Claud Briggs. *Courtesy of Harlow's Weekly*

The Oklahoma sterilization law's chief sponsor, Dr. Louis Ritzhaupt. *Courtesy of Harlow's Weekly*

McAlester prison, 1930. *Courtesy of Corbis*

Prisoners displayed wearing dresses as punishment, c. 1920s–30s. *Courtesy of Oklahoma Department of Corrections*

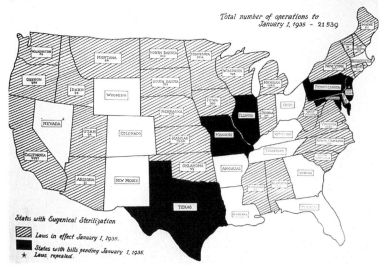

Total number of operations to
January 1, 1935 - 21 539

States with Eugenical Sterilization
Laws in effect January 1, 1935.
States with bills pending January 1, 1935.
★ Laws repealed.

Sterilization laws spanned America in 1935. *Courtesy of Harry Laughlin Papers, Truman State*

Skinner and his lawyers at his sterilization trial, October 1936. *Courtesy of* Muskogee Daily Phoenix, *1936*

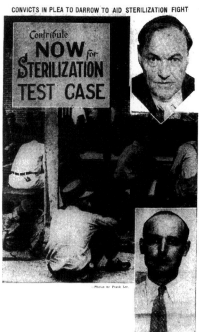

CONVICTS IN PLEA TO DARROW TO AID STERILIZATION FIGHT

Contribute NOW for STERILIZATION TEST CASE

Clarence Darrow declines to represent prisoners who protest inside McAlester prison to raise money for a lawyer, May 11, 1934. *Courtesy of Scripps Howard News Service*

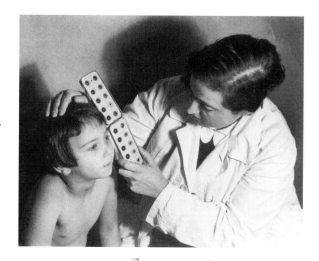

Eugenic examination of Jewish child, Berlin, Germany, c. 1936. *Courtesy of AKG*

Fascism haunts debate over FDR's court-packing plan. *Courtesy of* Collier's *magazine, April 17, 1937*

Data on crime and foreign-born races, from *Crime and the Man* (1939) by Harvard professor E. A. Hooton. *Courtesy of Harvard University Press*

Racial hierarchies of criminality, from *Crime and the Man* (1939) by Harvard professor E. A. Hooton. *Courtesy of Harvard University Press*

Warden Dunn with Claud Beavers, who led what the *McAlester News-Capital* called "a bloody break for liberty" in 1936. Both would die in the McAlester break of 1941. *Courtesy of AP*

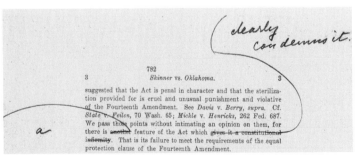

Justice Frankfurter makes a change on the draft opinion to emphasize equal protection, 1942. *Courtesy of Papers of Justice William O. Douglas, Library of Congress*

of criminology of the Harvard Law School and his associates over a period of—"

Briggs cut him off. "May I ask you before you quote figures, this Mr. Gluech [*sic*], is he a surgeon or physician, or is he a lawyer?"

"He is Professor of Criminology of the Harvard Law School."

Briggs persisted. "Of the Law School. He isn't even a doctor, a M.D. or surgeon?"

Now Ritzhaupt was on the defensive. "All right, I can go further on this research with V. C. Brown of New York, a New York physician."

Briggs asked whether Dr. Brown's study had concerned patients with mental disease. Ritzhaupt denied it.[20]

Briggs cut to the chase. "Do you know that . . . I have a certificate before me" from the Oklahoma State Penitentiary and it "discloses that . . . of 2034 first termers only twelve of those 2034 had parents or grandparents [who] had ever been convicted of crime," and that for those "serving second or [third], fourth, fifth, sixth and seventh terms, 1753 in number, . . . [it] shows not a single instance where the parent of any of the second or more termers had ever been convicted of crime—"

Ritzhaupt interrupted. "I would question the authenticity of that research—there were "insufficient expenditures of money . . . to trace the families."

Briggs replied that the "report [was] made and signed by the record clerk of the Oklahoma State Penitentiary."

Ritzhaupt was curt: "It would have no effect whatever [on my] analysis."[21]

Angered by Ritzhaupt's obstructionism, Briggs was reduced to sarcasm. Turning back to the Glueck study of 1,000 delinquents, he asked Dr. Ritzhaupt to explain "how one thousand children got into the penitentiaries and had criminal records?"

Ritzhaupt responded curtly, "I hold the record in my hand," even though he had shifted from the Glueck study to a different one. "This is a compilation of the Department of Social Hygiene [*sic*] of the Princeton League of Women Voters, Judge Briggs"—as if Ritzhaupt had become the lawyer and Briggs the judge. Finally,

Briggs, exasperated, attacked, implying that Ritzhaupt was biased: "Doctor, are you not confident of the accuracy of that report because it conforms to your opinion?"[22]

Briggs had an ace up his sleeve that he hoped would show Ritzhaupt to be a true partisan in the eugenics debate. This was the most recent independent report on eugenics and sterilization—by the neurologist Abraham Myerson, issued by the American Neurological Association—which, despite its ambiguities, was hailed by the *New York Times* as the work of a distinguished committee based on a "scientifically objective" study, one which raised significant doubts about sterilization. Briggs wanted Ritzhaupt to confront the report. "Did you know that . . . eminent specialists have been . . . conducting extensive research" on these questions under the auspices of the American Neurological Association?

"No, I did not know that," replied Ritzhaupt.

"Did you know," continued Briggs, "within the past three or four months, that Dr. Myerson, Abraham Myerson, . . . noted authority and chairman of this special committee" has "made the following statement—may I read it to you?"

Watts rose: "We object . . . incompetent, irrelevant and immaterial."[23]

Briggs had been treading on thin ice. The whole purpose of the 1935 law, a law whose passage he had presided over as president pro tempore of the Oklahoma Senate, was to prohibit a trial that would call into question whether criminal tendencies were inherited. Briggs's entire line of questions and answers had, in theory, been irrelevant. Now Watts saw the danger. The Myerson report was critical of sterilization and, in particular, of the idea that sterilization should be applied to criminals. Just as Briggs was about to read a key passage, Watts objected. Judge Higgins sustained the objection, explaining that "the reasons for the legislature enacting that law is not a matter for the jury."[24]

Briggs persisted. "Do you know that . . . Dr. Myerson's committee decided—"

Watts was on his feet again. "I object to Senator Briggs reading from the textbook . . . let him bring the doctor in."

Briggs was angry. "[Dr. Ritzhaupt] has not brought his society of women voters in here and he has quoted from them."

Judge Higgins sustained Watts again. "Books cannot be introduced, medical books, the books themselves."

But, Briggs insisted, "I want to know" whether Dr. Ritzhaupt "has read" the Myerson report.

Judge Higgins replied, "Doctors can testify from what is standard. He may not know anything at all about it, but he can say that the standard textbook writers so state."[25]

Briggs tried to reframe the question: "[D]o you not, Doctor, regard Dr. Abraham Myerson as a recognized authority of the subject?"

"I do not," said the witness.

"Why?" asked Briggs, knowing that Ritzhaupt was clearly over-reaching—Myerson was an expert in the field.

"Because I don't agree with his theory, because the preponderance of the evidence can be placed on the opposite side which he upholds," replied Ritzhaupt. Ritzhaupt had invoked the language of law, of preponderance and evidence; perhaps he knew enough about the law to know that if he denied Myerson was a legitimate authority, there was nothing that Briggs could possibly do (Briggs would later describe Ritzhaupt to the jury as a "fallacious attorney"). Lawyers cannot testify and, in any event, the book was hearsay. Briggs could not read the book into evidence and he could not make Ritzhaupt say that Myerson was an expert.[26]

Briggs's only recourse was to approach the bench and lay the record for appeal (allow the court reporter to record what the Myerson report would have said if it had been admitted). Speaking to the judge, Briggs was blunt: Dr. Myerson "is a well known and recognized authority on neurological matters." The American Neurological Association report was "wholly opposed to sterilization, believing it . . . a dodging of the issues and a shifting of responsibility from society to the germ-plasm." He went on to say that the British experts on whom Myerson had relied had concluded that there was "so little" known about heredity that "laws for the sterilization of the unfit can claim no justification whatever in science."

Finally, and if only for the judge, Briggs read from the Myerson report: "Sterilization made compulsory by the State is, of course, pure tyranny."[27]

Neither the Myerson report nor the prisoners' own study were admitted into evidence at Skinner's trial. Technically, the judge was right, that the law was not on trial; he was also right that books as a general rule are hearsay. What was Briggs to do? He persisted for some time in trying to make Ritzhaupt admit that the operation was harmful in some way, particularly if it was forced upon Skinner, that it would affect his physical and psychological condition by building up "a feeling of resentment and hatred." Again, Ritzhaupt refused to go along, testifying that he believed that the operation would be not only beneficial to society, but also to Skinner himself.[28]

Returning to examine the witness, Watts tried to repair the damage done by Briggs's implications that coerced sterilization would drive a man to insanity. "You talked with Mr. Skinner this morning, did you not?"

"Yes sir," replied Ritzhaupt.

"Did you observe anything extraordinary about his mental condition or mental attitude?"

"No sir, I didn't."

"Did he strike you as being a normal person mentally?"

Ritzhaupt was clear: yes, Skinner was "[v]ery normal, especially intelligent." (It was an ironic comment, given that sterilization of criminals had originally been based on the theory of their inherent lack of intelligence, their feeblemindedness.)

Returning for a final attempt to shake Ritzhaupt's testimony, Briggs asked the doctor whether he had tried to pressure Skinner into consenting to the operation.

"No, I asked him if he thought his children would follow in his footsteps whether he would not submit to the operation," answered Ritzhaupt.

"He let it be known very definitely he didn't want it done?" asked Briggs.

"Yes."

The witness was excused.[29]

———•———

Watts called T. H. McCarley, the McAlester town doctor and prison physician. With appropriate prompting, McCarley offered his qualifications, said that he had examined Skinner, and agreed that Skinner was a man of "over average intelligence" and "mentally alert." Watts continued, "Doctor, have you ever performed . . . an operation to make a person sexually sterile?"

McCarley testified that he had done about half a dozen operations on men and a "good many" on women, and that there was little inconvenience to the operation.

"From your experience and study, what would you say as to the proposition of whether or not the operation of vasectomy if performed upon the defendant, Jack T. Skinner, would impair or be detrimental to his general health?" asked Watts.

"I think it would not [a]ffect him unfavorably in the least," replied McCarley.[30]

On cross-examination, Briggs turned to the question of coercion, asking Dr. McCarley whether he had "ever had an opportunity to observe the effects or results upon one who had been forcibly required to submit to this operation?"

"I have not," said McCarley.

Briggs pushed on: if a man wanted to have children and he was "confronted with the fact that he [would] never be able to have children, to procreate . . . assuming that he becomes enraged and angered at the forces who compelled him to submit to this operation," would not his health suffer?

McCarley wasn't buying. He replied that "the effect of vasectomy on a man would just be equal to taking a child and extracting a tooth." The McAlester boys simply didn't understand. It is just like a child who can't "see the reason for having an extraction, and you have to hold that child and extract the tooth." And "that is all there is to it."[31]

Briggs couldn't let Dr. McCarley's characterization of the prisoners as children stand. "Now, Doctor, don't you think . . . that . . . any real virile, red-blooded, man would very keenly resent having his power of procreation taken away from him?" If Briggs was ever going to get the jury's support, he had to make them identify with the prisoners of McAlester. But McCarley would have none of it, insisting that the operation "has no effect whatever on a man's sexual nature." Briggs persisted: "But I say a man who through the performance of this operation has had destroyed and wiped from his mind all hope of becoming the parent of children—"

McCarley interrupted, sparring with Briggs: "they have an idea that it interferes with their sexual pleasure . . . and they are so firm in that belief that it is absolute[ly] impossible to convince them to the contrary."

Briggs refused to let McCarley evade the question again. "I am not asking you about that."

McCarley interrupted again: "you can't convince the convicts in the Oklahoma State Penitentiary of it . . . I have talked to them." McCarley had turned the moral question on its head—from a question of state compulsion to one of sexual license.[32]

Briggs shifted his attack, asking McCarley whether he was simply a hired gun for the state: "You are a State employee?"

McCarley replied that he was. Briggs asked whether he had ever had "any occasion to study or examine the authorities to ascertain what the leading medical authorities of the Nation had to say about the effect of vasectomy on those who were forced to submit to it against their will?"

McCarley was frank about his own indifference. "I have never studied that feature of it at all."

"Never sought any information?" asked Briggs.

"No sir."

"And it is just an opinion of yours, a private opinion of yours, without any experience to back it," pushed Briggs.

McCarley replied that his opinion "is based on . . . my textbooks where they tell me [that vasectomy] doesn't have any deleterious effects."

"Does your textbook also tell whether those who have been forced to submit to the operation of vasectomy have had any deleterious effects?"

McCarley capitulated. "No, I am not competent to pass on that except from my own personal individual opinion."[33]

The state called its last witness, Dr. D. W. Griffin, the head of the Norman asylum. Griffin's testimony was little different from that of the other doctors, except for one minor breach. During Watts's examination, Griffin noted that Skinner had started his criminal career "at fifteen or sixteen," and expressed open sympathy for Skinner's youthful straying: "it makes me believe there might be something back of this. I don't know what it is,—something."

Watts immediately steered Griffin back to the party line, reminding him that "you still would be of the opinion . . . that an operation of vasectomy . . . would not impair his general health?"

Griffin agreed wholeheartedly. "No, I certainly would not think it would at all."[34]

On cross-examination, Briggs returned to the question of coercion. "You have not had any observation where any [patients] were forced to submit to this operation?"

"No," replied Griffin, "we have never tied anybody down and forced them to it, we have been able to talk them into it."

"Then you are not able to say from any experience you have had . . . as to what the results might be on a normal man . . . who was forced to submit to such operation against his will?"

Griffin replied that there would not be any permanent effect, but Briggs probed further. "You stated a while ago . . . that . . . if you had [the] opportunity you might be able to uncover something in connection with this boy's case. Is it not true that this young man if he had had proper treatment in the beginning that he . . . never would have been involved in these other instances of trouble he got into?"

"Probably," said Griffin, "it might have been cut short had we known and handled him properly . . . when he stole the first six chickens."[35]

The door to Skinner's past having opened, Briggs pressed on. "Do you understand what the first offense was? The facts?" he asked Griffin.

"Yes," said Griffin, expressing dismay that Skinner had been treated so harshly by the courts for the stealing of chickens. "I feel like these youngsters when they do commit the first crime against the law they should be dealt with tenderly because there are so many of them that are not just right."

Sensing an opening, Briggs continued, "Did you understand at the time of the first crime that he had . . . an accident[,] lost one of his feet[,] and was in school and sent to the reformatory . . . for eleven months for . . . a childish prank?"

"Yes," said Griffin, "I learned that."

Briggs continued to press Griffin, trying to fit as much of Skinner's story into his questions as possible, stringing them out clause by clause: "Assuming the state of facts to be this, that his father died when he was quite young and when ten or eleven years of age his mother remarried and his step-father was unkind to him and he left home at fourteen or fifteen years of age . . . and was out away from home seeking work at fifteen or sixteen years of age when this accident occurred and his foot was injured and he lost it and then that his first offence or crime of chicken stealing occurred after he came home in that crippled condition and was attending school at Shawnee, for instance when he was nineteen years of age—"[36]

His curiosity piqued, Dr. Griffin interrupted. "He lost his foot before nineteen?"

"Yes, when fifteen, I believe."

Griffin was taken aback. "That is why I say I cannot answer that, I don't know enough about the case."

Watts objected. "I cannot see the materiality of this line of cross-examination."

Judge Higgins agreed. "I don't see where that throws any light on whether it would be permanent injury to his welfare, as to what some Judge did or where the parents were lacking."

The interruption seemed to remind Dr. Griffin of the party line; he shifted tack abruptly. "Mr. Briggs, pardon me, but I think he is the very kind of type that should be sterilized."

Briggs tried to return Dr. Griffin to his earlier sympathy, but the witness seemed to have awakened to the danger; he would even go so far as to offer an opinion that Skinner was "psychopathic."

On redirect, Watts returned to the state's main theme. "Do you feel that this operation of vasectomy is more or less in an advanced stage in the science of medicine?"

Dr. Griffin took the cue and this time supplied the expected answer: "It has been performed without any deleterious results." He even testified that the operation would "have a tendency to curb crime, that is what we believe and that is what gives rise to the idea . . . that we should continue to do sterilizations." The state of Oklahoma rested.[37]

—————————◆—————————

Briggs opened the defense with what the sinews of war—the canteen money—had bought: Dr. M. S. Gregory. Dr. Gregory was an Oklahoma City psychiatrist who had graduated thirty years earlier from the University of Michigan medical school. Gregory was a specialist in what he called nervous disorders, a man who had trained at the "Federal insane ward" at St. Elizabeth's Hospital in Washington.

"Have you examined the defendant in this case?" Briggs asked.

"I examined him a short time last night," replied Gregory.

"[W]hat, in your opinion would be the effects of an operation . . . of vasectomy, upon his general health?"

Gregory was blunt. "Very few men willfully and deliberately ask to be sterilized. A few do because of reasons of their own, but they do that voluntarily and when they do that voluntarily then you do not get the detrimental emotional upset that does come and will come, I believe will come, to any individual who is forcibly emasculated, sterilized or castrated. I believe it would be very serious because he will develop a chronic state of hate . . . of hate and fear, perhaps, disturbing the whole physiological system of the body."

Briggs asked Gregory to explain to the jury "how the effects of these emotions would manifest themselves." Gregory replied with a detailed and highly technical explanation of the sympathetic nervous system, at the end of which Briggs asked for a conclusion.

"Now, Doctor, in your opinion will the result of this hate . . . as a result of compulsory sterilization . . . will that ultimately [a]ffect his general health?"

Gregory replied that "he will develop so much hate that . . . he may be driven to more crime."

On cross-examination, Watts did little to shake Gregory's testimony, asking routine questions about the contrary opinion of the other experts; in rebuttal, Briggs asked Dr. Gregory to confirm the conclusions of the Myerson committee, which he did.[38]

The defense called the final witness, Jack Skinner, to the stand. Briggs began, "I want you to explain to the court and jury what your attitude is with reference to this attempted sterilization, in your own words."

"Well, I have a great resentfulness toward it," Skinner replied. "I hope when I have served the judgment of the court to be released and become an honest citizen and marry and settle down and raise possibly a child or maybe two." He added, "I don't hold any grudge against society for sending me to the penitentiary." He had confessed his wrongs, pleading guilty to all charges. He repeated, "I want to, when I get out, marry and be an honest citizen. I have always desired to do that."[39]

Briggs invited Skinner to tell his story. Skinner explained that, after he left the Granite reformatory in 1934, he married and moved to Oklahoma City. While in prison, he had saved up about "three or four hundred dollars" by "doing extra work for a manufacturer of pillow cases and pillow tops," and he and his wife lived off of that while he looked for work. "I walked all over town, I had been all over town trying at all the relief camps and everywhere trying to get a job, I didn't care what it was, my occupation is book-keeper and of course I couldn't find that kind of work and I agreed to accept anything, manual labor or anything, and I couldn't find a thing."

Briggs clarified it for the jury. "You had at that time exhausted your finances and spent three months in a desperate effort to get work."[40]

Watts interjected: "Your Honor, I cannot really see the materiality of this testimony."

"It goes to the moral turpitude of the crimes," replied Briggs, suggesting to the jury that Skinner was not depraved but, like others in the Depression, had done something desperate to feed his family.

Judge Higgins quickly put a stop to the testimony, warning the jury that "this is not for your consideration . . . whether the defendant in this case was rightfully or wrongfully sent to prison."

There was only one question left for Briggs to ask: "[Y]ou stated that you hoped and had ambition . . . that you might be able to . . . overcome this trouble of yours by living an up right [sic] clean life and rearing a family?"

"That is my hope," replied Skinner.

"Is it that [hope] that creates the resentment . . . that makes you intensely dread and resent the forceful performance of this operation?"

"Yes sir," replied Skinner: "I would be out and alone and could not marry and rear a family and would not have any inspiration, I would be by myself without inspiration."[41]

Briggs rested.

The county attorney, W. J. Counts, silent during the trial, now rose to deliver the state's closing argument. His statement was brief, a formality almost, warning the jury not to wander from the issues at hand. There was no question, Counts emphasized, about whether Skinner was a habitual criminal. The jury's only role was to decide whether or not the operation would be detrimental to Skinner's health. And on the question of health, the jury was to rely upon the experts, "men who have made it a study and know the result of surgery and its effects." The issue was narrow, Counts concluded, but the jury should not minimize its duty: "This is not a little tiny case, it is a case of great magnitude."[42]

Briggs rose. "I am indebted to the County Attorney for the frank admission to you gentlemen that this is a serious matter . . . it involves a good deal more than even the proponents of this law understand and appreciate. I think it involves a great deal more than Senator Ritzhaupt, who is the author of the Act, admittedly, understands and

realizes." Briggs invited the jury to imagine themselves in the prisoners' shoes. "[I]f this law is sustained by you under the evidence
in this case . . . then . . . the Legislature can pass [sterilization] laws
[that] . . . will [a]ffect every individual in the State. They are not
restricted to passing such laws as may [a]ffect the inmates of the State
Penitentiary, if this law stands up."[43] Wouldn't an "operation of this
sort . . . make you resentful, men, you red-blooded men on this jury,"
he continued. "I wonder what would be your attitude or mine if we
were . . . incarcerated in that institution out there . . . I wonder if it
would not build up in our minds a feeling of resentment and hatred
. . . which might . . . cause us to become enemies of society, most
desperate enemies of society."

Briggs turned to Skinner. "Gentlemen of the Jury . . . here is
a young man with ambition; look at him—he does not possess the
appearance of a hardened criminal . . . [W]hen he [has served]
this sentence he wants to go out and hunt up that little wife who
divorced him . . . and try to reconcile [with] her . . . and settle down
to raise a family." Jack Skinner "has paid the bitter price of his
wrongdoings and has paid for it dearly," and "now he is faced with
the danger . . . of paying the largest penalty that a red-blooded,
virile young man could be required to pay." "Why," Briggs asked,
"should he not resent it . . . if they take from him this hope and
ambition that he lives and thrives upon today. Why should he not
become enraged?"[44]

The state's attorneys had told the jury that the only question
for them to decide was one of health. Briggs confessed that the state
was right: the "only field of escape left for the poor boy . . . the only
avenue of escape that is left for him is for a jury or court to find it
might be detrimental to his general health." Briggs repeated himself: "that one question [of health] is the only avenue of escape under
the instructions of the court here." And, again, that the state had
"left only one avenue of escape and that is the slim avenue that [it]
might be possible for a jury . . . to find that it might be detrimental
to his health." Today, one wonders whether Briggs was conscious
that he used the word "escape" so often in his closing argument. It
had been only five months since the break of 1936. Perhaps Briggs

thought fear his best strategy. It was almost as if he was telling the jury: if you don't sympathize with these men, at least fear what they might do.[45]

The state, as the plaintiff in a civil case, was entitled to the last word before the jury retired. Watts began, "Gentlemen, [you] have got a duty to perform. . . . Mr. Briggs paints a very lovely picture of the ambitions and desires of this young man. He wants to go out, remarry and settle down and raise a family." But "he has had three opportunities to do that." Watts now attacked Skinner's defense. "Gentlemen of the Jury . . . Mr. Briggs has tried to impress you" that "if we sterilize this young man it will create in his mind . . . hatred and fear and rage to such extent . . . that it will affect his sympathetic nervous system and . . . that it will have a reaction upon his vital organs . . . [and] impair his general health." That was an absurdity, charged Watts; a man might worry about many things, including being vaccinated or going to prison, but we wouldn't say that it would upset his sympathetic nervous system and harm his health. "[Y]ou can see the absurdity and ridiculousness of a theory of that kind, Gentlemen." He concluded that "it is your solemn duty as jurors under the oaths you took to go out and enforce this law regardless of the fact that you might feel sympathetic toward this young man and four thousand others out there."[46]

———◆———

Some papers said the jury deliberated for less than thirty minutes before concluding that Skinner was to be sterilized. As they deliberated, six convicts, fearing sterilization, escaped from a prison labor camp south of McAlester. It was a minor disturbance compared to the May break, but one that seemed to vindicate Briggs's warning. The *Daily Oklahoman* editorialized that the fact that "several trusties have fled McAlester penitentiary because of the fear of sterilization" proved the law was a "genuine deterrent" to crime.[47]

CHAPTER 7

The Supreme Court in 1937

*Surely Mr. Roosevelt's mandate was to function as the President,
not as Der Fuehrer.*
　　　　　　—William Allen White, journalist, 1937[1]

Having lost at law, the prisoners would once more turn to the press. A month after the trial, on November 22, 1936, a feature story, "State Convicts Battle Sterilization Law in Courts," appeared in the *Tulsa Daily World*, explaining that Oklahoma had completed the first step toward "race betterment." It was an ironic reference, as the article was clearly sympathetic to the prisoners' fight. The reporter, Walter Biscup, who had helped bring Ralph Bainum, Convict No. 18051, to the people before, closed the piece by asking, "What do the 3,600 convicts in the state penitentiary think of sterilization?" The answer was provided by Bainum, in a series of extravagant rhetorical questions. By what "divine grace can . . . judges . . . discriminate between who should and who should not be permitted to reproduce?" "Is this the beginning of a new nationalism in this country?" "[W]hat good is this 'hitlerization' going to do?"[2]

Bainum's reference to Hitler may appear incendiary today but, in the year 1936, talk of "forms of government," such as nationalism and Fascism and socialism, were not academic matters. By 1936, droves of Americans had gravitated to Huey Long's "Share Our Wealth" society, with its demagogic promises to make "every man a king"; millions of voters had pledged their support to the vitriolic

radio priest Father Coughlin's proposals to nationalize key indus-
tries; and nearly a fifth of the nation's entire population would sign
petitions supporting the cockeyed economic plans of a once obscure
California sexagenarian, Dr. Francis Everett Townsend. As Franklin Roosevelt would tell one reporter, "I am fighting Communism,
Huey Longism, Coughlinism, [and] Townsendism."[3]

Revolution abroad made this talk of governmental form banal,
yet fearsome. By the end of 1936, when Bainum made his charge of
"hitlerization," totalitarianism had already marched into Europe and
Africa. In the spring, Hitler's troops had occupied the Rhineland,
defying Germany's treaty obligations; in May, Mussolini installed
Fascism in Ethiopia; and in July, General Franco waged a civil war
in Spain with arms and planes supplied by Hitler and Mussolini.
However much the Americans wanted to look the other way (and
they did), by the end of 1936, Europe's new forms of government
cast a frightening shadow on America's public life. In a world of
revolution, it was not surprising that the political issues of the day,
high and low, whether seemingly local like sterilization or national
like the New Deal, were debated in terms of grand governmental
transformation.[4]

On the very day Skinner's trial concluded, the Republican candidate for the presidency, Alf Landon, resorted to dire warnings,
insisting that Roosevelt's defeat was necessary to preserve our "form
of government," implying what other Republicans had been saying
all along, that the New Deal was the first step toward Fascism. The
next day, Roosevelt reminded people that in a world that had "gone
undemocratic," America was becoming more democratic, ruled less
by "selfish minorities." On November 3, 1936, the results were as
stunning to the president's supporters as they were to his opponents:
Franklin Roosevelt had carried all but two states, something that
had not been done in a hundred years. The *Chicago Daily Tribune*
wrote of a "new chapter in American history." The *Atlanta Journal*
compared Roosevelt to the Founding Fathers: the American people
had handed Roosevelt a "tribute of confidence unparalleled since
Washington was first chosen President." William Allen White, a
Landon supporter and well-known Republican columnist, did not

conceal his astonishment and admiration: "It was not a Roosevelt victory. It was not a Landon defeat. It was a revelation." History, said White, was in the making. "We are going on a great new adventure. It is not unlike the turning we took in 1776; again in 1861 . . . As the old hymn lines it out, it is 'a grand and awful time.'"[5]

In Oklahoma and elsewhere, Democrats and their admirers summarized the governmental transformation as a quiet revolution signaling a new equality. As the Republican White put it, "From this November day on, we should have a new America, an America in which . . . the Federal Government should be the strong coercive arbitrator between those who have and those who have not," a government which will curb "cunning greed and . . . balk the anti-social plans of the strong." Al Nichols, a leader in the Oklahoma Senate, told the press of the culmination of a progressive movement that had been building since the turn of the century: "On the 3d of this November, twenty-seven million voters registered their will at the polls that equality shall be more than a catchword and that government shall not be merely an instrument through which a few may reach their selfish ends. There is a new order. Humanity now rules in America." Not all shared this enthusiasm. Like many Republicans, William Randolph Hearst, one of the richest men in America and the outspoken owner of a vast publishing empire, believed that Roosevelt had thrown the Constitution to the winds in embracing the New Deal. And, yet, after the election, even Hearst sounded conciliatory, borrowing Lincoln's famous words and telling his readers that "[e]very once in a while a republic needs a 'new birth of freedom.'"[6]

———

Just months after the election, in February 1937, the electoral honeymoon was over. Franklin Roosevelt had announced a plan that would change the membership of the United States Supreme Court and with it launched a controversy the intensity of which was unparalleled by any legislative proposal of the twentieth century. As the newspapers put it, Roosevelt's plan to "pack" the Supreme Court had "precipitated the greatest constitutional crisis since slavery." It was a crisis that would make resolution of Skinner's lawsuit even more difficult than it might have seemed, for at stake was the content of the constitutional law that would determine the prisoners' case.[7]

The controversy had been brewing for some time. Two years earlier, at the end of May 1935, on what became known as Black Monday, the Supreme Court had declared unconstitutional a law that sat at the heart of the New Deal, the National Recovery Act. As *Newsweek* put it, the NRA decision "chucked 758 codes" of corporate conduct affecting 700,000 employers. With that decision, "[n]ine out of every ten wage earners lost Uncle Sam's guarantee of minimums in their pay checks." Black Monday, however, was nothing compared to the controversy that arose at the beginning of 1936. In January, popular magazines reported that the "whole New Deal house of laws shook and trembled." The Supreme Court blew to pieces, said one *Business Week* reporter, the second heart of the New Deal—the Agricultural Adjustment Act, an act that paid farmers to cut production and was the legal template for efforts at a national response to the drought. The Supreme Court, having angered labor in the NRA decision, now angered farmers who had expected "more than two billion dollars in AAA benefit checks" in the following year. The NRA and AAA decisions were not alone; between "January 7, 1935 and May 25, 1936, the Supreme Court voided more than a dozen New Deal laws."[8]

There was one final blow. In what appeared to be the reversal of a prior liberal decision, the Supreme Court, in the 1936 *Tipaldo* case, created "a national outcry against the Court" by holding a state minimum wage law unconstitutional. Under the NRA decision, the federal government had no power to control wages; now, the states had no power. Columnists and official writers rose up to vent their wrath upon Justice Owen Roberts, the swing vote in the case: "In this decision one man's opinion overturned the legislation of more than one-third of the states." The president, questioned about the decision, said that the government was now in a " '[n]o-man's land,' where no Government can function," with the Supreme Court denying power to both states and nation.[9]

In February 1937, Roosevelt proposed his solution to the crisis: a bill that would allow him to appoint, with the consent of the Senate, a new justice for every justice on the Court over seventy years of age. It was front-page news everywhere. One reporter wrote, "I had been on a good many trains during the last weeks of the bitterly-contested Presidential campaign of 1936, but had seen little like this—when people were so stirred and interested that they put down their knives and forks to give total strangers their political opinions." Signifying the apparent momentousness of it all, the self-conscious feeling that people were living through constitutional history, magazines and newspaper regaled the public with their constitutional past. It was remembered that Lincoln, at the beginning of the Civil War, had failed to amend the Constitution to free the slaves. Historians reminded readers about previous "court-packing" attempts by other presidents. Constitutional amendments that would compromise the entire affair dotted the editorial pages. There was even a virtual tutorial in the difficulties of the constitutional amendment process, in the frequent reminder that the child labor amendment (however popular) had been languishing in state legislatures since 1924 and all that anyone had to do to stop ratification was to gather a small minority of legislators in a small minority of state legislatures to block it. As Roosevelt told one correspondent, if he had the money to buy off a small number of state politicians, he "could stop a constitutional amendment cold."[10]

These lessons in constitutional history and process did little to blunt the public reaction to the president's plan, which was immediate and full of hostility. It was the character of the opposition that was most significant, shadowed as it was by the ghosts of foreign dictators. By friends and foes alike, Roosevelt was charged with seeking "personal control of the entire Government," undercutting all checks and balances. Even some of the president's men, like the Columbia law professor and brain-truster Raymond Moley, openly complained that the plan came "perilously near to a proposal to abandon Constitutional Government." The *Herald Tribune* went so far as to liken FDR to Louis XIV (who said, famously, "*L'Etat ç'est moi*"). By May, columnist Walter Lippman insisted that the purpose of the plan was no longer to liberalize the courts but to "master[ ]" them. In a nationally broadcast message, Senator Carter Glass of Virginia claimed that Roosevelt wanted to "rape" the Supreme Court, turning its members into a set of "subalterns," "wet nurses," and "marionettes to speak the ventriloquisms of the White House." Missouri's Senator Bennett Clark exclaimed that he would "rather put [his] back to a blank wall and be shot than vote for the President's proposal."[11]

Perhaps given the level of emotion involved, it was no surprise that references to Fascism and dictatorship appeared regularly in the talk of men high and low. William Allen White, who had written of Roosevelt's election as "revelation," would in February 1937 liken the president to Hitler:

> In a world-challenging democracy, in a day when tyrants, appearing as demagogs [sic], crying out against predatory wealth, have shattered Europe's democratic institutions, this court message of the President's seems strangely like the first looming American symptom of danger . . . Surely Mr. Roosevelt's mandate was to function as the President, not as Der Fuehrer.[12]

The president's supporters responded in kind. Who was the real dictator here, after all? The Supreme Court had essentially told the American people that much of what they had voted for in 1936 was unconstitutional. Did democracy mean anything if the people were rendered powerless by the decisions of judges appointed for life? Was it really a people's government if life and law depended upon "which side Justice Roberts will flop?" The president's supporters were right that the votes of November had not disappeared. The country had not changed its mind about child labor or social security or labor organizing. Despite their fear of court-packing, people still asked reporters why it was that the Supreme Court always seemed to "throw out laws designed to help the little fellow."[13]

Both sides of the debate invoked the same fears: the whiff of dictatorship and Fascism, "a government of men, not laws" (one of the most incessantly employed phrases of the period). It was simply that each side differed on the nature of the dictatorship. Some critics feared Roosevelt, but more feared the shadow of the future. What would the president's proposal mean in the hands of demagogues like Huey Long or empty-headed politicians like Warren Harding? If the president's opponents feared dictatorship, so too did his supporters. It was simply that they questioned why Justice Roberts seemed "to have more power than the President of the United States: Who elected him to be our dictator?"[14]

———•———

Inside the Supreme Court, things may well have looked entirely different. Cases portrayed in the press as matters of the New Deal raised issues lawyers found quite distinct, so distinct that no first-year law student would have failed to see the cleavage. Those who followed the Court knew, for example, that in a 1934 case called *Nebbia*, the Court had made significant strides toward affirming measures to control prices. Lawyers also knew, for example, that the Wagner Act labor law was far more likely to be upheld as constitutional than the Guffey Coal Act. (Strikes that interfered with the "stream of commerce" had a far stronger legal base than the direct federal regulation of coal mines.) But, for the press and the public, these expert distinctions were largely meaningless; *Guffey Coal* and *TVA* and *Tipaldo* and a variety of other cases were typically clumped together as "New Deal cases."[15]

This gap between how the people understand the Supreme Court and how the Court understands itself is not a failure, but a constitutional inevitability. As the Harvard law professor Felix Frankfurter put it at the time, "The evolution of our constitutional law is the work of the initiate. But its ultimate sway depends upon its acceptance by the thought of the nation." The Court exists to bind the public to the nation's founding commitments and history, and crafts its decisions as a specialist. But, in a democracy, people experience constitutional law in their lives. And, in the New Deal, this experience was as widespread as it was persistent; people lived the rulings of the Supreme Court in the crops they decided to plant, the hours of work they would endure, and their children's fate as laborers. In their letters to the justices, the people did not ask about the "stream of commerce" theory or businesses "affected with a public interest," the terms lawyers would use. Instead, they invited the justices to understand how the law was lived. They wondered whether it might not be fair to pass a law "compelling Supreme Court Justices to work a dirt farm three months out of every year," or drive a truck, before they ruled again in ways that appeared to be "favoring a few at the expense of many."[16]

This was not a battle between law and politics, but between two ideas of politics. The people did not demand that the Court capitulate to their will; they aimed to protect the Court from the president's political influence. The real battle was between a political theory entrenched by the Supreme Court in law and right, and another political theory voted by the people at the polls. For decades, the Supreme Court had struggled with wage and hour legislation even as it regularly affirmed regulation of business; the Court was particularly attuned to what it called labor laws because it feared that laws controlling wages and hours would turn the country toward socialism. But these larger, structural fears—fears of major governmental change—were distilled, melted down, into the technical common law rhetoric of the day, in the rhetoric of rights to property and contract. The justices wrote in their opinions that they were protecting the individual laboring man's right to work, and repeatedly implied that they were justified in fighting a battle against labor interests who were legislating "special benefits" for themselves. The Depression shed a harsh light on such claims, for it revealed that those thought to be gaining a special preference were not so terribly special, but rather ordinary working men, that the purported "few" were actually many, and that if labor was legislating itself a monopoly it was doing so in defense against capital's own forms of monopoly. As legal critics had been saying for some time, the Supreme Court had become so enchanted by the word "liberty" that it had forgotten to ask, "liberty for what and from what"? What good was liberty if it meant the "liberty to starve"?[17]

With the constitutional amendment process blocking even

popular amendments, such as the proposal to ban child labor, the Supreme Court faced a difficult choice: it could make new constitutional law, reversing course to support Congress's legislation, or it could continue to thwart large and vocal majorities, risking the possibility of deep changes in constitutional structure and restrictions on judicial power. Long before the president's plan was announced, as early as 1935, the risk to the Court's power was clear, but the form unknown. Would the president attempt to pack the Court, or would Congress deprive the Court of its basic powers (proposed constitutional amendments often undercut the Court's powers quite radically)? In the years from 1935 until 1937, these risks were spelled out in the editorial pages of popular magazines and newspapers for all to read. By 1937, the Supreme Court's actions showed that, consciously or unconsciously, it had chosen to save the constitutional structure (and its power of judicial review), making extreme remedies unnecessary, by reversing course and changing its own interpretation of the Constitution.

On March 29, 1937, the Supreme Court reversed itself in a state minimum wage case.[18] In short order, the trend continued, the Court's decisions falling like a house of cards. Two weeks later, Justice Roberts, who had been thought to be the major block against labor laws, joined in a five-to-four pro-labor decision upholding the constitutionality of the National Labor Relations Act. Two months later, the Court validated the federal social security law. To the public, the result appeared to be a legal revolution, performed by the Supreme Court itself. Opponents and proponents of the New Deal both claimed that the Constitution had been effectively "amended . . . by legal interpretation." A Court that had appeared to resist popular labor legislation aggressively was now set on a course to defer to legislative will. As *Literary Digest* put it, the justices had been transformed from nine old men into nine old "Santa Clauses."[19]

By August, the papers seemed to report a collective sigh of relief; the Court had given the people what they had demanded. Today, scholars still debate whether the Supreme Court's change in course was driven by the Court's legal doctrine or external political pressures. But it was neither the politics of Roosevelt nor the doctrine of the Court that was the most powerful factor in the debate. It was the shadow of governmental revolution. The people supported the Court not because they agreed with the results of its decisions but because they (rightly) feared basic, structural change. The Supreme Court, in turn, had to fear that, if it continued to block the will of the national majority, the president (or Congress)[20] would gain undue control of the Court, imperiling the constitutional structure of the nation and the Court's power to protect individuals from excessive state power.[21] Given the fear of dictators and demagogues of the day, the choice the Court made is really rather unsurprising: what was more dangerous, risking presidential despotism and control over the Supreme Court or deferring to controversial but majoritarian policies?[22] In an age of strong-men governors and foreign dictators, the Supreme Court's fears of socialism, nurtured in the nineteenth century, would yield to fears of Fascism in the twentieth.[23]

———•———

Except for the references to "hitlerization," all of this might have seemed irrelevant to Skinner's case. No large issues of labor and capital or the right to work or property were implicated in the question of sterilization. Yet there was one important way in which the New Deal constitutional revolution was significant for Skinner's case. If the constitutional theory that had "won" the New Deal revolution was Justice Holmes's theory of deference to majority will, then Skinner's case may well have looked even harder than it had before. In the new world of judicial deference to legislatures, one had to wonder how the Supreme Court would come to understand claims that the legislature could not trample on rights or disregard claims of equality. Holmes, after all, had dismissed the equality argument as the "usual last resort" of constitutional lawyers in the decision that appeared to control Skinner's case, *Buck v. Bell*.[24] If deference was now the rule, would every legislative venture, including sterilization, pass constitutional muster?

CHAPTER 8

Science in a Foreign Mirror: 1937–1941

[T]he growing sense of race egalitarianism . . . is, I think, a very unscientific position.

—S. J. Holmes, zoologist, 1939[1]

Congress was still thrashing away at FDR's court-packing plan when Claud Briggs traveled to McAlester for final legal arguments in Skinner's case. Lawyers in the Oklahoma legislature could postpone their cases when the legislature was in session, on the theory that citizen-legislators could not be asked to legislate and litigate at the same time. During 1937, Briggs had delayed judgment repeatedly, using his legislative immunity to halt action in the trial court. Now the legislature had recessed; time was up. Owen Watts, the assistant attorney general, confidently told reporters that Oklahoma's sterilization law would soon find its way to McAlester. As expected, Judge Higgins made the judgment final in Skinner's case on July 12, 1937, overruling Briggs's plea for a new trial. The state ordered that Skinner undergo the operation at the end of August 1937. At Briggs's request, the order was stayed pending appeal to the Oklahoma Supreme Court.[2]

———◆———

Three months later, on October 28, 1937, the *Oklahoma News* reported that "[t]he eyes of several hundred three-time losers at the

McAlester and Granite prisons turned toward the state Supreme Court today." Briggs had filed an impressive petition, eighteen counts long, in Oklahoma's highest court, listing every possible reason to reverse the jury's determination. The Oklahoma Supreme Court was likely to be the prisoners' best and last chance at law. Even if Briggs imagined that the case might make it to Washington, the odds were distinctly against it—if for no other reason than that the United States Supreme Court agrees to hear very few cases.[3]

Briggs had argued and briefed dozens of cases in Oklahoma's highest court. But Skinner's case was difficult, the law in flux, and his cause distinctly unpopular. The Myerson report, on which Briggs relied at trial, had been widely publicized but seems to have done little to change public opinion. In May 1937, one poll found that 84 percent of the nation favored "sterilization of the habitual criminal and hopelessly insane." *Fortune* magazine's 1937 poll was only slightly less favorable, finding that "sixty-three percent of Americans endorsed the compulsory sterilization of habitual criminals and that sixty-six percent were in favor of sterilizing mental defectives." A 1938 poll of 25,000 insurance policy holders found 88 percent of the men and 93 percent of the women supported "sterilization of habitual criminals."[4]

This unanimity was not based on ignorance of the possibility of abuse. In 1936 and 1937, few newspaper readers were unaware of the possibility that sterilization could be performed on unsuspecting and unconsenting persons; it was one of the leading stories of the decade—all because of a scandal involving America's best blood. In 1936, Ann Cooper Hewitt, heiress to the multimillion-dollar Cooper Hewitt fortune, filed a civil suit charging that her mother had had her sterilized under cover of appendectomy in order to steal Ann's inheritance (if Ann had no children, the money would go to her mother). That suit was in turn followed by a criminal case against the doctors who performed the operation. Day-by-day developments in the Hewitt case were reported from coast to coast throughout 1936. The question was whether Ann was feebleminded; to prove that, her mother emphasized Ann's improper erotic infatuations with people below her station. The judge in the case took the intelligence test administered to Ann and scored a mere twelve years old, but the doctors ultimately escaped criminal prosecution when the charges were dismissed for lack of evidence. After her mother tried to commit suicide, Ann dropped the criminal charges against her and ultimately withdrew the civil suit.[5]

The Hewitt scandal, however widely publicized, did little to change public enthusiasm for sterilization, which lasted well into the late 1930s and even beyond. In 1937, a sex crime panic brought a new round of sterilization legislation and proposals across the country in states including Indiana and Georgia and California. That year, Puerto Rico passed a eugenics law despite earlier cries of "legal lynching in Bermuda." Although experts were expressing more vocal doubts and some foundations were refusing to support eugenics research, the actual number of sterilizations increased in America from 1936 to 1937 and again from 1937 to 1938. E. S. Gosney's Human Betterment Foundation, the second most important eugenics organization in the country, remained tireless in its publicity efforts, repeating over and over again that "more than 150,000,000 civilized people are living under eugenic sterilization laws." The *Los Angeles Times* regularly ran Fred Hogue's "Social Eugenics" column, which extolled some facet of the science, well into the late 1930s.[6]

Given the state of public opinion, it should be no surprise that the prisoners' charges of "hitlerization" brought no grand outcry. Sterilization was not debated in ways we might find familiar today—as a matter of right and fundamental human dignity. Outside the Catholic Church, sterilization generated little public protest in Oklahoma. The Board of Affairs moved along, sterilizing hundreds in Oklahoma's asylums. For some, like Edith Johnson, the *Daily Oklahoman* columnist, the progress of sterilization was far too slow; as she reminded readers in January 1937, "If there is any one thing we, as a people, are sissy about it is in our failure to sterilize the unfit." Oklahoma had a sterilization law, she urged, but what use was it when "criminals and morons and the mentally sick . . . interfere with and prevent its administration?"[7]

———◆———

The essence of any appeal, whether in a state or federal court, is the law; the facts have already been determined by a jury. The art of the law is the brief, a document filed with the court explaining why the jury's determination should be reversed or affirmed. Briggs's opening brief in the Oklahoma Supreme Court listed claim after claim: that Skinner had not had a fair hearing, that sterilization was cruel and unusual punishment, that the law was a bill of attainder (an improper attempt by the legislature to punish an individual), that it imposed punishment "after the fact" (the sterilization law had not been passed until after Skinner committed his third crime), and that sterilization violated due process and equal protection. There were some new arguments, but for the most part Briggs seemed to be stuck on old claims, ones he had already lost. Briggs insisted on claiming that the law was "penal," not "eugenic." If the law were penal in nature, it would be suspect under a number of constitutional provisions, as punishment entails special constitutional protections. But before one reached such an argument, one would have to hurdle a significant barrier: why should the court overturn the people's judgment that the law was about eugenics, that it was like any other public health regulation?[8]

If stuck on an old argument, Briggs nevertheless made it with greater insistency and realism. The state's police power only extended to questions of health and safety. Briggs repeatedly challenged the idea that the law could possibly be about health, since its terms simply did not match the declared purpose. As if imagining the men of McAlester, Briggs argued that the law would allow sterilization of "aged inmates" (J. J. Kelly was over fifty) and "inmates who are serving life sentences" (Bainum was in for life). Such men, Briggs urged, could not possibly pose a "eugenic" threat. And, if these men posed no threat, then their sterilization was "sheer brutal punishment." The only problem with this argument was that Skinner wasn't Kelly or Bainum.[9]

Absent from Briggs's opening brief was any sustained claim that Skinner had a right not to be sterilized. Although this might seem extraordinary to lawyers today, who are versed in a constitutional law that emphasizes right, the entire structure of constitutional law was different then. Constitutional law aimed to limit governmental power not by defining the affirmative content of rights but by defining the limits of governmental power (what was called the police power). Legal analysis focused on whether the law served a health or safety or public purpose. In some contexts, most notably rights to property and contract, rights could be strong enough to overcome the police power argument. But in a vast number of cases, claims of right were defeated by the common welfare.[10] Eugenics had always had a set of progressive followers who thought it appropriate that the rights of individuals should be subordinated to the collective whole; and, for some, the New Deal seemed to prove the wisdom of placing the public's rights above those of individuals. Harry Laughlin, sterilization's great crusader, would proclaim that eugenics was the "inherent right" of the community, invoking the notion of the community's right of self-defense against the harms imposed by the "unfit."[11]

The Oklahoma attorney general's brief was a far easier argument to craft; all the state of Oklahoma needed to tell the court was to defer to the Oklahoma legislature. The legislature had said the law was about health, and that conclusion was entitled to deference. The proposition was thought so elementary that the state's brief to the Oklahoma Supreme Court was largely a string of block quotations from basic law books and, of course, *Buck v. Bell*. As the state's brief put it, "Courts are not at liberty to declare statutes invalid although they may be harsh . . . or are oppressive or are mischievous in their effects." Acting in the name of the public, "the state, in the exercise of its police powers, may always impose reasonable restrictions upon the natural and constitutional rights of its citizens." *Buck v. Bell* had held that such laws, laws aimed at health, fell squarely within the police power.[12]

The last word in the battle of the briefs belonged to Briggs; the petitioning party, the one who has lost in the trial court, has the final opportunity to reply to the claims of his opponent. Briggs's reply brief verged on the intemperate. He did not write that sterilization was "cruel and unusual," but that it was "vicious," even "brutal, disgusting and revolting" to impose such a burden where there was no evidence of genetic taint. Ever insistent that the law was penal in nature, Briggs claimed that his nemesis, Dr. Ritzhaupt, had proven it so by testifying at Skinner's trial that the law's purpose was to deter crime. Angrily, Briggs wrote that legislature had "swept aside all caution and restraint" in its "ardent desire to improve our racial stock." He even argued that the state was going to sterilize "*en masse*" a large portion of Oklahoma's prison population. "Mass" or "wholesale" sterilization was how they referred to Hitler's program at the time, to distinguish it from American laws.[13]

The prisoners' reply brief ended as Briggs had at Skinner's trial, with a warning. This was not a warning of escape, but a warning about the politics of eugenics. If this legislation was sustained as a eugenic measure, one for health and safety, then:

> the next step will be a law providing for the sterilization of some other portion of our population, perhaps all persons who have demonstrated an inability to earn over $200.00 per year and are compelled to live in abject poverty. The time may come when the legislative halls will become a battle ground, where class will strive against class to obtain legislation that one class is of such excellent stock that it should be selected to carry on the propagation of the race and that the inferior class should be taken out and sterilized.[14]

This charge may have reflected powerful fears; it certainly reflected Briggs's lifelong support for the "masses against the classes." But it was poorly framed as a legal objection. The claim that the legislature might, in the future, target an inferior class was an appeal to what many knew of eugenics and its aristocratic pretensions, but it was not a legal argument. Briggs had not tied his claims of inequality to the law he was arguing against.

———•———

In August 1938, as Briggs prepared to argue Skinner's case before the Oklahoma Supreme Court, President Roosevelt, like the rest of the world, worried about armies beginning to move on European soil. Months earlier, in the spring of 1938, Hitler had swept into Austria, annexing the country in the name of German race and blood. By September, the crisis would reach fever pitch as Hitler demanded and achieved control of the Sudetenland, the Czechoslovakian home of ethnic Germans. France called up half a million reservists and the British dug air-raid shelters even as their leaders averted war by bowing to Hitler's demands. On November 9, in what would become known as Kristallnacht, the night of broken glass, Hitler's men ransacked synagogues and terrorized Jews. Just months later, in March 1939, Hitler would motor through a captive Prague and set his sights on Poland. However much Americans might have wanted to stay out of the conflict, as 1938 turned into 1939, the prospect of major war in Europe was hard to ignore.[15]

Germany's famed efficiency and economy and safety—lauded by the American press in the early days of the Nazi regime—now lost ground to Hitler's militarism, oppression, and racism. Today, we associate all of this with Hitler's obsession with the Jews but, at the time, Americans conceived of Nazi oppression in far more general terms. It was Nazi persecution of Catholics, Protestants, and Jews that was discussed; the treason trials of prominent ministers and efforts to tar priests as sex offenders were decried, along with the new "pagan" Nazi faith that openly sought to embrace a national, anti-Christian Teutonic religion. As early as 1936, Anne O'Hare McCormick, the Berlin correspondent for the *New York Times*, asked, "What strange impulse drives a government to create unnecessary enemies by proceeding in one whirl of combat against Jews, Protestants and Catholics all at once?" By 1938, there was an apparent answer: the Nazis had conquered entire populations in the name of preserving the Aryan race.[16]

Once thought a matter of science, race in the hands of Hitler would become not only a politics but also a secular religion; American newspapers dubbed it a "new holy trinity" of blood, race, and soil. In 1935, at a German "Miracles of Life" exhibition, the Nazis proclaimed that a shocking 189,677 sterilization operations had been performed in just fifteen months. The number was quickly revised downward to 56,244 in a year (still 1,000 a week, as many as were performed in six months in the United States). Those shocked by the numbers were told that they showed how quickly the German public grasped the need for "eugenic purity." As the Nazi expert on sterilization in the Ministry of the Interior, Arthur Guett, explained, "The mixture of races causes the swelling of congenitally unsound elements." Before the end of 1936, the Nazis had moved to consolidate the racial order, promulgating the infamous Nuremberg laws against racial pollution by Jewish blood, and threatening Catholics with "heavy penalties" for anti-sterilization "propaganda." As time passed, these concepts were extended; in July 1938, the Italians had "gone Aryan," issuing a manifesto declaring that races and nations were biologically synonymous and that there now existed a "pure" and "Aryan" Italian race.[17]

Germany's racism extended not only to religion but also to science. In 1936, the German physicist and Nobel Prize winner Philip Lenard had declared that Jewish physicists stole their ideas from the Aryans. In 1937, the theoretical physics of Einstein and Planck was publicly indicted as "Jewish physics." Lenard would write in the preface to his *Deutsche Physik*, "Science, like every other human product, is racial and conditioned by blood." Nobelists like the great Werner Heisenberg faced off against Lenard and his fellow Aryans. But, by then, the Nazi Minister of Education had already declared that race was the new "objectivity" of science: "The old idea of science based on . . . abstract intellectual activity has gone forever"; in its place was a science driven by the Nazi concepts of "race, blood and the like" as "ultimate and indispensable principles."[18]

As Nazi territorial ambitions became clear, Americans began to speak out about the dangers of this strange brew of science and race. Reporters wrote that *Mein Kampf* linked Aryanism and sterilization, and magazines reprinted Nazi primers. Senators quoted German texts in order to impale the Nordic ideal, declaring that, for Nazi science, "there is no concept of 'human being' ('man') in contradistinction to animals . . . the only existing differentiation is between Nordic man, on the one hand, and animals as whole, including all non-Nordic human beings, or sub-man, who are transitional forms of development." American scientists began to issue their own decrees. Twelve hundred scientists, in December 1938, signed a manifesto defending democracy and seeking to educate the public about false and unscientific racial doctrines.[19]

In February 1939, on the day we celebrate the birthday of the great liberator of races, Abraham Lincoln, Roosevelt's Secretary of Agriculture, Henry Wallace, a man knowledgeable about genetics (and soon to be Roosevelt's vice president), lashed out against the race prejudice embedded in Nazi science in a lengthy speech: "never before in the world's history has such a conscious and systematic effort been made to inculcate the youth of a nation with ideas of racial superiority as is being made in Germany to-day." The Hitler Youth handbook taught that the Nordic race was superior in all things: in intelligence, in judgment, in the search for truth and progress. Nordic men were true men, strong, persistent, energetic, and gifted in warfare—the ideal of manliness personified. By contrast, the "Western Race" was inferior. They were "loquacious" and acted "more by feeling than by reason," they were mentally "excitable, even passionate," and yet lacked creative power; in other words, they exhibited all the attributes of femininity. The subtext was clear: the great racial tropes of eugenics, the sticky traits of unmanliness, excessive sexuality, and animality, had been turned on America itself.[20]

The *New York Times* editorial page called them the "minute men of science"—those who in 1939 would begin to openly dispute the claims of Aryan science.[21] Their fight was not the beginning of the battle, but the beginning of the end, for it reflected views that had begun to emerge much earlier. This was no sudden shift in criticism, but a swelling chorus that had been emerging in public discourse for at least three years. The Nazis' disrespect for religion and their caustic racism had become the subject of increasing public concern, finding its way into speeches by university presidents and governors and labor leaders. Columbia University's premier cultural anthropologist, Franz Boas, insistently reminded reporters that there was no scientific evidence of inherent racial superiority. His students and colleagues at Columbia—Ashley Montagu and Otto Klineberg and Ruth Benedict among them—produced books and empirical studies aiming to prove what the humanist Jacques Barzun had written in 1937: that the Nazi idea of a pure Aryan race was nothing but "superstition."[22]

The politics of race had become just that, a politics rather than a science, and with that change, the public debate about the "racial science" of eugenics began to shift. In 1934, the announcement of Hitler's eugenics program had done little to change American practice.[23] Now eugenics had run up against a greater challenge. Scientists had been quite skeptical of grand eugenic claims for some time, some emphasizing that calculations showed it would take thousands of years to rid the population of dangerous recessive genes, but this had done little to change the public taste for eugenics. Politics is typically viewed as the enemy of science but, in this case, it was the perverse politics of race that would begin to change people's minds about science.

American eugenics was becoming publicly associated with racism. As one editorialist put it, "when we study the efforts of American experts on heredity to improve the stock by law it is clear that we, too, have our prejudices." Waldemar Kaempffert, the *New York Times* science editor, wrote that unless geneticists "curb the 100-percenters [those who believed only in '100 percent American' blood] who see no good in any one who is not white, Protestant and 'Nordic,' we might as well abandon [eugenics] altogether as a guide in improving the social quality of humanity." Speaking at the World's Fair in October 1939, after European war had begun, Secretary Wallace did not mince words; there was no such thing as a pure race, as the "fanatic" Nazi racialists claimed. He warned that in America, too, there remained those wedded to false and dangerous ideas that "certain races or racial strains are mentally superior or inferior."[24]

Wallace was not without his opponents. In a 1939 speech reprinted in the prestigious journal *Science*, S. J. Holmes, a prominent zoologist and president of the American Eugenics Society, defended eugenics against claims of snobbery and classism, cruelty to the poor, and racism. Holmes was quite open about the fact that eugenics was based on the notion of the "natural inequality of man." His major defense was to turn the tables, to declare that his

opponents were under the "influence of emotional bias." The growing "sentiment in favor of race egalitarianism," said Holmes, was a
political ploy, something for which there was no scientific basis.[25]

For years, even the critics of eugenics had held out hope for a
"true" science of eugenics, free of abuse. The Myerson report exco-
riated punitive state legislation, yet concluded that the feebleminded
and the epileptic might be sterilized. In 1936, Waldemar Kaempffert,
the *New York Times* science editor, had heartily decried genetic chau-
vinism but insisted, "Genetic research must teach us to identify the
hereditary defectives in our midst, whether they are Americans or
Chinese, black or white." Even the great and celebrated critic Franz
Boas, who led the charge against racism in science, told reporters
in 1937 that sterilization might be appropriate in certain circumstances. By August 1939, however, fears of racism were beginning
to eclipse such ambivalence. As the world's geneticists met in Edin-
burgh, Scotland, and saw their colleagues rush home because of the
threat of war, their most prominent members—among them the
brilliant British scientist J. B. S. Haldane and the American Nobelist
Hermann Muller—issued a manifesto imploring the world to reject
the "unscientific doctrine that good or bad genes are the monopoly
of particular peoples."[26]

By the end of 1940, polls showed that a substantial number
of Americans believed that Hitler's Fascism would enslave all of
Europe. Now, the embrace of things German carried risks. The
ever zealous Human Betterment Foundation would aim to "steer
clear" of the German eugenics they once embraced. Eugenics enthusiasts would begin to reframe their claims in the political rhetoric of the day. When Frederick Osborn, a nephew of the
prominent eugenicist Henry Fairfield Osborn, wrote a book rejecting many of his uncle's assumptions, *Time* magazine called it a
"eugenics for democracy." The book, *Preface to Eugenics*, was lauded
as a "new, environmental eugenics." Eugenicists were said to have
finally given up their enchantment with heredity as predestination
and taken a more moderate position (though this merely solidified

a move already underway since the early 1930s, when the "social reasons" for eugenics had been touted—that is, the bad behavior of badly situated parents). Now, said *Time*, Osborn the younger had "presented the scientific evidence to demolish the last remnants of his uncle's fancy." There was no "menace" of the feebleminded, reported Osborn. The thin red line between the super-procreative feebleminded and the under-procreating gentry was really a good bit thicker than eugenicists had predicted; the birth rates of the mentally afflicted were, in fact, quite low.[27]

One might have thought that a "democratic eugenics" was impossible. The great eugenic popularizers—Albert Wiggam and Michael Guyer, Madison Grant and Lothrop Stoddard—had all railed against democracy, calling its egalitarian premises naïve, unscientific, unsound and weak, the "rule of the worst." The Harvard geneticist Edward East dubbed equality a "cult"; the Berkeley zoologist S. J. Holmes called democracy a "fetish." The zoologist Michael Guyer wrote that equality was "beautiful" but "misleading"; the popularizer Paul Popenoe went so far as to write that "democratization" of the country might be "dangerous." Even in 1939, S. J. Holmes was prepared to insist that one of the great virtues of eugenics was that it was a science of "natural inequality."[28]

Yet, in 1940, even eugenicists were bowing to the political forces of the day, trying to make eugenics consistent with American ideals of equality and democracy and individualism. Voluntary sterilization and birth control, Osborn urged, were the appropriate forms of eugenics in a democracy. This move to a "democratic eugenics" did little, however, to resolve the question of sterilization. Osborn was a eugenicist, even if a reformed one. He rejected the notion of wholesale, compulsory sterilization—but took the position that sterilization was appropriate for individual cases of the feebleminded. Organized eugenics may have wrapped itself in the rhetoric of democracy, but sterilization would not die.[29]

———◆———

As foreign racism shed increasing darkness on eugenics, Claud Briggs and the prisoners of McAlester waited. Although the parties had completed briefing Skinner's case by the end of 1938, there was no word from the Oklahoma Supreme Court throughout 1939 and 1940. The press speculated that Skinner's case had been pending longer than any other case on the Oklahoma Supreme Court's docket (the list of cases waiting for decision), and that the justices seemed to be having an extraordinarily difficult time reaching a decision. In 1938, the newspapers announced that Jack Skinner would be eligible for release long before the case was to be decided on appeal, implying that Skinner would win his case by default. But the claim was soon refuted; Owen Watts, the assistant attorney general, publicly warned that Skinner could not win by delay: the law would be enforced against habitual criminals whether inside or outside McAlester prison. Briggs was still waiting for a decision when his partner, former Chief Justice Lester, who had gone with him to that first meeting at McAlester prison, died in July 1940.[30]

Finally, on February 18, 1941, the Oklahoma Supreme Court issued its decision. As in *Main*, the court concluded that the law was a proper exercise of the state's police power. Briggs's arguments about punishment were rejected on the grounds that it was not for the court to second-guess the legislature and its purposes; the law was "eugenic," not "penal." When it came to due process and equal protection, the court asked whether the law was a "proper exercise of the police power," warning that if reasonable, the law would be sustained, even if it affected "constitutional rights." The only significant difference between *Main* and *Skinner* was that—befitting the general legal trend following the court-packing incident—there was a good deal of talk about deference to the legislature, the court stating that the law would be upheld under any state of facts showing that sterilization furthered the "welfare" of society. In the end, the Oklahoma Supreme Court seemed to suggest that its hands were tied, that it was unwise for it to overturn the judgment of a democratically elected majority.[31]

There was, however, one unusual note: Justice Monroe Osborn, a judge noted for his independence of mind, who had voted for sterilization in the *Main* decision, had changed his position and brought with him three other justices to dissent from the majority's opinion.

The dissent was brief, just over a page, and the dissenting judges struggled to present a unified front, announcing their result more firmly than they explained the rationale behind it. The basic thrust of the opinion was that Skinner simply had not had a fair hearing. Almost as an aside, the dissenters made reference, without citation, to the fact that the right to beget children was "one of the highest natural, inherent rights."[32]

CHAPTER 9

Deciding *Skinner*

[B]ack of it all, at the bottom of it all, as the biologist views it, lies the integrity of the racial blood. No ethics, religion, art, democracy, idealism, philosophy, or any other dream of man can long succeed unless blood currents of the race be kept rich, regnant and alive.

—Albert Wiggam, popular science writer, 1925[1]

In the town of McAlester, families were getting ready for church on the morning of August 10, 1941. At the prison, warden Jess Dunn was working on a new communications system with an engineer named Herschel Fentriss. Fentriss had brought along his boss, R. W. Murray, and the boss's twelve-year-old son; Dunn allowed the father and son to tag along. By 1941, Warden Dunn was a McAlester veteran. He had served as deputy to two prior wardens, Brown and Kenny. When Kenny was ousted over differences with the Board of Affairs, Dunn was elevated to the post. He was reputed to be a "two-fisted" disciplinarian, but he abolished the rod and offered more opportunities for work, education, and recreation than any prior warden at McAlester.[2]

Fentriss, Dunn, Murray, and the boy were standing in the prison yard as Dunn pointed out where he wanted the speakers on the cell houses. Four convicts crept out from under the stairs near the mess hall. Dunn felt a razor at his throat. Claud Beavers, the man who had led the great break of 1936, was holding the razor. Beavers screamed to "get that [expletive] kid out of here"; Murray and his son ran. Dunn and Fentriss, weapons at their throats, were shoved toward the prison's east gate. The deputy warden, H. Ben Crider, ran to the yard and saw blood trickling down Dunn's neck. Crider screamed at the convicts that they would never get away with it, that they would be killed. With the knife at his neck and a civilian at his side, Dunn yelled: "My God, Ben, don't let them shoot now. There's an innocent man here." The guards lowered their rifles and opened the gate.[3]

Outside, the men commandeered a car belonging to a prison guard, the prison siren howled, and the local sheriff, Bill Alexander, led the chase. A bridge was out, and the inmates were forced to turn back the way they came when Alexander spotted the convicts' vehicle and leaped out of his car, blocking their path. Dunn yelled to Alexander, "Let us pass, Billy." "Well you can pass, Warden," replied Alexander, but "those convicts have got to fall out of that car." The ringleader opened fire; Alexander shot him through the head and the convicts' car backed up and screamed off in a different direction. After fleeing about a quarter of a mile north, the convicts leaped out of the badly damaged car and hid in a ditch. Alexander, who had been following, saw Warden Dunn's body inside the abandoned car, slumped over with "blood running from his head." Alexander leapt out of his vehicle and "kept on shooting until all of the convicts gave up."[4]

Later, the newspapers would say it was the "bloodiest quarter hour" in the history of McAlester prison. "Black Sunday" left the warden, Jess Dunn, dead; he had been shot at close range after freeing himself from his bonds. Three inmates were dead; the fourth, Hiram Prather, would be tried and executed for Dunn's murder. The next day, the break was front-page news across the country, page one *New York Times* material. Bill Alexander, the sheriff who thwarted the break, became a celebrity, recounting events on the CBS radio network. A group of prisoners wrote to the local paper expressing their sorrow for the loss of a man who had given them "the hope of self-redemption." The new warden, Fred Hunt, a 200-pound man fond of his ten-gallon hat, announced that Dunn's pet project, a prison rodeo that brought thousands to McAlester, would proceed in Dunn's honor.[5]

The newspapers said that history had repeated itself in the 1941 McAlester break. Five years earlier, in the great break of 1936, Jess Dunn had headed the posse that spent days in the Kiamichi mountains tracking Claud Beavers. At the time, some speculated that Beavers had escaped McAlester to avoid sterilization, but Warden Kenny denied it. Five years later, as sterilization menaced McAlester for the last time, Claud Beavers broke again. Once more he faced Dunn; this time both would die.[6]

For much of the spring and summer Briggs had stalled. Although courts rarely rehear cases, Briggs asked the Oklahoma Supreme Court for repeated extensions of time to file a rehearing petition. He had little choice; the case had lingered so long in the Oklahoma Supreme Court that Briggs's original clients were all gone from McAlester, although they could still be sterilized (the terms of the law applied to habituals both inside and outside the prison). Bainum, Hyde, and Kelly had all been paroled or pardoned; Skinner had completed his term.[7] When asked by the press about the case, Briggs appeared ambivalent; he explained that, five years earlier, he had taken a $1,000 retainer to pursue a trial and appeal and he had done that. Briggs added almost as an afterthought, "I won't let the boys down."[8]

October 8, 1941 was the last possible day for an appeal; the Oklahoma Supreme Court had denied Briggs's request for a rehearing and its stay of the sterilization order was about to expire. That day, the headlines in the *McAlester News–Capital* were of the death penalty verdict in the Dunn murder trial. Buried in the middle of the page, in an exceedingly brief two-paragraph story, was other, rather extraordinary, news: lawyers were racing to Washington to save Skinner's right to appeal to the United States Supreme Court. The *Daily Oklahoman* reported that two McAlester attorneys, Guy Andrews and H. I. Aston, had entered the case at the last moment and that "Aston left Monday by airplane for Washington to arrange for appeal before the deadline."[9]

Lawyers Andrews and Aston were new to the case, but not to

McAlester. Aston was a former schoolteacher and long-time court clerk. His partner, Guy Andrews, then almost seventy years old, was one of the leading lawyers in eastern Oklahoma. As a young man, Andrews had set out from Texas to find his fortune in Oklahoma, and landed in the coal mines near the town of Wilburton. Like Briggs, with grit and hard work he made himself a prominent lawyer, even though he had never attended law school. Unlike Briggs, Andrews had experience in the United States Supreme Court. He had fought, and lost, a fairly well-known case, the *Oklahoma Ice* case, a decision celebrated today for its dissent by Justice Brandeis, seeking deference to the states as a "laboratory" of experimentation.[10]

Today, one wonders why, suddenly, the lawyers from tiny McAlester, Oklahoma, were flying (a rather extreme step at the time) to Washington to save the prisoners' appeal. For much of September, McAlester had been preoccupied with the fallout from the prison break and Dunn's death—charges of politics at the prison and the trial of Dunn's killer.[11] As Briggs's court papers reveal, the Board of Affairs was blocking further appeal, refusing to release the prisoners' canteen funds. Once more, however, history appeared to repeat itself. Days after the 1936 break, Warden Kenny had released $1,000 for the prisoners to appeal their case. So, too, it was only after the 1941 break that money was disbursed to pursue Skinner's case. On October 6, 1941, the very day that Fred Hunt was confirmed by the Oklahoma Senate as McAlester's new warden, funds were released for the filing of Skinner's case in the United States Supreme Court.[12]

Two days and a plane flight later, lawyer H. I. Aston appeared before Justice Stanley Reed in his chambers in Washington. He would argue that the death of Warden Dunn and the prison break had prevented the lawyers from filing for Supreme Court review. As the prisoners' formal papers explained it in one long run-on sentence, as if dictated on the fly: "due to conditions arising from an outbreak by some of those within the penitentiary that resulted in the death of the Warden . . . and the resulting necessity of adjusting anew conditions resulting from such outbreak, the appointment of another Warden who naturally would want to acquaint himself with matters involved in the litigation . . . delayed action upon the request for allocation of the money for the purposes of this appeal until Monday, the 6th day of October." Before Aston returned home to Oklahoma, Justice Reed granted the last extension of time that could or would be granted in Skinner's case.[13]

———◆———

Two months later, on January 12, 1942, the justices of the United States Supreme Court met in their chandeliered and wood-paneled conference room to discuss, as a preliminary matter, whether even to hear the arguments in Skinner's case. The eminences of old— Justices Brandeis and Holmes and Cardozo—were all gone. The Supreme Court's members were terribly new and some (like Justice Douglas) almost young. Roosevelt may have lost the battle to pack the Court, but he won the war. Due to death and retirement, Roosevelt had made seven new appointments since the Court clash in 1937: first, Hugo Black in 1937, then Justices Reed, Frankfurter, Douglas, Murphy, Byrnes, and Jackson in quick succession. The justices were almost all New Dealers. Black had been one of Roosevelt's stalwarts in the Senate, Douglas was a former chairman of the Securities and Exchange Commission, Frankfurter was a member of Roosevelt's closet cabinet, Reed was a former solicitor general, and Jackson and Murphy had both been attorney general. Only Chief Justice Harlan Stone, the former dean of the Columbia Law School and elder statesman of the Court, had been there when *Buck v. Bell* had been decided.[14]

Skinner's was but one of many cases to consider. The case had been late, full of technical problems, and presented by obviously inexperienced lawyers who could not decide who was in charge. Despite Aston's mad rush to Washington, there was no assurance that the Supreme Court would even hear the case; all the lawyers had obtained, up until this time, was simply the right to file for review. At such conferences, the justices sit to discuss the legal merits of the claims. The discussions are largely secret, recorded only in the notes of individual justices. The vote was unanimous to grant a writ of certiorari, to at least hear the lawyers' arguments in Skinner's case that sterilization was unconstitutional.[15]

The grant of the writ was an unexpected victory in a case in which there had been few. This minor victory posed its own problems, however. The arguments in the case had to be reevaluated. The Supreme Court is the last legal battleground; this is the time when lawyers must become their own harshest critics, questioning the best and worst arguments in their case. Briggs's claims that the law was aimed at punishment rather than health had repeatedly failed. The new lawyer, Andrews, decided to shift focus. He would argue due process and equal protection, emphasizing the law's arbitrariness. This was a risky strategy given *Buck v. Bell*, which appeared to reject both arguments out of hand.[16]

Andrews went back to basics; arbitrariness had been the touchstone of equal protection and due process arguments for decades before 1937. And so he focused on the irrationalities of Oklahoma's sterilization scheme. Briggs had foreshadowed the crux of the argument in his claim (borrowed from the prisoners' own arguments) that the worst criminals—such as Capone and Zangara (who attempted Roosevelt's assassination)—would not be sterilized under Oklahoma's law if they hadn't had three convictions. Why did inheritance of criminal tendencies follow from three convictions but not two? Deference is owed to legislatures, urged Andrews, but they may not "enact an arbitrary or unreasonable standard."[17]

In his petition for the court to hear the case, Andrews revealed his own emotion, writing in the first person (and thus violating the unwritten rules of brief-writing):

> I have wondered upon what rational basis the Legislature could have arrived at the conclusion that all those committing minor offenses would transmit to their progeny only vices; while the dishonest financier who appropriates trusting depositors' monies in the banks, or trustees who convert funds of confiding clients, and the saboteur, and the inciter of treason could spew from his loins only progeny blessed

with virtues. The terms of the Act exclude from its penalties the Capones, the Ponzis and the Benedict Arnolds.[18]

From this premise came a legal argument raised, but never emphasized, by Briggs: Oklahoma's law violated equal protection. The law created "classes," urged Andrews, of habitual and nonhabitual criminals—and the line between those classes was arbitrary. It was not simply the line between two and three crimes; it was the law's exemptions for liquor and tax offenses, as well as embezzlement and political crimes. In short, the tax cheats and inciters of treason could commit eight crimes and still not run afoul of the sterilization law, but those convicted of three lesser crimes (chicken stealing, for example) would. When he wrote the principal brief, Andrews was not shy about outlining the implications of the law's exception; he wondered aloud whether the legislature intended to establish an "aristocracy of crime, relieving favored [criminals] of the burdens borne by those less fortunate."[19]

Inside McAlester, the prisoners echoed Andrews's brief, the prison newspaper inveighing against the "pro-sterilization gentry," who sought to treat men as if they were guinea pigs. Even the prisoners recognized, however, that in a nation at war, resources were scarce; the canteen money was paying for the lawyers' expenses, and Andrews and Aston had their law practices to run. In early April 1942, Andrews negotiated a deal with the Oklahoma attorney general to minimize the cost; the parties agreed that the case would be submitted "on the briefs," which meant that the lawyers agreed not to appear in Washington.[20]

———•———

On April 11, 1942, the justices met again in their conference room to consider the motion to decide Skinner's case without oral argument. Chief Justice Stone presented Skinner's case almost as if he were lecturing law students, remarking that "there is a *Harvard Law Review* article on this." The reference was to an article that had come to dominate Stone's view—as it had Holmes's—of the Constitution. The article was by the Harvard constitutionalist James

Bradley Thayer, and was known for its argument that the constitutionality of legislation should be presumed. The "presumption
of constitutionality" was an old but practical idea that it is for the
people, and not the courts, to decide the nation's course. In Skinner's case, however, Stone noted the presumption less to apply it
than to suggest that it posed a problem—a rather large one.[21]

For Stone, it had been the majority's refusal to abide by the presumption that had endangered the Supreme Court as an institution
and led to the court-packing crisis. At least since 1937, Stone had
been pondering how to reconcile the presumption with a role for
the court in protecting individual rights. In a footnote in an otherwise nondescript case, the 1938 *Carolene Products* decision, Stone
would write that the presumption of constitutionality might not be
applied in three types of cases: one, where the Bill of Rights was
clearly invoked (free exercise of religion, for example); two, where
the political process was itself involved (as in election and free speech
cases); and three, where majorities could not be relied upon, as in
the case of laws burdening religious, national, or racial minorities.*
As Stone made clear to a friend to whom he wrote on the day after
the *Carolene Products* opinion was issued, the state of the world had
helped him reach such an accommodation:

> I have been deeply concerned . . . about the increasing racial
> and religious intolerance which seems to bedevil the world,
> and which I greatly fear may be augmented in this country.
> For that reason I was greatly disturbed by the attacks on the
> Court and the Constitution last year, for one consequence

---

* The footnote reads in part: "It is unnecessary to consider now whether legislation
which restricts those political processes which can ordinarily be expected to bring
about repeal of undesirable legislation, is to be subjected to more exacting judicial
scrutiny under the general prohibitions of the Fourteenth Amendment than are
most other types of legislation. . . . Nor need we enquire whether similar consid-
erations enter into the review of statutes directed at particular religious, . . . or
national, . . . or racial minorities; . . . whether prejudice against discrete and insular
minorities may be a special condition, which tends seriously to curtail the operation
of those political processes ordinarily to be relied upon to protect minorities, and
which may call for a correspondingly more searching judicial inquiry." (citations
omitted).

of the program of "judicial reform" might well result in breaking down the guaranties of individual liberty.[22]

Carolene's footnote four would not only become the most famous footnote in constitutional law; it actually rewrote history. In the note, Stone listed various cases that he thought exemplified its propositions. Cases that had once made sense in the old lingua franca of police power and property rights were now redescribed as ones of discrimination on the basis of race and nationality. The old theory that the Supreme Court's job was to police mob-like majorities yielded to a new theory that its job was to protect minorities from majorities.[23]

It was a moment of what the legal scholar Derrick Bell calls convergence—when the majority finds it in their interest to protect the rights of the minority. From 1938, when *Carolene* was decided, until 1942, the Supreme Court heard numerous cases involving the Jehovah's Witnesses, then considered a "small" and "obnoxious" minority religion. In Texas, Witnesses were run out of town on the theory of their supposed Nazi sympathies; in Australia and New Zealand, the Witnesses were banned; in Germany, they were executed. In case after case, the Supreme Court reached out to hear the Witnesses' claims of oppression regarding saluting the flag, door-to-door solicitations, handing out tracts, and violent altercations.[24]

It was not only religious minorities but racial ones who benefited from the fear of majority intolerance. From 1938 until 1942, the Supreme Court heard almost a dozen cases involving discrimination against African-Americans. For the first time since the passage of the Fourteenth Amendment more than half a century earlier, the Supreme Court began to take an interest in the constitutional claims of racial minorities. In a series of criminal cases, the court reached out to attack lynching by indirection, striking down confessions obtained by force and fear of the mob, refusing to uphold convictions where there had been no due process of law (biased juries, no lawyers, torture). These were small steps in a segregated world, taken far too late, but steps that would mark the beginning of the long march toward the most famous equality decision of the twentieth century, *Brown v. Board of Education*.[25]

At first, America's entry into the war intensified this concern. Soon after Pearl Harbor, the president implored the nation to reject the anti-immigrant hysteria of World War I. Be wary, he said, of those trying "to breed mistrust and suspicion between . . . one group and another, one race and another, one government and another." The nation's most famous anti-Semite, Henry Ford, formally denounced bigotry, declaring that "hate-mongering" against any racial group undermined America's unity. Even the tiny *McAlester News–Capital*, in little-Dixie Oklahoma, editorialized that "[t]here is no place in great cosmopolitan America for this group-against-group, race-against-race business at any time . . . for there[in] lie failure and defeat." But the public's tolerance had its limits. Just as the nation appeared unified in its quest to resist Nazi racism, Washington announced plans to regulate the movement of the Japanese on the West Coast. At the Supreme Court, the cases lawyers today associate with the war—the Japanese curfew and Nazi saboteur cases—were months away. But, before the Court was faced with a stark conflict between liberty and security, there was one more case that would profit from pre-war convergence: *Skinner v. Oklahoma*.[26]

Ironically, it was Chief Justice Stone, the author of *Carolene*, who had doubts in Skinner's case. His principal aim in *Carolene* was to reconcile the apparently irreconcilable: a role for the Court in overruling legislation and, at the same time, a strong presumption of constitutionality. It was one thing for Stone to take the lead in a variety of cases expanding the right of free speech, which could be justified as enhancing political debate, or religion, which was protected by the Bill of Rights. It was another for the Chief Justice to reverse his own position in *Buck v. Bell*, in which he had voted with Holmes. As Murphy's notes of the conference state, "The technical difficulty with this case is that we always indulge in some constitutional [presumption] and if we indulge that, we haven't anything to go [on]."[27]

Enter Felix Frankfurter, the former Harvard professor, the man who held the "scholar's seat" on the Supreme Court. Frankfurter relished legal battle. He positively enjoyed lecturing his fellow justices on the finer points of law; his condescension was almost stunning. Precisely because of this trait, Frankfurter's opinion carried with it the aura of a refined and technically correct result. Although they would later become archenemies, at the time Douglas would say that Frankfurter "was our hero. He was indeed learned in constitutional law and we were inclined to take him at face value." Frankfurter insisted that, in Skinner's case, Oklahoma's law violated equal protection. As Murphy's notes report, "FF" said, "I would invalidate on section 24 [the section that exempted tax cheats and embezzlers]. It does offend equal protection."[28]

Not all were convinced. Roberts, like Stone, was worried; if this was a "eugenic" law, he said, "we are bound to give credence to what [the] legislature did." Stone agreed but emphasized the failure to give Skinner a full hearing: "Civil rights are involved and if this man has a right to the protection of these civil rights then he has a right to be heard. The state should have to defend its statute. I would set this down for argument and issue a stay." Stone stated that the issue was not "cruel and inhuman punishment. This is eugenic legislation." Roberts added that if the attorney general "comes up here and says it is a penal statute," then "we deal." On April 14, 1942, the Supreme Court restored the case to the oral argument schedule; Oklahoma's attorney general was to appear in Washington. The prisoners' lawyers would stay home.[29]

———◆———

Three weeks later, on May 6, 1942, Mac Q. Williamson, attorney general of Oklahoma, climbed the long flight of white marble steps into the Supreme Court building. Completed at the height of the Depression, the classical structure was quickly dubbed the "marble palace" (a deliberate Depression-inspired mocking of the Court's motto, emblazoned on its classical frieze, "Equal Justice Under Law"). But for the fact that he had been specially called to Washington, Oklahoma's attorney general might have climbed the steps with confidence. The state's briefs had all been rather rote affairs, almost copies of claims made earlier. The state's case wasn't terribly difficult to explain: the Supreme Court should simply defer to the state's position; in matters of health and safety, the legislature had broad police powers. As reporters later summarized Williamson's argument, the law was a "eugenic measure" to "maintain the purity and the virility of the race."[30]

Yet, as the newspapers also reported the next day, the attorney general's apparently easy case quickly turned sour. Chief Justice Stone dogged Williamson about genetics: was there any scientific evidence "which would indicate that 'criminal propensities' are transmitted?" And, if there was not, why should the Court apply the standard rule that laws are presumed to be constitutional? Williamson wobbled, conceding too much. "I am not prepared to say that that presumption must be indulged here," he said, then backtracked. "But I don't know that the court should assume there was no such evidence" before the legislature. Jackson asked whether environment was more responsible than heredity for crime, and Williamson waffled again, saying that "[p]erhaps the greater weight gives the environment as the motivating cause of crime," but that there was a "division of opinion" on which the legislature might justifiably rely.[31]

"Several justices," according to the papers, asked Williamson the question that Andrews had asked in his brief, that the prisoners had themselves raised, and that had been given constitutional legitimacy by Frankfurter: why "stealing chickens was included and embezzlement excluded" from the law? Williamson replied, "There are elements of violence in stealing chickens." "Not if done surreptitiously," Stone replied. The state's attorney general was at loss. By the end of the argument, he was forced to admit that the law's exceptions "are very difficult to reconcile." As one Oklahoma newspaper explained, the attorney general had virtually conceded that the exemption for embezzlers and political crimes raised "serious doubts" about the law's constitutionality.[32]

———◆———

The next day, May 7, 1942, the Justices met once again in their conference room to consider Skinner's case. Stone remained skeptical of the equal protection claim. Stone revered Holmes and, as he once wrote Stone, Holmes took "no stock in a priori human rights or in the passion for equality." According to Douglas's notes, Stone had insisted at the first conference that "moronic minds" were different, suggesting that he would not overrule *Buck*. And yet, that was an apparent virtue of Frankfurter's equality argument; a narrow equality argument focused on the precise language of the statute in *Skinner* might allow the Chief Justice to leave *Buck* alone but strike down Oklahoma's eugenic effort.[33]

It is not too hard to believe that Frankfurter, as the Court's only Jewish justice, felt the sting of Oklahoma's blood laws in ways not shared by his colleagues. The brilliant Frankfurter, who had arrived at Ellis Island at the age of twelve, and who as early as 1934 had corresponded with Columbia professor Franz Boas about the racism of the Nazis, cannot have been insensible to the power of Aryanism to brand entire groups as inferior races. Frankfurter believed in the power and duty of judges to find the meaning of legislative acts; he believed that reading law required "reading life," for it was life, not dictionaries, at which legislators aimed their laws. He was reared in Holmes's view that statutes were "live but groping attempts to express ideas, and that what one must look for are the ideas behind the words." For Frankfurter, the "life" of Oklahoma's statute—the "idea behind the words"—was not what his hero Holmes had seen when he wrote *Buck v. Bell* in 1927. Then, eugenics was, publicly at least, synonymous with health; by 1942, the claims of health had been revealed as a "cloak for class snobbery, ancestor worship and race prejudice."[34]

In the end, Stone relented and agreed to "go along" with Frankfurter's equal protection argument. He may well have relented because Frankfurter was the source of the argument. Stone and the rest of the Court knew that Frankfurter was even more wedded to the presumption of constitutionality than Stone himself. Frankfurter had staked his reputation on it; he had authored one of the Supreme Court's most controversial opinions of the day, upholding the state's right to force the children of Jehovah's Witnesses to salute the flag. The result was public uproar and violence: Witnesses were attacked, jailed, and fired from their jobs. If Frankfurter—so wedded to the presumption of constitutionality that he would risk extreme unpopularity—was willing to ignore the presumption in Skinner's case, Stone may not have wished to cause more dissension on the Court than there already was.[35] It was the end of the term, and the unruly Roosevelt Court was beginning to show how unruly it could be; Murphy and Douglas were about to denounce Frankfurter's flag salute opinion, which would soon be overruled. Stone was no eugenics enthusiast; he thought that the Oklahoma legislature knew absolutely nothing about genetics; that he was not happy with the equality rationale did not mean he would vote to affirm Oklahoma's sterilization law. Roberts, the only other potential dissenter, indicated that he would defer to the others. At the end of the May 7 conference, the Chief Justice assigned the youngest (although not the newest) of the justices, William O. Douglas, to write the draft opinion.[36]

———◆———

The spring was a busy season for the justices winding up their term before a summer break. Soon Douglas would find himself at graduation day, warning young faces that the "class of 1942, like the class of 1861," would emerge from ivied halls into war. But before the speeches of the day could be imagined or spoken, there was constitutional work to be done. Douglas took to his assignment, the *Skinner* case, soon after the May 7 conference. In pencil on a yellow pad, he focused on the exemption section which provided that "offenses arising out of the violation of the prohibitory laws, revenue acts, embezzlement, or political offenses, shall not . . . be considered within the terms of this Act." It took about two pages to set out the inequality argument. Douglas emphasized the arbitrariness of the statute's limits: "A person who enters a chicken coop and steals chickens commits a felony; and he may be sterilized if he is thrice convicted"; not so the clerk who "appropriates over $20 from his employer's till." The former is a common thief and will be sterilized, while the latter, the embezzler, will not. Douglas explained at length the arcane lines drawn by the criminal law between different forms of larceny—lines that would, under Oklahoma's law, spell the difference between those who would and those who would not be sterilized.[37]

Today, constitutionalists find the emphasis on the statutory exemption and the criminal law pedantic and even irrelevant. But at the time, arbitrariness remained the basic test for equal protection claims. A statutory exemption was precisely where an expert like Frankfurter, trained in the old (now largely lost) arts of equal protection law, is likely to have gone. Lawyers, when they are trying to convince, pick old arguments, not new ones. And the argument Frankfurter used was old. From before the turn of the twentieth century, lawyers had argued that laws were unconstitutional if they contained an arbitrary exemption or discrimination, often picking on a statutory exemption as evidence of legislative favoritism. The classic example was *Connelly v. Union Sewer Pipe*, in which an agricultural exemption to an antitrust law was found to be arbitrary, or the more recent *Truax v. Corrigan*, in which Chief Justice Taft found that exempting labor from injunction remedies violated the equal protection clause of the Fourteenth Amendment. Even into the 1930s, this kind of equality challenge was common, frequently added to claims that a regulation violated the right to property or contract. Although no longer the law today, at the time, these justices had grown up on the class legislation controversies of the day.[38]

Given the old law of equality, it made perfect sense for Douglas to emphasize the statutory exemption in Skinner's case, and to seize upon the exemption chosen. Seen in its best light, the class legislation theory was a theory of failed governance. The fear was that an exemption showed that the legislature had improperly favored the exempted—in Skinner's case, those who committed the high-class crimes of the banker and the lawyer, the politician and the doctor— and burdened the lowly chicken thief. This was the "aristocracy of crime" that Guy Andrews had identified. The idea was that the exemption section did precisely what the nineteenth-century purveyors of the class legislation idea aimed to prohibit: it violated the rule of generality promoted by the legal scholar Thomas Cooley (who borrowed it from John Locke) that there ought to be "one rule for rich and poor, for the favorite at court and the countryman at plough."[39]

In Skinner's case, the risk of unjust preference was significantly amplified by the liberties at stake. A eugenics law is not only a law that might favor the rich and disfavor the poor, it is one which makes that economic distinction permanent by placing it within body and blood. As Douglas explained, a sterilization law assumes certain "biologically inheritable traits"—that the chicken thief has bad blood, while the embezzler does not. That made the law's lines, drawn by the common law of crimes (a common law that is the product of history and reaches back, in America, to the eighteenth-century jurist Blackstone), seem terribly arbitrary. As Douglas explained, "We have not the slightest basis for inferring that . . . the inheritability of criminal traits follows the neat legal distinctions" between embezzlement and theft. At the time, the scholar Walter Wheeler Cook explained: " 'criminality' is a legal and sociological and not a biological term . . . its definition depends upon the social, cultural, and political traditions and practices of a given community. Fascist Italy and Nazi Germany regard as 'criminal' many types of conduct which we regard as praiseworthy."[40]

As Justice Douglas concluded in *Skinner*, the common law of crime could not possibly announce a "rule of human genetics." To emphasize the arbitrariness, Douglas wrote that the law was "as invidious a discrimination as if it had selected a particular race or nationality for oppressive treatment." Today, such references seem mysterious to lawyers because the prisoners challenging the law were not known to be African-American. But such references made perfect sense in a day when race was still a question of blood and was commonly used to demean "white" races. When Justice Douglas was writing, the culture still viewed many whom we today would call "white" as races: the "Jewish race," the "Italian race," the "Aryan race," were quite common references of the day (likely, given the war, very common).[41] As Justice Douglas wrote in a draft he never circulated or published, the law "hardly has a firmer con-stitutional basis than if in dealing with particular offenses it drew a line . . . between Nordic and other racial types."[42]

In 1942, America was at war against an Aryan racism that was as capable of delineating "races" of criminals and Communists as of paupers. The notorious Nuremberg laws (by 1942, they were notorious) defined a Jew by blood. America's own racial laws, its laws against miscegenation (promoted heavily by eugenicists), defined race in terms of blood. Not surprisingly, professional academics in 1942 seemed to find it easier to relate sterilization to questions of race. Harvard's Thomas Reed Powell, one of the great Court-watchers of his generation, explained how Justice Douglas had elaborated on the statute as a tool "of discrimination against a particular race or nationality." Professor Powell explained that the cases cited by Justice Douglas were ones about the "Chinese and colored races," and argued that the judges who joined the opinion must have been primarily concerned "with the desirability of setting up a barrier against legislative *race discrimination.*" He even noted that habitual criminality was in the South often associated with race.[43]

Today, most lawyers who read *Skinner* focus on none of this, preferring the lines that begin the published opinion. In a large cloud-shaped bubble at the top of his penciled draft, Douglas added the lines for which the case would become famous: "This case touches a sensitive and important area of human rights. Oklahoma deprives certain individuals of a right which is basic to the perpetuation of a race—the right to have offspring."[44] Today, these lines have become embroiled in the most controversial of constitutional questions surrounding the "right to privacy," as *Skinner*'s "right to procreation" is thought to support the right to abortion. That, however, creates a puzzle, since if these lines created a right, in the sense that moderns understand a right—as capable of trumping the common welfare— the lines should not have been added as an afterthought, but should have ended the case, leaving the rest of the opinion and its emphasis on equality irrelevant. It also fails to explain why no one, whether the justices in conference or the litigants, emphasized the question of right.

The solution to this puzzle lies in recognizing that, for decades before 1942, basic constitutional law was very different from what it is today. At the time, rights claims had a different relationship to equality claims. They were not competitors, but allies. The law applied the same standard, arbitrariness, to both due process and equal protection clauses. Today, constitutionalists view rights as trumps (winners despite claims of public purpose), but then the general doctrinal rule was that legal rights could be defeated by claims of the general welfare, known as the police power.[45] Under the old law, to say that Skinner's case involved basic human rights was not to end the case: the police power could easily defeat such a claim, as it had in *Buck v. Bell. Skinner*'s innovation was not the invocation of right, but the idea that rights married to inequality could trigger "strict scrutiny"—a term used for the first time in *Skinner* and one which would become central to the future of constitutional law.[46]

———◆———

Days after Douglas put pencil to yellow-lined pad, there was a printed draft ready to circulate to other members of the Court. The response was quick and approving.* On the back of his copy of the draft, Black wrote, "really great job!" "Very good and I agree," wrote Murphy. Frankfurter commented, "Yes, gladly, with a slight suggestion on page 3." Douglas had written that "there is another feature of the Act which gives it a constitutional infirmity." Frankfurter's "slight suggestion" added emphasis to the equality point, striking "gives it a constitutional infirmity," and replacing it with "clearly condemns it."[47]

Only one justice remained unconvinced: Chief Justice Stone.[48] Stone would write his own opinion in *Skinner*, agreeing with the result but offering different reasons, urging that Oklahoma had failed to give Skinner a full enough hearing on whether he would pass on his "criminalistic" genes. Stone argued that the law violated Skinner's right to procedural due process. This was the cautious approach of the judge's judge. Today, lawyers tend to admire Chief Justice Stone's opinion for its opening: "If Oklahoma may resort

---

* There was no indication from any of the justices that the opinion was in the least controversial—that it "created" new rights, or had anything to do with what we today call "substantive due process" (a term with extremely negative connotations and one which is most often used by modern lawyers to describe *Skinner*).

generally to the sterilization of criminals on the assumption that their propensities are transmissible to future generations by inheritance, I seriously doubt that the equal protection clause requires it to apply the measure to all criminals in the first instance, or to none." This was a rhetorical move once made by Holmes almost as routine, a move that presumes a thin logical idea of equality. But there was nothing in that argument that answered the majority's claim that the legislature was self-dealing, foisting burdens onto others that it would never apply to itself. Moreover, there was something hypocritical about the remark's logic; it assumed that it was perverse to extend sterilization, yet the Chief Justice was unwilling to brand sterilization itself unconstitutional. The answer to Stone's argument is to turn it around: if sterilization was impermissible or cruel, what good would a fuller hearing do?[49]

The last opinion in the case was written by Justice Jackson, who concurred in the result, arguing that Stone and Douglas were both right, and that their opinions were sounder together than apart. The dangers of the act exacerbated, and reinforced, each other. The lack of a hearing on the question of inheritance reinforced the notion of legislative hypocrisy and self-dealing, where majorities exploit public prejudices against minorities by distributing burdens only to those deemed "other" or "different." Jackson borrowed the terms of the day, the idea of the *Carolene Products* decision that constitutional scrutiny of legislation was particularly important to protect minorities from the "experiments" of dominating majorities: "There are limits to the extent to which a legislatively represented majority may conduct biological experiments at the expense of the dignity and personality and natural powers of a minority—even those who have been guilty of what the majority define as crimes."[50]

The great dividing line between the justices' opinions reflected their visions of equality. The Chief Justice saw the danger as one of individual injustice, the failure to give Skinner a more intensive, personalized hearing. Justices Douglas and Frankfurter and Jackson saw the problem as what the lawyer Andrews had called an "aristocracy" of blood. It was a fear not only of individual injustice but of structural failure, even genocide: "The power to sterilize, if exercised, may have subtle, far reaching and devastating effects. In evil or reckless hands it can cause races or types which are inimical to the dominant group to wither and disappear."[51]

—◆—

The day after *Skinner* was decided, June 2, 1942, the headlines were all of the bombs dropped on Cologne the night before. Buried on page 15, the *New York Times* story read, "High Court Voids Sterilization Law: Hits Oklahoma Discrimination, Applying Statute to Chicken Thief, Not Embezzler." *Skinner* was likened to two other cases decided the same day, *Hill v. Texas* and *Ward v. Texas*, cases in which African-American defendants were granted constitutional relief from bias-infected criminal trials. Calling all three cases decisions involving "personal liberties," the reporter explained that "the Supreme Court unanimously invalidated today the Oklahoma law for sterilization of habitual criminals on the ground that it was discriminatory." The *Washington Post* explained that the Court "struck down the statute because it singled out only certain types of criminals," a "clear, pointed, unmistakable discrimination." The *Christian Science Monitor* concluded that the law was overturned because it failed "to meet the requirements of the equal protection clause." The *Daily Oklahoman* was emphatic: "U.S. Tribunal Holds Law Is Discriminatory." An editorial entitled "Because of Exemptions" cried political foul: "It may be considered good politics to penalize chicken thieves and exempt bootleggers and embezzlers, but it is a violation of the federal constitution," doing "open violence to the equal protection clause of the fourteenth amendment." The *Tulsa Daily World* wrote that the Court had declared the act "discriminatory" and the editorial staff wrote that the "discrimination of the act was its fatal defect," chiding the judges for evading the underlying issue—whether sterilization was ever constitutional.[52]

Only one major paper, the *New York Herald Tribune*, wrote of the case as at all momentous, calling it "one of the most important sociological decisions [the Court] had ever delivered." The article's use of the term "sociological" was hardly odd at the time (eugenicists themselves increasingly used it in the 1930s); its reference to the momentousness of the decision was to the Court's departure from *Buck v. Bell*, the dozens of states that still had sterilization laws on the books, and the references to "human rights." But when it came to the ultimate rationale of the decision, the *Herald Tribune*, like so many other papers acorss the country, acknowledged that the Supreme Court based its rationale on inequality. The *New York Times* mentioned liberty, the *New York Daily News* referred to right, and the *Los Angeles Times* used the term "human rights," but each concluded that the law was struck down because of "discrimination."[53] Of the law review articles that would emerge in the next five years, not a single one wrote of the Supreme Court's decision as focused on the right to procreate (the proposition for which *Skinner* is known today). At the time, one law review article complained that the notion of a natural or fundamental right to procreate was a faulty religious claim.[54]

Today, *Skinner* is viewed by its critics as radical in its reasoning, inventing new rights that do not exist in the text of the Constitution as it was written in 1787 (the right to procreate). In 1942, however, *Skinner* was viewed as too timid—none of the opinions denounced sterilization as inherently unconstitutional (without regard to inequality). A number of commentators thought the Supreme Court was sitting uncomfortably on the fence between *Buck* and *Skinner*, one case affirming the right of the state to sterilize and the other rejecting it. As the Harvard professor Thomas Reed Powell wrote in 1943, the "interesting thing about the decision is that seven members of the Court refrained from passing any judgment on the underlying issue"—that is, the constitutionality of sterilization itself. Powell would go on to speculate, without further explanation, that the case revealed the justices' concern about race.[55]

Skinner led to no avalanche of letters to the justices. One lawyer wrote to Justice Jackson to commend him for his opinion limiting the power of a majority to experiment at the expense of the "natural powers of a minority." The lawyer thought it good that "there are Courts to point out to legislatures (and eugen[ic]ists) that . . . men cannot experiment with them as men have experimented with cattle." Sterilization was a "powerful weapon" as objectionable in Hitler's hands as in America: "In a single generation our self-constituted supermen can eliminate Jews, Communists, Democrats, Bankers or any other group or class, by the gratuitous grafting of Mendel's Law with personal prejudice." For all we know, the lawyer continued, they might even follow Shakespeare's character Dick the Butcher, who thought to "kill all the lawyers."[56]

The last comment—about sterilizing the lawyers—was meant as a joke. But it was a joke which had been made before, by governors who vetoed laws and legislators who refused to pass laws lest they themselves be sterilized.[57] The joke was no joke; it reflected precisely what the Supreme Court had held—that it is far easier to oppress others when the remedy is not applied to oneself. As Justice Jackson would later explain in a Supreme Court case now famous for these lines: "nothing opens the door to arbitrary action so effectively as to allow those officials to pick and choose only a few to whom they will apply legislation and thus to escape the political retribution that might be visited upon them if larger numbers were affected." The founders knew, wrote Justice Jackson, "that there is no more effective practical guaranty against arbitrary . . . government than to require that the principles of law which officials would impose upon a minority must be imposed generally." Generality was essential to the "linkage" of fate between majorities and minorities.[58]

When news of the Supreme Court's decision reached McAlester prison, the papers reported that there was jubilation in the cells and trusty buildings. Only one of the original "brain trust" was there to celebrate. The lawyer Hyde had been pardoned and fled to Alaska; Kelly had been paroled and disappeared; Skinner had completed his term, remarried, and left for California. Only Ralph Bainum, Convict No. 18051, the man the *Tulsa Daily World* claimed was the state's leading expert on sterilization, would learn of his vindication from inside his cell—eight years after he had sat at the counsel's table in the first sterilization case. Bainum had been paroled in 1940 to a family friend in California, in part because of his work on the sterilization issue. Claud Briggs had made a special plea for him, writing that Bainum had helped prevent "atrocious crimes" and had even brought to an end "a reign of terror" among the prisoners. Briggs's letter to the parole board did not explain how Bainum had prevented the terror or even precisely what was meant by such a term, but made clear that Briggs took it quite seriously: "These matters . . . have very firmly and indelibly impressed themselves upon my mind." In 1941, Bainum was returned to McAlester, his parole revoked based on what would turn out to be a false claim that he had impersonated a federal officer (to acquire moonshine).[59]

Official Oklahoma circles seemed less than astonished at the Supreme Court's decision. The attorney general acknowledged difficulties with the case, but the law's sponsor, Dr. Ritzhaupt, was less resigned. Sounding as if he were still arguing against Claud Briggs, Ritzhaupt claimed that the law was sound from the "eugenics standpoint," and that these men were "psychiatrically unfit" to be "the parents of normal children." But the papers were doubtful, suggesting that there were more important things to worry about when the world was at war. Oklahoma, they predicted, would wait until peacetime "before trying another experiment" in biology.[60]

Foreign experimentation was evident immediately. On the very day the decision was rendered, the *Norman Transcript* reported on page one not only the outcome in Skinner's case, but also that Hitler's agents had killed 200,000 Jews in what was prematurely described as "the most terrible racial persecution in modern history." Later that week, American papers revealed that Nazi authorities in Hungary had ordered the sterilization of all male gypsies (the population of gypsies in Hungary was estimated at 250,000). On August 6, Americans learned that the Germans were ordering the sterilization of all children arrested in a roundup of 18,000 Parisian Jews. And, in Norway, Nazi doctors were advocating the immediate sterilization of mental patients and the "mercy killing" of the "incurably insane."[61]

Today, as we read the Supreme Court's words in *Skinner*, words about the withering of races, it appears a prescient warning of a Holocaust then under way, but still unknown in America. In fact, the justices were referring not only to events of the day but also to those of the past. By the time Skinner's case reached the Supreme Court, eugenics had already been branded as a cloak for prejudice,

whether of class or race. *Skinner* consolidated this public view, and
helped to further it, but did not invent it. It would be wrong to
romanticize the Supreme Court's opinion. *Skinner* did not overrule
Buck v. Bell. It is one of the great oddities of constitutional law that
Buck v. Bell has never been explicitly overruled, and is occasionally
cited for ancillary propositions by the Supreme Court to this day,
including its lines about "equality" as the last resort of a constitutional lawyer.[62]

Precisely because *Buck* was not overruled in *Skinner*, sterilization continued in asylums and welfare offices in America long after
the case was decided; precisely because its notion of race was lost,
it was forgotten and reborn in predictable guise. In the 1970s, for
example, one federal court found that over 100,000 people had
been sterilized under federal health and welfare programs, and one
study found that over half of them were black.[63] Consent had been
obtained, but by fraud or coercion: doctors told some women in
labor that their babies would not be delivered unless they consented
to sterilization; welfare authorities insisted that, if their young
clients were not sterilized, they would lose their welfare benefits.
Before World War II, Jim Crow had served as accidental protection
for African-Americans who, in some Southern states, were excluded
from the asylums where most sterilizations took place.[64] As early as
the 1940s, however, it became obvious that the racism of eugenics
would not die; it was simply transferred to those who have always
borne the greatest burdens of racism in America.[65] As the historian William Leuchtenburg recounts, "In 1983, a North Carolina
jury took only forty-five minutes to decide that state officials had
not violated the rights of a fourteen-year-old black girl when they
sterilized her because she was allegedly 'promiscuous' and 'feeble
minded,' though at the time of the trial, fifteen years later, she held
an associate degree from New York City Technical College and a
job in a department store."[66]

That constitutional pronouncements fail to realize their aspi-
rations is a truism among legal scholars, but it should not obscure
what the Supreme Court's decision in *Skinner* did do. At a minimum, after *Skinner*, legislative expansion of compulsory steriliza-

tion was suspect. Far more importantly, *Skinner*'s "strict scrutiny" would almost immediately change the Supreme Court's approach toward questions of race; in 1944, in the Japanese exclusion case, *Korematsu v. United States*, the Court would assert that any law curtailing the "civil rights of a single racial group" was now subject to the most "rigid" judicial scrutiny. Four years later, *Skinner*'s opening lines—that the Court was dealing with an important area of "civil and human rights"—would provide the means to attack the other great racial enthusiasm of eugenicists, anti-miscegenation law. The first important case to use *Skinner* to help overturn a law was Justice Traynor's 1948 opinion in the California Supreme Court striking down California's law banning the marriage of black and white. (The United States Supreme Court would reach that result as a matter of federal constitutional law, but not for decades.)[67]

In theory, *Skinner* would usher in one of the most important concepts in constitutional law of the last part of the twentieth century: that, in some cases, legislation was to be "strictly scrutinized" by courts—an expression used for the first time in *Skinner* to strike down a law, and which now is central to constitutional law, appearing in cases as varied as affirmative action, sex equality, and race discrimination. This was *Skinner*'s great innovation. Before *Skinner*, no one argued against sterilization as a matter of right, because civil and personal rights could in theory be too easily defeated by a constitutional law whose doctrine celebrated the common welfare and police power. After World War II and in the shadow of Hitler's horrors, human rights would take on an entirely new character in constitutional law, a transformation often legally accomplished by invoking *Skinner*'s "strict scrutiny."

REQUIESCAM

Jack T. Skinner was paroled from McAlester prison in November 1939. In 1940, he married Jane Skinner and moved to California, where he had a dry-cleaning business. In 1977, at the age of seventy, Skinner died in Tulare County, California. He was survived by his wife, a step-daughter, "six grandchildren and 10 great-grandchildren."

F. C. Hyde, the youngest member of the "brain trust" and an ex-lawyer, was paroled in 1940 at the age of thirty-two, and four years later was officially pardoned for his offenses by the governor of Oklahoma. He traveled to Ketchikan, Alaska, where he remarried and became the owner and captain of a commercial fishing vessel. He died in Alaska in 1981 at the age of seventy-seven.

Ralph Bainum was reparoled from McAlester in 1947. Two years later, he took to drink again, was found in violation of the conditions of his parole, and landed back in McAlester. In 1958, at the age of sixty, Bainum would die in McAlester's prison hospital.[68]

———◆———

Guy Andrews never argued another case in the United States Supreme Court. He died in the town of McAlester in 1955.

Dr. Louis Henry Ritzhaupt ran unsuccessfully for governor of Oklahoma. When he left the Oklahoma Senate, he had been one of its longest-serving senators; his legacy included legislation on behalf of "crippled children." He died at the age of seventy-three in 1964.

Claud Briggs argued over two hundred cases in the Oklahoma Supreme Court. His obituary explained that the Oklahoma Negligence Lawyers' Association, which he helped to found, was an important precursor for the American Trial Lawyers' Association. He died at the age of seventy-three in 1965.

Jess Dunn, the warden who was killed in 1941, is remembered every year, to this day, at McAlester prison for the rodeo he helped to create.[69]

Epilogue: Failures of Modern Memory

Science has supplied [us] with a true technique of righteous-
ness . . . It is filled with warnings of wrath . . . for the biological
ungodly, as well as with alluring promises for them who do His
scientific will. These warnings should first make you tremble;
they should, secondly, make you pray; they should, thirdly, fill you
with the militant faith of a new evangel.
　　　　　—Albert Wiggam, popular science writer, 1925[1]

It was an extraordinary intellectual seduction: a scientific faith that promised to rid life of crime and insanity and delinquency. In the days of public enemies and Depression, the promise seemed irresistible. Today, the story reeks of danger. Will we be seduced again? In fear of crime, will we be enticed to savagery? Will the constitution's sense of right once more yield so easily to claims of the common welfare? Will scientists insist again that they have discovered in nature the idea that democracy is folly? If there is an answer to these questions, it lies in a refusal to forget, in the recovery of modern memory.

———◆———

In retrospect, we can see how sterilization led, over and over again, to violence and escape at McAlester prison. The lawyers and the wardens knew this and tried to stop it, but the doctors and the politicians were indifferent to the warning signs. Prison officials and lawyers warned of riot and death and escape—and men did escape in 1934, again in 1936, and again in 1941. Meanwhile, not one but three laws were passed in the name of eugenics from 1931 until 1935, and the state pursued trials and appeals through 1941. Men died because of this policy, something that was evident to wardens and lawyers and prisoners alike, but was ignored in the great halls of public and scientific debate.

Skinner's history offers a profound lesson about the arrogance of ideas of nature married to those of criminality. As Stephen Jay Gould once wrote, few "tragedies" can be deeper "than the denial of an opportunity to strive or even to hope, by a limit imposed from without, but falsely identified as lying within." For over 150 years, scientists have searched for signs of crime within the body. They have given us theories that measured skulls and calibrated physiques; they have declared that criminals are born and that they have defective minds. More recently, scientists have given us overblown and ultimately false findings of extra Y chromosomes and genetic abnormalities leading to crime; they have even offered evolutionary theories of rape, all of which have been rejected as failed science.[2]

Skinner's history is testimony to what the great anthropologist Mary Douglas reminds us of: society's tendency to project its central social relations onto nature. If Douglas is right, we have failed, over and over again, in the search for crime's nature for a simple reason: neither social relations nor law exist within the body. This is precisely what the Supreme Court held, and was right to hold, in *Skinner v. Oklahoma*: that the arcane law of crime cannot possibly announce "a rule of human genetics." In short, *Skinner* offers a cautionary tale: history has shown over and over again that claims of a nature for crime are not only false but that they invariably reinscribe existing social inequalities, branding those society already detests. Any study in the sciences or social sciences that aims to search for a bodily solution to crime must remember that crime itself is defined by law, not nature, and that crime, violence, and aggression may as easily be found in the corporate boardroom or the trial court or the sporting arena as in the ghetto and the prison.[3]

During the late 1930s, a *New York Times* editorial branded eugenics "statistical gossip." In some ways, the label still fits. For all the hype surrounding the mapping of the human genome, we now know that much of the hoped-for success in genetic prediction of behavior and psychological disease has not materialized; widely publicized studies of genes "for" everything from criminality to schizophrenia, manic depression, alcoholism, homosexuality, risk-taking, and religiosity "have either been retracted, rebutted, or have yet to be replicated successfully." The truth is that the determinism implicit in the popular idea of the gene is false; behavioral genetics is a science of statistical correlation, not determination. The false popular concept of the gene-as-determiner (the same idea the eugenicists had) has led to panic and widespread misunderstanding about new technologies like cloning and "designer babies." The heritability statistics which fuel ideas like the "God gene" and the "gay gene" routinely trade on public misunderstanding. Despite the name, heritability statistics cannot prove inheritance. Like stock markets and hemlines, they deserve no greater respect than the claims of any correlational study.[4]

The eugenicists of old were not chary about claiming for their science the status of both religion and political theory. As we have seen, Depression-era genetics texts leapt with ease from ideas of nature to failed democracy. If scientists today are more wary of such dramatic moves, they must still remember what Stephen Jay Gould found in *The Mismeasure of Man*: that even when scientists aim consciously to avoid such claims, they may unwittingly recreate them. There was nothing about the discovery of the gene in Thomas Hunt Morgan's fruit-fly laboratory that required eugenics; for that, the gene would have to exit the lab and be translated into the public realm and applied as a solution to public problems of crime and insanity and economic depression. That possibility has not gone away. There is no claim of nature that cannot be transformed, in the public sphere, into a claim of political and social reality, for nature itself has two meanings: one which describes that which is, and the other which describes that which should be. It is the slippage between the two that makes for the public paradox of science—a science that may be no science at all once it leaves the lab and enters the arena of public debate.

In a few decades, we will look back, I believe, at the end of the twentieth and the early twenty-first centuries—at the heyday of the mapping of the human genome—as a day when a new form of eugenics was revived, a "soft" eugenics (to borrow a term from the geneticist Francis Collins). This soft eugenics was not coercive, but falsely predicted that the gene would solve the great public problems of the day. We will look back and wonder why we were so intellectually greedy as to believe that genes could determine everything from spirituality to risk-taking to shyness. No one today is looking for genes that make us happy, or genes that put women in the White House; they are looking for genes to solve social controversies, they are looking for gay genes and god genes. If Mary Douglas is correct that society finds its most sacred commitments in nature, we have once more generated false public hope that the gene will offer solutions to grave public problems, just as the eugenicists did when they aimed to solve the problems of crime and insanity that led to *Skinner v. Oklahoma.*[5]

———————◆———————

These lessons about crime and genetics are important. But they have been obscured for legal experts because, for them, *Skinner* evokes an entirely different, but equally explosive, controversy. *Skinner* is not associated with great debates about genetics, crime, and nature, but instead with grand modern controversies of constitutional law and right. For constitutionalists, *Skinner* sits in the shadow of the abortion and gay marriage debates—because its opening lines refer to rights of procreation and marriage. *Skinner* is a perpetual font of controversy among legal experts. Liberals extol *Skinner* as the beginning of a trend that resulted in the right to privacy in *Roe v. Wade*; conservatives recoil, believing, as Judge Bork has written, that *Skinner* begins the road toward the end of all restraint in constitutional law.[6]

Eugenics poses a real dilemma for both conservatives and liberals. If there is no right to procreation, as conservatives claim in order to resist its logical corollary (a right not to procreate), does anti-abortion require the constitutional embrace of eugenics? If there is a right to procreation, as liberals contend, where did it come from, as the Founding Fathers could not have imagined the possibility of eugenics in 1787? Adding to these difficulties is the fact that neither the liberal nor the conservative position has a good account of the equality aspects of the case. Neither explains what most laypeople in America would find obvious: that a racial science must be constitutionally offensive, at least in part, because it has something to do with racism and equality—as well as interference with individual liberty.

If this book has anything to say about the standard debates about *Skinner*, it is that both liberals and conservatives have made a historical mistake. *Skinner* was neither argued nor decided as a case about rights in the sense that we use the term "fundamental right" today. Top constitutionalists feel compelled to embrace the rights interpretation of the case because they believe that *Skinner* cannot be a case about equality (today, an economic distinction between high-class and low-class criminals is thought not to render laws unconstitutional on the theory that to make "economic distinctions" unconstitutional would imperil a vast array of tax and welfare laws).[7] And yet, if this history is correct, equality was precisely how the justices and the commentators saw *Skinner* in 1942. This historical puzzle is important for both the past and the present. Today, many, including Justices Ginsburg and O'Connor, have argued that hot-button issues like gay rights and abortion would be less controversially decided by the Supreme Court if they were addressed in terms of equality rather than of right (thus avoiding, at least preliminarily, the question of whether the Court is inventing rights not found in the Constitution). If *Skinner*'s equality rationale can be resurrected from its current state of disrepair, it may support the claims of those like Ginsburg and O'Connor who find in equality a more moderate resolution of otherwise resiliently polarized battles.[8]

———◆———

Conventional wisdom among lawyers holds that *Skinner* is an activist opinion, written by the irresponsible and highly liberal Justice Douglas, who had a very bad habit of creating rights out of thin air (Douglas is famously ridiculed for declaring that a "penumbra" surrounds the Bill of Rights). Yet, had *Skinner* been decided as a case about right alone, it would have done precisely what the justices aimed not to do—return to the kind of substantive due process theory they had just rejected.[9] *Skinner*'s equality rationale was the work not of the great activist Douglas but the great avatar of judicial restraint, Felix Frankfurter.[10] If we are to brand the opinion a relic of judicial activism, we must tar not only the great champion of restraint, Frankfurter, but everyone else who voted for it, including the strict constructionist Justice Hugo Black and the modern hero of moderates, Justice Robert Jackson.

It would take the postwar explosion of human rights discourse to cause us to reread *Skinner*'s lines about procreation and marriage as the only lines in the case. In 1942, there were many good reasons for lawyers to avoid rights arguments other than the incentive to avoid association with the "bad" property rights decisions that were thought to have precipitated the court-packing plan. Not only were rights arguments, in the case of sterilization, considered vaguely and improperly religious, but there were rights arguments arrayed on the other side of the political debate: the right to be well-born, for example, and the right of the community to defend itself against bad "germ plasm" (highlighting the almost infinite plasticity of the notion of a right in political discourse). More importantly, rights claims were legally weaker than we now imagine. It is commonplace for lawyers to read cases of the past and to insert within them today's idea of right, but in the days when *Skinner* was argued, rights claims did not trigger special constitutional scrutiny and could be quite easily defeated by claims of the common welfare.[11]

Lawyers, conservative and liberal alike, feel forced to read *Skinner* as a rights case because they believe it a failed equality case[12]—but this too rests upon historical fallacy. Contrary to conventional wisdom, *Skinner* fits standard legal models that put the prohibition of "caste" legislation at the core of constitutional equality protections. The problem in *Skinner* was not with the distinction between the chicken thieves and embezzlers *simpliciter*. The problem was with a criminal law as a rule of genetics, as a rule of blood—this was class made permanent. The eugenicists, as we have seen, believed poverty was inbred, that the family histories of the Jukes and the Kallikaks were, as they put it, histories of races of paupers. Oklahoma's law created a line between privileged and unprivileged blood, the sign of caste and aristocracy. Social inferiority that is permanent and biological—inferiority that is naturalized and thus cannot be overcome—is the hallmark of distinctions that are racial in character; it distinguishes them from class distinctions, which are thought of as easily transcended. Racial classifications require "strict scrutiny" in American constitutional law, because there can be no permanent inferior castes in a democracy.[13]

If this argument rationalizes *Skinner* with modern equality law, it fails to explain why, in 1942, the justices reached out to equality. In part, they reached out as an imperfect alternative; any other rationale would have been more activist. As Justice Jackson would later explain in his *Railway Express* decision, striking down a statute as a violation of equality is a less intrusive means of judicial review than striking it down as a matter of right. The equality rationale invites the legislature to return to the statute and thus enhances democracy; the legislature may repass the statute if it solves the equality problem (in this case, applies the law to itself). By contrast, a rights decision is more likely final; the subject matter is off-limits, and there is no way for the legislature to cure the error. This is precisely why Justices Ginsburg and O'Connor have suggested that matters like abortion and gay rights would be less controversially decided had the Court focused on equality first, before right.[14]

It was not only relative restraint that led the *Skinner* Court to reach out to equality in 1942. A history of equality law led them there—a history that has largely been forgotten. Today, lawyers think of equal protection cases as ones of race or sex, but, prior to 1937, equality claims were typically about property, taxes, and the right to work. Contrary to scholarly myth, equal protection did not die at the beginning of the twentieth century. The history of class legislation lived on in cases that focused on exemptions in statutes as a proxy for political favoritism, on the theory that law should be general, not partial.[15] The class legislation principle should make *Skinner* a good deal less controversial for conservatives who emphasize the original meaning of the Constitution, since it reaches as far back as the founding generation.[16] If there is one thing that is clear about the founding of our republic, it is that it aimed to prevent aristocracy, rule by blood. The notion of a government "by the people" rather than by inherited elites was embedded in the representation and electoral provisions of the document and specifically memorialized in provisions denying the power to grant titles of nobility or to punish by "attainting" of blood.[17] The theory of "class legislation" has always been about the fight against aristocracy—or, to put it differently, to prevent one set of rules, as the constitutionalist Cooley put it, for the courtier and another for the "countryman at plough."[18]

One need not invent rights to strike down a law that prefers some blood to other blood on the theory of its innate superiority; even the founding generation would have considered such a theory antithetical to its fight against British aristocracy. This would be true whether the law invoked fundamental rights or not (for example, "inferior blood" taxes should be unconstitutional for this reason as well). Those who claim *Skinner* forsakes original understandings have forgotten that the American Revolution and the Civil War were both fought to end forms of blood aristocracy, one known as monarchy, the other as slavery; the laws of eugenics were simply known by a different name, that of science.

Justice Jackson was in the end correct; today, *Skinner* is a case in which the liberty at stake is essential to the equality rationale. This is not the result of logic, but of governance. Far from being opposites, as is sometimes claimed, liberty and equality go hand in hand when we look to the incentives of legislatures. In politics, the more serious the invasion of liberty, the greater the likelihood that legislators have imposed that burden on those deemed "other" or "lesser" in some way. Rulers always have the temptation to self-deal, to exempt themselves and others they deem similar from the obligations they impose on others. Temptation only increases with the seriousness of the deprivation: the greater the deprivation, the greater the risk of inequality. It is a crude presumption about governance, one that can be defeated, but a presumption that suggests at the very least a second look, a stricter scrutiny. As the libertarian

Richard Epstein has argued, equality serves as an important back-stop to protect rights, particularly where we do not know the extent of the right. There is reason for this. Equality is a comparative concept; it requires us to find a baseline, and often that baseline reflects our judgments of shared liberty.[19]

What this reading of *Skinner* suggests is the great error of the modern literalism of equality law. Today, lawyers like to put equality cases into legal pigeonholes based on classification—this is a case of economics, that one of race. But this process decontextualizes the distinction from the statute and can lead to error. In *Skinner*, it is only by decontextualizing the distinction (economic) from the meaning of the act (sterilization only makes sense if it is attempting to eradicate dangerous blood) that one has trouble with the equality aspects of the case.[20] More importantly, the tendency to try to divide cases of equality from questions of liberty with false precision has led to a failure to appreciate how these concerns are intertwined in real, political, life as they were in *Skinner* (blood distinctions not only harm individuals but demarcate groups). This is the contextualist lesson in the majority's reference to genocide; this is the contextualist lesson in Justice Jackson's common law intuition that the greater the interference with liberty, the greater the risk of legislative oppression. This is the "reading of life" into law that Justice Frankfurter insisted upon so intensely.

This brings me to the most controversial aspect of *Skinner*'s history for lawyers, but an aspect of the case which, if credited, would make it far more intelligible to both liberals and conservatives and which helps to explain why the lay view—that a coerced racial science offends both equality and liberty—is correct. There is nary a lawyer today who thinks *Skinner* a case about race; a law student is likely to get an F on her exam if she even mentions it, because there is little evidence that the men litigating the case were black and the law did not say "Negro."[21] And yet this creates a historical puzzle: no lawyer thinks the case is about race, but no historian of science thinks eugenics was anything but a racial science. A student of history should then have to accept her F if she were to write on her history exam that eugenics was not a racial science.

Skinner's most significant constitutional passage refers to race: "When the law lays an unequal hand on those who have committed intrinsically the same quality of offense and sterilizes one and not the other, it has made as invidious a discrimination as if it had selected a particular race or nationality for oppressive treatment."[22] Did the justices simply miss this passage, or did they leave their minds behind when they signed on to the draft? History helps to supply the answer, for it reminds us that our contemporary notion of race as skin color is a contemporary notion. Indeed, the easiest way to see this is to remember that the most common application of the word "race" at the time—to the Nordic race or the Aryan race—was to a white race. As African-American critics of sterilization knew then, the claim that the "unfit" should be sterilized carried a social meaning that frightened black and white alike, as unfitness lay in imagined stupidity and real poverty.[23] During the 1930s, the term "race of paupers" had meaning not only for eugenicists but also for the average newspaper reader—and its meaning depended upon the notion of a culturally devalued trait embedded and made permanent by inheritance.

When Justice Douglas compared the statute in *Skinner* to one that distinguished by race, he did so because eugenics shared the deep structure of the concept of race: an idea of naturalized social inferiority injected into the body and blood. One of the greatest questions that remains unanswered about eugenics is why, if eugenics was a racial science (as historians agree), those sterilized in the 1920s and 1930s were generally white. The answer is that the history of eugenics is a history of racial formation: races we no longer see as such (including white races) were formed in a crucible of prejudices now long forgotten. When we look back at the justifications used by eugenicists to identify the "unfit," we find standard cultural tropes of inhumanity and natural inferiority: charges of animality, excessive sexuality, inherent criminality, and unmanliness. There is no coincidence in this particular set of cultural indictments; over long periods of time, these same tropes have been applied to Asians and Jews, Italians and Irish, not to mention African-Americans who continue to suffer from such slurs—all for the purposes of making inferiority appear inevitable and natural, for the purpose of constructing a category that carries with it the natural and permanent inferiority embedded in body and blood.[24]

To see *Skinner* as a case with a family resemblance to one of race should put it on much firmer ground for both liberals and conservatives, as both agree that racial classifications are clearly barred by the Constitution. But it still fails to explain the intuition that there is something about individual right, as well as equality, at stake in *Skinner*. In my own view, rights are vessels of history, in two senses of the word. They are vessels in the sense that they are lessons of the past that help guide our future; they are also vessels in the sense that they are containers, containers of memory, and in particular memories of grave political danger.[25] The rights invoked in the early part of the twentieth century condensed fears of socialism and Communism (that wage and hour restrictions and support for labor unions would lead to state-sponsored socialism); the rights invoked after World War II were reflections of entirely different political fears—fears of Fascism's racism, religious persecution, and suppression of speech. Enshrining history in right makes the right appear incontrovertible, but forgets that rights are the product of experience; they require us to "read life," as well as law. Today, it seems incontrovertible that compelled sterilization violates individual right, but, as this book shows, there is nothing in logic or language that demands this; brilliant men like Justice Holmes and vast majorities once dismissed such claims with the back of the hand.

To understand why forced sterilization raises important questions of right, we must consider history and experience. What does the state do when it commands that some cannot have children on the theory that their blood is tainted? If one were to look for such an experience in the history of America prior to *Buck* and *Skinner*, one would have to look at a history both grave and deeply embarrassing—the history of slavery. Orlando Patterson has explained that the essence of slavery was not the question of property but natal alienation and social death—the fact that slaves had no families that law would recognize, that their children could be sold upon a whim, and that this "alienation of the slave from all formal, legally enforceable ties of 'blood' " gave "the relation of slavery its peculiar value to the master."[26]

Such history provides an important cautionary tale for any attempt by the state to enforce a rule of deliberate natal alienation, like the one Oklahoma sought to enforce in *Skinner*. After all, what was it that *Skinner* said at his trial, that he would be alone and without inspiration? What was it that the prisoner Martin said as he lay dying, that he did it "for his wife"? Why did one prisoner's mother say that sterilization could "ruin a man" for life? Why did the men and women of Vinita asylum claim that they just wanted to die? There was more at stake than children in eugenic sterilization; there was future and past, wives and loved ones, social life and social death.

Historically, the most appalling of masteries have involved control not only over individuals' work and property but also over family and social life; this was true in antebellum America as well as Nazi Europe. In 1942, Americans knew that Hitler meant to enslave Europe, and they knew that this was a racial slavery; they also knew that this slavery traded in selection of blood, and sterilization and eugenics were one means of this mastery. *Skinner*'s terrible compromise, its failure to overrule *Buck v. Bell*, was a failure to recognize this mastery—a failure to recognize that "moronic minds," as Chief Justice Stone put it, were no different, for the problems of mastery are not only in the treatment of those demeaned or deprived, but in the moral hazard to those who presume to define the mental or moral unfitness of others.

———•———

Democracy entails a paradoxical attitude toward claims of nature; democratic governments have been extraordinary laboratories for ingenuity and scientific progress. At the same time, there are some "natural" ideas that cannot be accepted by a democracy without it becoming something else altogether. There are no predestined failures or successes in a democracy; there can be no aristocracy of blood, no genetic pariahs (this is the meaning, after all, of the great statement in the Declaration of Independence that "all men are created equal"). It follows from this that, in a democracy, citizens must continually strive to treat each other as equals. This is not because we are physically equal; we are genetically unique. To live in a realm in which some are deemed officially "elect" is to live in a different form of government, an aristocracy. This is true whatever nature tells us.

The philosopher Michael Walzer has urged a theory of justice in which equality may demand different things in different contexts—in which some spheres, such as the home or the public sphere, are quite separate from others.[27] Some forms of knowledge simply do not translate well into other realms; the claims of religious truth, for example, are constitutionally incommensurable with the claims of governance. This is not because we choose to ignore faith, or because we are deep relativists, but because we decide that our public life in a democracy will be better if we choose to act toward other human beings without regard to their religious affiliations. These assumptions have served us well for over two hundred years, even as they require us to struggle with new claims of equal dignity and respect.

This is the important lesson of *Skinner*'s tale. A democratic theory of genetics, as the "minute men of science" once proclaimed it in 1939, must be one which rejects the claim by the discoverer of the double helix, James Watson (a claim shared by eugenicists), that the "gene is fate."[28] As citizens, scientists must recognize that in this, as in religion, there must be a basic separation, a separation of science and state.[29] In the case of conflict and uncertainty, science cannot establish itself as "above" the demands of constitutional order. At a minimum, no science may establish its definition of humanity as more orthodox than the demands of a constitutional order in which we must assume we are equal citizens, without regard to our genes. Today, we live in a world where science regularly risks politicization in debates ranging from global warming to designer babies.[30] May the lesson of *Skinner* be one in which scientists and all who revere science (myself included) remember how great an incentive politics has to manipulate science and how easily science may capitulate to the very politics it aims to conquer.

Acknowledgments and Method

This book has been an exercise in what the historian of law Lawrence Friedman calls "dirty" history, mucking about in local archives where most fear to tread. Seven years after I began piecing together this story, there is much more that I would like to know about *Skinner*'s history, but there is also much more in this history than one would have hoped about a case that once smelled vaguely obscene, was brought by self-made lawyers, and originated inside a prison during the Depression. After reading the trial transcript in *Skinner*'s case, I sent a research assistant to Oklahoma and she came back saying there was nothing to be found. Given what I knew, I found this unsatisfying and so, one hot Oklahoma summer, I packed up my children and babysitter and took a look for myself. The index at the Oklahoma Historical Society (compiled by the WPA) turns out to be wrong; there are hundreds of articles on sterilization in dozens of Oklahoma newspapers, but at the time I was there you had to read them page by page on an old machine that takes quarters for copies.

This story differs from much history of science in that it aims as far as possible to engage those who were science's subjects, rather than its authors. A history of crime and eugenics has never been written, in part because we have very bad records from inside prisons, and in part because popular sources (including eugenicists) falsely reported that few states had laws covering inmates (it takes a lawyer, curiously, to reveal the history of science, as it requires one to actually read the statutes). This story also differs from some standard accounts of eugenics; there remains the misconception that eugenics was a late-nineteenth/early-twentieth-century science, in America, only later pursued with enthusiasm by the Nazis. America was, however, the great leader in eugenic legislation, and its support for sterilization laws remained strong throughout the 1930s.

This story differs from standard legal histories, as well: it foregrounds the ordinary men who brought the case to the Supreme Court rather than the great men who decided it. The narrative resists the tendency of lawyers to spotlight what the legal historian Bob Gordon has so charmingly called the "mandarin texts." Law's texts do matter; they cannot be completely submerged within larger interests or social phenomena. Unlike poetry or idle conversation, legal opinions are public acts, they are attempts to "do" things in the world in a particular context. Without the context (and the ways in which the context is "condensed" within law), we are left reading the present into the past, recreating our own dramas in period costume. This is after all the tale of *Skinner v. Oklahoma*, a case in which modern notions of right and equality are read into the document, notions that make *Skinner* both incomprehensible and the object of perpetual controversy for constitutionalists, even if the great moments and meanings of the past—of science and war, fascism and race—make the text quite comprehensible in its own time.

Piecing together this story required the aid of countless librarians and people in Oklahoma, as well as a fleet of research assistants. Special thanks to those in the newspaper archive in the Oklahoma Historical Society, without whom this book could not have been written. So, too, my gratitude goes to the Oklahoma Department of Library Archives in Oklahoma City, where librarians showed me to the files that gave me prison poetry, the transcript from the Winkler hearing, Claud Briggs's correspondence with warden Jess Dunn, and the secretary of state's records on pardons and paroles. A good deal of background information was obtained from the Western History Collection at the University of Oklahoma; special recognition goes to the outstanding Carl Albert archive, which houses the papers of a number of Oklahoma politicians, including those of Alfalfa Bill Murray, where I first found the *New York Daily News* article which forms the basis of chapter one. Finally, I owe a great debt of gratitude to Professor William Savage, who as a member of the department of history at the University of Oklahoma, on one of my early trips to Oklahoma gave me a copy of the memoir "Beyond the Door of Delusion," written in 1932 inside the Vinita asylum.

This book's early versions were written for and only because of the support I received at the Yale Law School, where I was a visiting professor in 2003. Daniel Kevles, of Yale's history department, was of invaluable assistance and patience, in urging me to pursue a story that had never been told in the history of eugenics. At Yale Law School, special thanks to Bill Eskridge and Bruce Ackerman and Vicki Shultz, who encouraged the work and read too many bad early drafts. I am forever in their debt. Thanks as well go to the librarians of the Yale and Wisconsin law schools for their assistance, to the Burrus–Bascom family for funding a chair at the law school of the University of Wisconsin that has allowed me to do this work, and to the university as a whole, which granted me the funds to take time to teach myself something about genetics. The original draft of this work was supported by the American Council for Learned Societies. Particular thanks to Martha Nussbaum and Cass Sunstein for recommending that Norton publish the book. Finally, to my agent, Cecilia Cancellaro, and to my editors at Norton, who made me drop all my fancy legal pretension so that this story could reach a wider audience, you have my utmost thanks.

The colleagues—past, present, and future—who read various versions, and parts, of this book, offering their time and advice, include Jane Schacter, Arthur McEvoy, Marc Galanter, Neil Komesar, Stewart Macaulay, Jim Jones, Martha Fineman, Beth Mertz, Jane Larson, Alta Charo, Pilar Ossorio, Brad Snyder, Bill Buzbee, and Robert Schapiro. Special thanks to Bill Novak of the University of Chicago Law School and the American Bar Foundation for help on questions of historiography, and Joshua Landis for help navigating the history department at the University of Oklahoma (not to mention his extraordinary hospitality during years of traveling to Norman). My deep gratitude to my Wisconsin colleague Frank Tuerkheimer for referring to me Tom Marquardt, an ex-FBI agent, who helped track down Jack Skinner himself. Finally, to my research assistants—Mike Duchek, Anfin Jaw, Kat Kaufka, Jill Priluck, and Jason Postelnik—my debt is incalculable.

This book was written in part because of an odd collection of strangers, who in small and large ways, at various points in my career, and from various positions of power, encouraged me to believe that I had abilities others failed to see. My thanks to Judge Edward Weinfeld and his family, Arthur Liman and his family, Senator Joseph Biden, Bruce Ackerman, Philip Bobbitt, Bill Nelson, Bill Eskridge, and most recently, but certainly not last, Martha Fineman, for their divine interventions on my behalf. To my friend, the Stanford constitutionalist Jane Schacter, endless kudos for her support, patience, and willingness to accept one more note before another plane ride telling her that, if I should die, to please publish my last manuscript (a grim joke of sorts).

To say a book is written for a family is to lie: families want the author's presence, not her words. The day that I was born, it was hardly thought that I could be the someone I am now. History would make that girl-child in an image that she might never have chosen but could not escape. To my family, Rick Cudahy, and my children, Mia and Jack, know that you are my great protection against history, and my great hope for the future. Your patience and love allows me the courage to say on a regular daily basis what vast populations of women before me could not: to paraphrase the great Texas congresswoman and scholar Barbara Jordan, this is my country and my constitution, too.

Notes

Archives and Manuscript Collections

Cal Tech Archives, Gosney Papers	GP
Dep't of Library Archives, Okla. City, Okla.	DOLA
Harvard Law Library	HLL
Papers of Thomas Reed Powell	
Papers of Sheldon Glueck	
Papers of Felix Frankfurter	
Library of Congress, Manuscript Div., Wash. DC	LOC
Papers of Justice William O. Douglas	WDP
Papers of Justice Felix Frankfurter	FFP
Papers of Chief Justice Harlan Stone	HSP
Papers of Justice Frank Murphy	FMP
Papers of Justice Hugo Black	HBP
Papers of Justice Robert Jackson	RJP
Library of the U. S. Supreme Court, Wash. DC	LSCT
National Archives, Wash. DC	NA
Oklahoma Department of Corrections	DOC
Oklahoma Historical Society Archives	OHS
Princeton University Archives, ACLU Papers	PA
Univ. of Okla. Carl Albert Archive	CA
Univ. of Okla. Western History Collection	WHC

Newspapers

Atlanta Journal:	Atl. J.
Blackwell (Okla.) Morning Tribune:	BMT
Chicago Tribune:	CT
Daily Oklahoman:	DO
Los Angeles Times:	LAT
McAlester (Okla.) News–Capital:	MNC
Muskogee (Okla.) Daily Phoenix:	MDP

New York Daily News:	NYDN
New York Herald Tribune:	NYHT
New York Times:	NYT
Norman Transcript:	NT
Oklahoma City Times:	OCT
Oklahoma News:	ON
St. Louis Dispatch:	St. L. Dis.
San Francisco Examiner:	SFE
Shawnee (Okla.) Morning News:	SMN
Tulsa Daily World:	TDW
Washington Post:	WP

Magazines

American Medicine:	Amed.
American Mercury:	Amerc.
Business Week:	BW
Christian Century:	CC
Collier's:	Coll.
Current History:	CH
Harlow's Weekly:	HW
Literary Digest:	LD
New Republic:	TNR
News Week:	NW
Pictorial Review:	PR
Reader's Digest:	RD
Review of Reviews:	RR
Scientific American:	SA
Time:	Time
World's Work:	WW

Books Frequently Cited

Canadian:	Oklahoma History South of the Canadian (J. Gilday & M. Salt eds. 1925)
East:	E. M. East, Heredity and Human Affairs (1927)
Harlow:	Rex F. & Victor E. Harlow, Makers of Government in Oklahoma (1930)
Kevles:	Daniel Kevles, In the Name of Eugenics: Genetics and the Uses of Human Heredity (1995 ed.)
Landman:	J. H. Landman, Human Sterilization: The History of the Sexual Sterilization Movement (1932)

Larson: Edward J. Larson, Sex, Race, and Science: Eugenics in the
              Deep South (1995)
Laughlin: Harry H. Laughlin, Eugenical Sterilization in the United
              States (1922)
Paul: Diane B. Paul, Controlling Human Heredity 1865 to the
              Present (1998)
Thoburn: Joseph Thoburn, 5 Oklahoma: A History of the State and
              Its People (1929)

Trial Transcripts

WT: Winkler Transcript, Okla. Penitentiary Case No. 1, files of
              Jesse Ballard, AAG, DOLA, RG1
ST: Skinner Transcript, Okla. Pitts. Co. Dist. Ct. No. 15734
              (1936)
MT: Main Transcript, Okla. Okla. Co. Dist. Ct. No. 75080,
              DOLA (Sup. Ct. files) (1932–33)

Epigraphs

1 Felix Frankfurter, *Justice Holmes Defines the Constitution*, Atlantic at
   484 (Oct. 1938).
2 James Willard Hurst, *Themes in United States Legal History*, in Felix
   Frankfurter: A Tribute 199 (Wallace Mendelson ed., 1964).

Prologue: An Intellectual Seduction

1 Francis Galton, *Studies in Eugenics*, 11 Am. J. of Sociology 11, 25 (1905).
2 Clarence Darrow, *The Eugenics Cult*, 8 Amerc. at 129, 130 (1926) (quoting Walter).
3 Editorial, NYT, May 16, 1937, at 66.
4 Clarence Darrow, *supra* note 2, at 131.

Chapter 1: The Justice, the Governor, and the Dictator

1 Albert E. Wiggam, The Next Age of Man 399 (1927).
2 Behind the Door of Delusion by "Inmate Ward 8" [Vinita Memoir]
   125–26, 134 (William W. Savage, Jr. & James H. Lazalier eds., 1994,
   1932).
3 Id. at 125–26, 128, 133–34.
4 Julia McCarthy, *Sterilization—How It Works*, NYDN at 31 (Dec. 22,
   1933).

5 RD at 49 (Mar. 1932); Time at cover, 15–16 (Feb. 29, 1932); NYT at 12 (July 28, 1934); Keith L. Bryant, Jr., Alfalfa Bill Murray 184 (1968); James R. Scales & Danney Goble, Oklahoma Politics: A History 170 (1982).

6 *See* Time at cover, 14–16 (Feb. 29, 1932); HW at 9 (Oct. 31, 1931); Oklahoma's Governors, 1929–1955 54 (LeRoy H. Fischer ed., 1983); Bryant, *supra* note 5, at 190.

7 Time at 14–16 (Feb. 29, 1932); HW at 5 (Feb. 7, 1931); Bryant, *supra* note 5, at 215.

8 RD, *supra* note 5, at 49, 51–52 (Mar. 1932); NYT at E6 (Dec. 10, 1933); Time at 15 (Aug. 3, 1931); Time at 9 (Aug. 17, 1931); Time at 9–10 (Aug. 31, 1931); Oklahoma's Governors, *supra* note 6, at 63; Scales and Goble, *supra* note 5, at 167.

9 1931 Okla. Sess. Laws ch. 26, sec. 1, at 80; Time at 14 (May 4, 1931); TDW at 13 (Apr. 23, 1931); LD at 20 (May 23, 1931); Edwin G. Conklin, *The Purposive Improvement of the Human Race*, in Human Biology and Racial Welfare 577 (Edmund V. Cowdry ed., 1930); Steven Selden, Inheriting Shame: The Story of Eugenics and Racism in America 48–49, 64 (1999); The Wellborn Science: Eugenics in Germany, France, Brazil, and Russia (Mark B. Adams ed., 1990); Eugenics and the Welfare State: Sterilization Policy in Denmark, Sweden, Norway and Finland (Gunnar Broberg & Nils Roll-Hansen eds., 2005).

10 McCarthy, *supra* note 4. Laughlin, at 15–34, enumerates many pre-1922 sterilization laws which included habitual criminals and those convicted of rape and perversity (Indiana, Washington, California, Nevada, Iowa, New Jersey, New York, North Dakota, Kansas, Wisconsin, Nebraska). Landman, at 63–87, demonstrates that post-1922 laws did the same (North Dakota, Michigan, Nebraska, Oregon, Idaho, and Utah). This is true despite the fact that, at the time, it was often said that these laws were inactive.

11 HW at 6 (Apr. 25, 1931); HW at 14 (Apr. 18, 1931); LD at 20 (May 23, 1931).

12 Madison Grant, The Passing of the Great Race 5 (1921); Margaret Sanger, The Pivot of Civilization ch. 4 (1922); Margaret Sanger, Motherhood in Bondage 100–01 (1928); Paul at 102–3 (quoting Roosevelt); Larson, at 73–74, 132–33 (groups); LAT at A6 (May 1, 1934); NYT at 7 (Dec. 29, 1934); ON at 2 (Nov. 4, 1934) (Kiwanis); W. A. Plecker, *Virginia's Effort to Preserve Racial Integrity*, in A Decade of Progress in Eugenics 105–12 (1934); Bartlett C. Jones, Prohibition and Eugenics: 1920–1933, 18 J. Hist. Med. 158, 160 (Apr. 1963). On Catholic opposition, Syracuse Herald at 2 (Dec. 24, 1933); ON at 2 (Oct. 10, 1934).

13 Time at 14 (May 4, 1931); William Murray, 3 Memoirs of Governor Murray and True History of Oklahoma 639 (1945).

14 Leon Whitney, The Case for Sterilization 53–54 (1934); Harry Laughlin, *Further Studies on the Historical and Legal Development of Eugenical Sterilization in the United States* at 96, GP, 11.7 (1936);   Michael F. Guyer, Being Well-Born, preface (2d ed. 1927) ("right of rights"); Fred Hogue, *Social Eugenics*, LAT at I23 (Apr. 10, 1938) ("just what are the rights that would be infringed upon. It would be the right to function as a carrier of venereal diseases or the right of the feebleminded to reproduce their kind.").

15 Editorial, *Blood Will Tell*, Sat. Even. Post at 30 (Mar. 21, 1925); Guyer, supra note 14, at 1; Francis Galton, *Eugenics: Its Definition, Scope and Aims*, Nature at 82 (May 26, 1904) ("it must be introduced into the national conscience, like a new religion"); Francis Galton, *Studies in Eugenics*, 11 Am. J. of Sociology 11, 20, 24 (1905).

16 LAT at II, 1 (Mar. 9, 1915) (eugenic babies); *Over Thousand Babies In Eugenic Congress*, LAT at II, 7 (Mar. 7, 1915) ("eugenic congress" of babies); Fred Hogue, Social Eugenics, LAT at 31 (Jan. 5, 1936) (housing); id. at 30 (Mar. 22, 1936); Paul Popenoe & Roswell Johnson, Applied Eugenics 200–01 (1920) (marriage and divorce); Paul A. Lombardo, *Eugenic Sterilization in Virginia: Aubrey Strode and the Case of Buck v. Bell* 114 (Ph.D. diss. 1982) (poetry); Popular Eugenics: National Efficiency and American Mass Culture in the 1930s (Susan Currell & Christina Cogdell eds., 2006) (art).

17 Frances Corry, ON at 1A (Nov. 5, 1933).

18 Edith Johnson, DO at 8 (Feb. 3, 1933).

19 ON at 1, 7 (Feb. 15, 1933) (farmers); TDW at 12 (May 24, 1931) (California deports to other states); DO at 4A (Jan. 1, 1933) (banishment paroles); TDW at 4 (Jan. 2, 1933) (overcrowding); HW at 16 (Jan. 10, 1931) (asylums).

20 Phillip Reilly, The Surgical Solution 39 (1991) (sixteen states passed laws between 1907 and 1913, but four vetoed); Landman at 290–93 (bills, App. B); *id.* at 252 (mayhem); Paul Popenoe, *Eugenical Sterilization: A Review*, 14 J. of Heredity 308, 309 (1923) ("dead letter").

21 *Buck v. Bell*, 274 U.S. 200 (1927).

22 Kevles at 110; Paul A. Lombardo, *Three Generations, No Imbeciles: New Light on Buck v. Bell*, 60 N.Y.U. L. Rev. 30, 52–53, 61 (1985); *id.* at 54 (based on Lombardo's interview with Buck, Carrie was raped by the nephew of her foster mother, Mrs. Dobbs). J. David Smith & K. Ray Nelson, The Sterilization of Carrie Buck 1, 3–6 (1989).

23 Lombardo, *supra* note 22, at 54 (epileptic claim); *id.* at 32 n. 10 (nine-

year-old on the Stanford–Binet); Lombardo, *supra* note 16, at 203 (quoting Harry Laughlin) (incapable of "self-support and restraint," "a record of immorality, prostitution and untruthfulness").

24   *See* Henry H. Goddard, Feeble-Mindedness: Its Causes and Consequences (1920); Paul at 59 (tiered system).

25   Paul at 67 ("half of the white draft"); Daniel Kevles, *Testing the Army's Intelligence: Psychologists and the Military in World War I*, 55 J. of Am. Hist. 565–81 (1968).

26   When the psychologist and eugenicist Goddard administered intelligence tests to immigrants at Ellis Island, he found that 40 percent of recent immigrants were feebleminded. The foreign-born were at the time often charged with causing crime. Paul at 108 (Goddard); *id.* at 99 (crime and foreign-born); Goddard, *supra* note 24, at 571–572; 3 Murray, *supra* note 13, at 639 (1945) (feebleminded causing Depression); *Eugenics As the Cure for All the Race's Ills*, 114 LD 22, 23 (Sept. 10, 1932) ("forced on our attention").

27   Paul at 59 (Brigham quotation, right and wrong per Goddard); Heredity and Eugenics: A course of lectures 280–81 (William E. Castle et al. eds., 1912) (Davenport lecture) (feeblemindedness is a "lumber room" that includes the inability to "appreciate moral ideas" and inability to "control the appetites and passions"); *Feeblemindedness*, 6 J. of Heredity 32, 32 (1915) ("incapable of performing duties"); John Lewis Gillin, Criminology and Penology 177 (1926) (feebleminded as no different from children); on the equation of social inadequacy and feeblemindedness, *The Unemployables*, Eugenical News 128 (Sept.–Oct. 1934); Lombardo, *supra* note 16, at 163 ("socially inadequate classes").

28   Henry H. Goddard, The Kallikak Family 77 (1931 edition, reprinted 1973, first edition 1912) ("unmistakable look of the feeble-minded"); *id.* at 78 ("glance sufficed to establish"); Stephen Jay Gould, The Mismeasure of Man 171 (1981); Whitney, *supra* note 14, at 110.

29   Paul A. Lombardo, *Medicine, Eugenics, and the Supreme Court: From Coercive Sterilization to Reproductive Freedom*, 13 Contemp. Health L. & Pol. 1, 9 (1996); Lombardo, *supra* note 16, at 189 ("a look about it"); Lombardo, *supra* note 22, at 51 ("shiftless, ignorant").

30   Lombardo, *supra* note 22, at 40–45 ("Priddy suit"); A. S. Priddy to Harry Laughlin, in Smith & Nelson, *supra* note 22, at 56 ("grave doubt"); Lombardo, *supra* note 16, at 143, 154.

31   Lombardo, *supra* note 22, at 35; *id.* at 33 (collusive suit); *id.* at 56–58.

32   Prior to 1922, only one of seven challenges upheld a sterilization law: (1) *Smith v. Board of Examiners*, 88 A. 963 (N.J. 1913); (2) *Davis v. Berry*, 216 F. 413 (S.D. Iowa 1914) *found moot*, 242 U.S. 468 (1917); (3)

Haynes v. Lapeer, 166 N.W. 938 (Mich. 1918); (4) *Osborn v. Thomson*, 169 N.Y.S. 638 (N.Y. Misc. 1918), *aff'd*, 171 N.Y.S. 1094 (N.Y. App. Div. 1918); (5) *Mickle v. Henrichs*, 262 F. 687 (D. Nev. 1918); (6) *Williams v. Smith*, 131 N.E. 2 (Ind. 1921); but *see* (7) *State v. Feilen*, 126 P. 75 (Wa. 1912) which upheld a sterilization law. *See also* the 1921 decision in *State Bd. of Eugenics v. Cline* (Or. Cir. Ct. Marion Co. Dec. 13, 1921) (unreported opinion) in Laughlin at 287–89 ("the 1917 Statute . . . clearly violates the provisions of the state and federal constitution prohibiting class legislation.").

33 When Buck's case reached the Supreme Court, six courts had struck down these laws (Iowa, Indiana, New York, New Jersey, Nevada, Oregon) and two had upheld them (Michigan, Washington). *Smith v. Command*, 204 N.W. 140, 145 (Mich. 1925); *In re Salloum*, 210 N.W. 498 (Mich. 1926); *State v. Feilen*, 126 P. 75 (Wa. 1912).

34 *Davis, supra* note 32, at 416–17 (humiliation and degradation, "Dark Ages," "mental torture"); *Mickle, supra* note 32, at 691 ("brand of infamy," "strange methods of repression"); *Osborn, supra* note 32, at 640, 645 ("class of people," "beyond . . . comprehension").

35 Of the six reported cases to strike down sterilization laws in the pre-*Buck* period (*Smith, Davis, Haynes, Osborn, Mickle,* and *Williams,* all *supra* note 32), not a single one refers to the right to procreate or to the notion of a fundamental right. *Davis* refers to marriage as a "civil right" but strikes down the law as a cruel and unusual punishment and a bill of attainder. The only pre-*Buck* court to refer to natural or fundamental rights is *Smith MI, supra* note 33, which *rejects* the argument. The most consistent rationale was equal protection; see *Smith NJ, Osborn, Haynes,* and the unpublished *Cline, supra* note 32. See also governor's and attorney general's messages vetoing laws during this period. Laughlin at 38–39 (Pa: violates equal protection); *id.* at 45 (Vt: "inexcusable discrimination"); *id.* at 50 (Id: class legislation).

36 *Smith NJ, supra* note 32, at 966 ("not the only persons," "racial differences," "permanent and paramount"); *Osborn, supra* note 32, at 643–44 (following *Smith NJ*); *Haynes, supra* note 32, at 940–41 (Mich. 1918) (following *Smith NJ*). Laughlin at 265, 267, 280–81 (briefs referring to class legislation); *Sterilization Studies of the Committee on Cacogenic Control,* 9 J. Crim. L. & Criminology 596, 597 (1919) (class legislation); Stephen A. Siegel, *Justice Holmes, Buck v. Bell, and the History of Equal Protection,* 90 Minn. L. Rev. 106, 115–16 (2005) ("In most cases, equal protection was either the sole ground or among the prominent grounds of decision . . . The courts never relied on substantive due process.").

37 *Buck v. Bell,* 274 U.S. 200, 202 (1927) (counsel: "new classes . . . even

races may be brought within the scope of such regulation"). The racial fear may explain Holmes's description of Buck as a "white woman." *Id.* at 205.

38   Brief for Plaintiff, *Buck v. Bell*, No. 292 at 6–7 (U.S. Oct. Term 1926) (invoking the "inherent right to go through life with full bodily integrity, possessed of all those powers and faculties with which God has endowed them"). Buck's lawyer, Whitehead, specifically denied the possibility of a right to procreate. See *id.* at 13 ("We concede that the State has the right to segregate the feeble-minded and thereby deprive them of the 'power to procreate.'"). In rejecting bodily integrity, Holmes wrote: "It seems to be contended that in no circumstances could such an order be justified." *Buck v. Bell*, 274 U.S. at 207.

39   East at 248–49 (waste of war); Richard Hofstadter, Social Darwinism in American Thought 41 (1944) (quoting Spencer).

40   Stephen Jay Gould, The Flamingo's Smile 312–13 (1985) (quoting Holmes); *Buck v. Bell*, 274 U.S. 200, 207 (1927); Albert W. Alschuler, Law Without Values: The Life, Work, and Legacy of Justice Holmes 27–28 (2000).

41   274 U.S. 200, 207 (1927) ("imbeciles"); *id.* at 208 ("usual last resort," "shortcomings"); WP at M4 (Feb. 12, 1928) (Butler Catholic).

42   Jacob Aronoff, *The Constitutionality of Asexualization Legislation in the United States*, 1 St. John's L. Rev. 146, 152 (1926–27) (Holmes likely to influence opinion on humanity of sterilization); J. H. Landman, *The History of Human Sterilization in the United States—Theory, Statute, Adjudication*, 63 U.S. L. Rev. 48, 50 (1929) ("realism, humanity and progress"); LD at 36, 37 (Jan. 23, 1932) ("Pages would be needed"); Lawrence Friedman, American Law in the Twentieth Century 110 (2002) ("progressive").

43   Landman at 113 ("*Buck v. Bell* has now definitely committed"); *id.* at 105 (eighteen states new bills, four more passed laws); *id.* at App. B (listing laws passed after 1927); Larson at 28 (citing Robitscher) (number of operations jumped).

44   The cases arising after *Buck* deferred to Justice Holmes's opinion, although some state procedures were deemed insufficient. *See, e.g.,* *State v. Schaffer*, 270 P. 604 (Kan. 1928) (upholding law); *Davis v. Walton*, 276 P. 921 (Utah 1929) (upholding law, but insufficient evidence to apply); *State v. Troutman*, 299 P. 668 (Ida. 1931) (upholding Idaho law); *In re Main*, 19 P.2d 153 (Okla. 1933) (upholding law); *In re Clayton*, 234 N.W. 630 (Neb. 1931); *Brewer v. Valk*, 167 S.E. 638 (N.C. 1933) (insufficient procedure); *In re Opinion of Justices*, 162 So. 123 (Ala. 1935) (same); *Garcia v. State*, 97 P.2d 264 (Cal. App. 1939).

45 CDT at 1 (Dec. 21, 1933) (400,000 in Germany); CDT at 10 (Jan. 1, 1934) (same); Reilly, *supra* note 20, at 40 (1,422 in U.S.); Jonas Robitscher, Eugenic Sterilization App. 2 (1973) (2–3,000 in U.S.).

46 Editorial, NYT at 16 (Aug. 8, 1933) ("Some 15,000 unfortunates"); NYHT at 11 (Dec. 21, 1933).

47 McCarthy, *supra* note 4; LD at 17 (Jan. 13, 1934); NW at 12 (Aug. 5, 1933); NW at 11 (Dec. 30, 1933); NYHT at 1 (Dec. 24, 1933); LAT at 3 (Dec. 21, 1933); LAT at 2 (Jan. 1, 1934); CDT at 5 (Jan. 5, 1934); Whitney, *supra* note 14, at 7; J. H. Landman, *Race Betterment by Human Sterilization*, SA at 292–95 (June 1934); E. S. Gosney, *Eugenic Sterilization: Human Betterment Demands It*, SA at 18–19, 52–53 (July 1934); C. Thomalla, *The Sterilization Law in Germany*, SA at 126–27 (Sept. 1934); Ignatius W. Cox, *The Folly of Human Sterilization*, SA at 188–90 (Oct. 1934). The quotation is taken from the trailer for *Tomorrow's Children*, a melodramatic film about a girl who escapes sterilization when it is discovered that she was adopted. *See* NYT at 16 (May 18, 1938).

48 *See* P. W. Wilson, *The World Watches Germany*, RR at 22 (Dec. 1933) ("understand," "scold"); *id.* at 24 (Dec. 1933) (decrying Nazi "crushing of minorities," suppressing speech); Roger Shaw, *Visiting the Third Reich*, RR at 37 (Jan. 1934) (ridiculing Hitler's 1933 elections); Edith Johnson, DO at 12 (Dec. 8, 1933); *id.* at 8 (Nov. 24, 1934).

49 Alan Brinkley, Voices of Protest: Huey Long, Father Coughlin, and the Great Depression (1982); RR at 48 (Oct. 1934) (NRA Fascist).

50 Shaw, *supra* note 48, at 37 ("gets things done"); TDW at 18 (Jan. 12, 1935) ("crime . . . done away with").

51 McCarthy, *supra* note 4, at 31 (quoting Leon Whitney, Hitler "greatest statesmen"); LAT at 2 (Jan. 1, 1934) (application to criminals); Richard F. Wetzell, Inventing the Criminal: A History of German Criminology 1880–1945 256–57 (2000) (coverage of law to specific categories of diseases and persons), *id.* at 258 (castration of sex offenders). The original Nazi law did not include criminals but "it emerged that Hitler himself was eager to see 'habitual criminals' sterilized." *Id.* at 257. That aim was fulfilled "when the Ministry of Justice issued a circular requesting that all courts, prosecutors, and prison officials report criminals who might suffer from a 'genetic disease' . . . for a sterilization hearing." *Id.* at 258–59; *Nazi Decree Revives Sterilization Debate*, LD at 17 (Jan. 13, 1934) (physician must refer); NYT at 19 (Jan. 9, 1934) (voluntary confinement as alternative).

52 As early as 1931, the Nazis were reported to seek "Nordic dominance," to "sterilize some races," and ban miscegenation. NYT at 1 (Dec.

8, 1931). Hitlerian Nordicism was the topic of Dorothy Thompson's popular work I Saw Hitler (1932); NYT at BR5 (Mar. 5, 1932) (review of Thompson's book); NYT at E1 (Oct. 9, 1932); NW at 13 (Apr. 15, 1933) ("Hundreds of Jews have been beaten or tortured"); NW at 14 (May 20, 1933) ("Holocaust: Down Unter Den Linden" marched 5,000 young men burning books; Goebbels says "Jewish intellectualism is dead"); *id.* at 15 (65,000 protesting German anti-Semitic policies); NW at 12 (June 3, 1933) ("ruthless persecution of the Jews"); NW at 10 (Sept. 9, 1933) (Jewry as "a ferment of decomposition").

53 Waldemar Kaempffert, *The Week in Science*, NYT at XX7 (Oct. 22, 1933); *see also* NYT at 2 (Aug. 12, 1933) (*Nature* magazine feared abuse by Germans).

54 NYT at 10 (Jan. 5, 1934); NYT at 10 (Jan. 4, 1934). The fine for doctors was 150 marks, close to half the monthly salary of the average official, NYT at E3 (Jan. 14, 1934); NYT at 4 (Feb. 8, 1934) ("Negroid children").

55 Gary Gerstle, American Crucible: Race and Nation in the Twentieth Century 161 (2001) ("in the 1930s and 1940s, many spoke of the Jewish and Italian races as being something other (and lower) than the white race"); Matthew Frye Jacobson, Whiteness of a Different Color: European Immigrants and the Alchemy of Race (1999). On Supreme Court usage, *Hill v. Texas*, 316 U.S. 400, 402 (1942) ("white race," "colored race"); *Stewart v. Keyes*, 295 U.S. 403, 415 (1935) (equating "Indians" with a "race"); *Morrison v. California*, 291 U.S. 82, 85 (1934) ("Japanese race"); *Nagle v. Loi Hoa*, 275 U.S. 475, 478 (1928) ("Chinese race"); *Gong Lum v. Rice*, 275 U.S. 78, 80 (1927) ("Caucasian race"); *id.* at 82, 83 ("colored races"); *United States v. Thind*, 261 U.S. 204, 215 (1923) ("white races"); Juan Perea et al., Race and Races: Cases and Resources for a Diverse America (2000).

56 S. J. Holmes, The Trend of the Race 8 (1921) ("breed an albino race"); *see, e.g.*, Stanley Powell Davies, Social Control of the Mentally Deficient 82 (1930) ("feebleminded race"); E. Wake Cook, Betterment: Individual, Social, and Industrial 8 (1906) ("race of criminals").

57 Grant, *supra* note 12, at 5, 50–51 ("native American aristocracy," "rigid system of selection"); *id.* at 18 ("primitive," "lower type"); Paul at 104 (quoting Grant on "moral perverts, mental defectives, and hereditary cripples"); Lothrop Stoddard, The Revolt Against Civilization 5 (1923) ("pacific penetration"); Lothrop Stoddard, The Rising Tide of Colour 5 (1920, 1981 reprint) ("not politics, but race"); *id.* at 169 (quoting Grant that race is "everything").

58 Paul at 104 (Grant's favorable reviews); W. E. Castle, Genetics

and Eugenics: A Text-Book 290 (1921) (immigrants pose threat to democracy); Heredity and Eugenics, *supra* note 27, at 309 ("from one thousand").

59 S. J. Holmes, Human Genetics and Its Social Import 357 (1936) ("becoming bleached"); Popenoe & Johnson, *supra* note 16, at 284 (1924) ("placed very near zero"). On the feebleminded "passing," Paul at 68.

60 NYT at 6 (Jan. 22, 1934) ("good example"); Thomalla, *supra* note 47, at 126 (referring to American laws in defense of German law); NYT at E3 (Jan. 14, 1934) (one billion marks).

61 See McCarthy, *supra* note 4, at 31 (Jewish leaders do not object to sterilization but fear abuse); Editorial, *New German Administration Adopts Sterilization Law to Build Up Race*, GP 22.2 (Aug. 1, 1933) ("outstanding accomplishment," "keynote in social welfare"); Editorial, ON at 6 (Jan. 2, 1934).

Chapter 2: The Brain Trust

1 Conklin, *supra* ch. 1, note 9, at 566.

2 ON at 1 (Apr. 18, 1934) ("call of science"); DO at 1 (Apr. 19, 1934) ("standing mute," "showed little interest," "incurable").

3 DO at 1 (Apr. 19, 1934) ("record of associating"); *Oklahoma Puts Sterilization Law into Effect*, LD at 17 (May 12, 1934) ("It's all right with me"); ON at 1 (Apr. 18, 1934) ("I was just a little kid").

4 DO at 1 (Apr. 19, 1934) (Cloyd "raised no objections"); Editorial, ON at 6 (Apr. 18, 1934) ("Why would anyone protest"); LD *supra* note 3, at 17 (May 12, 1934) (Marrs); LAT at 8 (Apr. 19, 1934) ("long and carefully planned").

5 OCT at 1 (Apr. 19, 1934) ("pretty"); NT at 1 (Apr. 19, 1934) ("sad-eyed girl," "logical answers"); DO at 8 (Apr. 20, 1934) ("over-study in school"); MDP at 7 (Apr. 20, 1934) (same); MDP at 9 (Apr. 22, 1934) (McAlester, funds "running low"); SMN at 10 (Apr. 21, 1934) ("greatest steps forward since statehood").

6 Edith Johnson, *Proposed Marriage Measures*, DO at 8 (Jan. 2, 1933) ("red tape"); ON at 1, 2 (Apr. 18, 1934) (300 eligibles, Brown order); MDP at 1 (Apr. 18, 1934) ("most comprehensive sterilization programs").

7 The WPA Guide to 1930s Oklahoma 299 (1986) (Wilburton); WT at 90 (July 30, 1934) (Briggs trip in May); TDW at 1 (Aug. 9, 1936) (desperado country).

8 DO at 1 (Dec. 12, 1934) (Briggs's background); HW at 11 (Nov. 17, 1934) (pleasing personality); 3 Canadian at 1064–66 ("earliest ambition," "home course"); Claud Briggs, WPA Questionnaire 284–85,

OHS; Harlow at 331; Who Is Who in Oklahoma 61–62 (Lyle & Dale Boren eds., 1935) (county atty., state rep.); Latimer Co. News–Tribune at 1 (July 3, 1936) ("masses against the classes").

9 The Briggs amendment appears in Okla. Senate Journal, 13th Legis. at 1811 (Mar. 19, 1931) ("any other State Institution"); HW at 5 (Feb. 7, 1931) (Murray's emotion and Briggs); HW at 7 (Aug. 4, 1934) (Murray opposed Briggs).

10 HW at 3 (Jan. 31, 1931) (man of the people, "stickler"); HW at 7, 15 (July 5, 1925) ("of the old school"); *Lester Picked to Top Welch in Court Race*, undated article, CA, Elmer Thomas Coll., Legis. Series, Box 8, at 43; HW at 10–11 (Feb. 20, 1932); DO at 1 (Aug. 8, 1927) ("Christian Citizenship"); WPA Index, Eugene Fay Lester, OHS.

11 *Kansas v. Schaffer*, 270 P. 604, 604 (Kan. 1928) (U.S. Supreme Court decided the issue); *id.* at 605 (general welfare supports sterilization, upholding constitutionality); *In re Main*, 19 P.2d 153, 156 (Okla. 1933) (upholding constitutionality based on common welfare); *State v. Troutman*, 299 P. 668 (Ida. 1931) (upholding constitutionality); *In re Clayton*, 234 N.W. 630 (Neb. 1931) (same); *Davis v. Walton*, 276 P. 921, 922 (Utah 1929) (upholding constitutionality—"the rule announced by . . . the case of *Buck v. Bell* . . . is a complete answer" to the Fourteenth Amendment claims—but finding insufficient evidence); *Brewer v. Valk*, 167 S.E. 638 (N.C. 1933) (holding that sterilization cannot be accomplished without a hearing, which was not provided, and distinguishing the case from *Buck*, North Carolina subsequently amended its law); *In re Opinion of the Justices*, 162 So. 123, 128 (Ala. 1935) (advisory opinion ruling that sterilization was within the constitutional police power but required a hearing).

12 MT at 9–11 (doubts about diagnosis), 40–44 (social workers' report) (May 27, 1932); *id.* at 41 ("charges of cruelty and abuse to his wife and children"); *id.* at 44 ("afflicted with a hereditary form of insanity") (Board finding). Even though Main consented, at the time, it was believed the operation might still qualify as a crime. *In re Main*, 19 P.2d 153, 156 (1933) (police power to sterilize).

13 1931 Okla. Sess. Laws ch. 26, sec. 1, at 80 (House Bill No. 64) (approved Apr. 22, 1931); 1933 Okla. Sess. Laws ch. 46, sec. 1, at 85 (Senate Bill No. 275) (approved May 5, 1933).

14 Ritzhaupt WPA Questionnaire, OHS Archives (No. 421); The Logan County History, 1889–1977: Logan County, Oklahoma 562 (Ritzhaupt family); HW at 11 (May 23, 1934) (candidate for governor); Okla. Senate Journal, 14th Legis. at 718–19, 752, 1468, 2575 (1933); Who Is Who in Oklahoma, *supra* note 8, at 428 (Ritzy, poultry).

15 Ritzhaupt, *The Doctor in Politics*, J. Okla. Med. Assoc. at 198 (June 1934) ("red ruin"). In the early years, eugenicists themselves noted the role of doctors in sponsoring sterilization laws. *See, e.g.*, Bleeker Van Wagenen, in Problems in Eugenics: First International Eugenics Congress at 477 (1912). For early and enthusiastic statements by doctors, 8 Amed. 192 (Mar. 1913) ("public right"); for medical skeptics, Dr. Morris Fishbein, NYT at N1 (Mar. 3, 1935); NT at 1 (Apr. 17, 1934) (Ritzhaupt offers to perform first operation); DO at 12 (Apr. 17, 1934) (Jails "growing larger," "curtail this expense").

16 *See, e.g.*, CDT at 2 (Apr. 24, 1934) (Dillinger); CDT at 2 (May 1, 1934) (same); MDP at 1 (May 6, 1934) (same); NYT at 3 (May 6, 1934) (same); LD at 7 (Bonnie and Clyde); NYT at 40 (Nov. 6, 1933) (Hamm); NYT at 1 (Apr. 27, 1934) (Robles); NYT at 4 (Sept. 29, 1933) (Urschel); TDW at 1 (May 15, 1934) (Robles). Mass crime panic was old news by this time. At the close of World War I, the nation and even the world suffered what appeared then to be "crime waves." *See, e.g.*, NYT at 93 (Oct. 10, 1920); NYT at 10 (Apr. 1, 1920); NYT at 2 (Dec. 24, 1920). The major difference by 1932 was that crime was broadcast by radio as a national event (in part because of the Lindbergh kidnapping) and that the federal government under Roosevelt, unlike earlier administrations, took responsibility.

17 CDT at 1 (Feb. 16, 1933); NYT at 1 (Feb. 17, 1933); NYT at 1 (Feb. 17, 1933); NYT at 1 (Nov. 26, 1930) (Hoover's war on crime); CDT at 5 (Nov. 26, 1930) (same); LAT at 1 (Nov. 26, 1930) (same); NYT at 1 (Dec. 13, 1934) (FDR's war on crime); NYT at 1 (Apr. 24, 1934) (same).

18 William E. Leuchtenburg, Franklin D. Roosevelt and the New Deal 334 (1963) (Dillinger); LAT at 3 (Apr. 14, 1934) (Zeitlow); NYT at 1 (Apr. 18, 1934) (Lockhart mob); LAT at 1 (Apr. 18, 1934) (same); LAT at 1 (Nov. 28, 1933) (California lynching); NW at 6–7 (Dec. 9, 1933) (Governor Rolph's statements); NYT at 1 (Nov. 11, 1933) (kidnapping of twenty-two-year-old Brooke Hart).

19 LAT at 2 (May 19, 1934) (FDR on crime); NYT at 1 (Apr. 24, 1934) (same); NYT at 1 (May 19, 1934); DO at 1 (May 19, 1934); Whitney, *supra* ch. 1, note 14), at 233 ("crime bill"); CDT at 2 (Apr. 25, 1934) (Nazi paper proposes sterilization for America's gangsters).

20 *See* NYT at 3 (Apr. 25, 1934) (airplanes); NYT at 2 (May 24, 1934) (army); NYT at 1 (Apr. 24, 1934) (bills); Claire Bond Potter, War on Crime (1998).

21 Landman at 104 ("acute current crime wave," "criminologists and eugeni[cists]"); Sheldon & Eleanor T. Glueck, Five Hundred Criminal

Careers (1930); Sheldon & Eleanor T. Glueck, One Thousand Juvenile Delinquents 151 (1939) ("88.2% of our juveniles recidivated");
V. F. Nourse, 39 Tulsa L. Rev. 925, 930 (2004) (Baumes laws in more
than twenty states); Clayton J. Ettinger, The Problem of Crime 303
(1932) (Baumes laws); Julia E. Johnsen, VI The Reference Shelf No. 3
(1929).

22 Edwin H. Sutherland, Criminology 622 (1924) (doubting efficacy but
sterilization was "clearly desirable" for those with inherited abnormal
traits). Sutherland cited the great eugenics popularizers of the day,
including Harry Laughlin; *id.* at 622 n. 4. In the 1934 edition, Sutherland took out the "clearly desirable" language, but also stated that
sterilization "might have other advantages." Sutherland at 582 (1934);
Ettinger, *supra* note 21, at 519 (linking feeblemindedness and crime);
Harry Best, Crime and the Criminal Law in the United States 274–75
(1930) (same); Nathaniel F. Cantor, Crime: Criminals and Criminal
Justice 423–24 (1932) (professing doubts about sterilization, *id.* at
423–24, but indicating that sterilization can be applied to insane and
feebleminded prisoners and others, *id.* at 424).

23 Sheldon Glueck, Crime and Justice 266, 267 ("reduce the reproduction"); Sheldon Glueck to Human Betterment Foundation, Glueck
Papers, HLL, Reel 54, No. 704 (Apr. 26, 1932) ("I am seriously con-
sidering the recommendation of sterilization legislation for Massachusetts"); Sheldon Glueck to E. S. Gosney, *id.* Reel 54, Nos. 704–07;
Sheldon & Eleanor T. Glueck, Five Hundred Delinquent Women 310
(1934) (stating that the evidence was overwhelming that "persons of
the kind so largely represented in our group are unfit to care properly
for children" and are "irresponsible and prolific breeders").

24 Heredity and Eugenics, *supra* ch.1, note 27, at 282 ("many criminals
. . . feeble-minded"); Goddard, *supra* ch. 1, note 28, at 58 (1973 reprint)
("criminality is often made out of feeblemindedness"); Horatio Hack-
ett Newman, Evolution, Genetics and Eugenics 459 (1932) (Juvenile
criminals as feebleminded); East at 243 (feeblemindedness was the
"best material" from which criminals were made); John Lewis Gillin,
Criminology and Penology 178, 855 (1926).

25 Percy R. Parnell, The Joint 4–5, 18, 24, 27, 36 (1976) (memoir of former McAlester prisoner who as a child knew the prison during this
period and was later incarcerated there); Robert Park, History of the
Oklahoma State Penitentiary 5 (1914); HW at 8 (Feb. 6, 1932).

26 Editorial, TDW at 4 (Jan. 2, 1933); HW at 7 (Apr. 30, 1932) ("seething
mass"); DO at 9 (Jan. 4, 1933) ("the hallways are filled with cots").

27 DO at 13 (Jan. 1, 1933) (Kimes); NYT at 3 (May 14, 1936) (Terrill);

NYT at 14 (May 24, 1936) (Lovette); HW at 8 (Feb. 6, 1932) (forty percent, "chicken stealing"); NT at 10 (Apr. 26, 1931) ("mixed blood aliens"). Warden's Annual Report, Oklahoma State Penitentiary, McAlester, Fiscal Year 1934, DOLA, Ex. G (almost half of sentences two years or under).

28 NT at 10 (Apr. 26, 1931); HW at 8 (Feb. 6, 1932) ("an hour"); *id.* at 16 (cutting costs).

29 The Prison Labor Problem in Oklahoma 36 (1937) DOLA (schooling data); 1934 Warden's Report, *supra* note 27, Ex. J: Occupations.

30 DOC Nos. 21466, 28404; DO at 11 (Jan. 9, 1930); Ponca City News at 1 (Jan. 5, 1930) ("the jury may convict me"); DO at 18 (Feb. 12, 1932) (trap laid); BMT at 1 (Jan. 18, 1930) ("send this man to prison"); Howard K. Berry, He Made It Safe to Murder (2001).

31 DO at 4 (Jan. 11, 1930); DOC Nos. 21466, 28404. The forgery was the alleged motive for the attempt to murder Collins, NYT at 14 (Aug. 20, 1929); CDT at 3 (Aug. 17, 1929); Information, *Oklahoma v. Hyde & McHone*, Okla. Logan Co. Dist. Ct. (Aug. 28, 1933).

32 TDW at 11 (May 12, 1927) ("superiority of mind," "aristocrats," "responsible position"); DOC No. 18051 (wife in Vicksburg, parents in St. Louis); Okfuskee County News at 1 (May 5, 1927) (King "has a criminal record" and is brought from the "Crystal county jail at Ozark, Mo., where he was being held on charges of bank robbery at Billings Mo."); *cf. id.* at 1 (Apr. 28, 1927) (Bainum was suspected of robbing a bank at Ozark); *id.* at 1 (Sept. 8, 1927) (Bainum brought from county jail in Missouri, arrested on charges of robbing a bank in Missouri). Bainum's Oklahoma Dep't of Corrections record indicates that he served a previous term as #7435 in the Lansing, Kansas, penitentiary; his co-conspirator, Harrison, was retrieved from there. *See id.* at 1 (Apr. 14, 1927); according to newspapers, officers testified at Bainum's trial that Harrison and Bainum "knew each other intimately in the Kansas penitentiary." *Id.* at 1 (Sept. 29, 1927). Efforts to retrieve Bainum's records at Lansing were unavailing and the FBI reported that they have no record of Bainum.

33 DOC No. 18051; TDW at 11 (May 12, 1927); Okfuskee County News at 1 (May 5, 1927) *id.* at 1 (Apr. 28, 1927); *id.* at 1 (Sept. 29, 1927); TDW at 16 (Apr. 8, 1927) (Grandpa Harrison aged twenty-two, looks fifty); Petition in Error, No. A–6886, *Ralph Bainum v. Oklahoma*, Ct. Crim. Appeals (date illegible) ("dudes from the city"); *Purdy v. State*, 287 P. 840 (Okla. Crim. App. 1930); *Ralph Bainum v. State*, 282 P. 903 (Okla. Crim. App. 1929).

34 DOC No. 10072; *Oklahoma v. Roach et al.*, No. 1391 (Okla. Craig Co. entry of judgment); *Roach v. State*, 214 P. 563 (Okla. Crim. App. 1923). Of the 2,136 prisoners received in fiscal year 1934, 108 were Catholics. 1934 Warden's Report, *supra* note 27, Ex. E. DO at 4 (Dec. 10, 1919). I uncovered no evidence that Kelly was in fact a lawyer.

35 DO at 5 (July 30, 1934) ("Warden Sam Brown, worried over prison unrest, was outspoken in his opposition to the law"); MDP at 1 (July 30, 1934) (same); MDP at 1, 2 (Apr. 18, 1934) ("Brown . . . said he fears riots"); ON at 1, 2 (Apr. 18, 1934) (riots); *In re Main*, 19 P.2d 153 (Okla. 1933). *Main* Brief, DOLA (Okla. Dist. Ct. No. 75,080) (filed Nov. 2, 1932) (seven pages, two and a half of which were introduction); MDP at 1 (Apr. 18, 1934) (Cloyd student of "social and eugenic reform"); DO at 1 (Apr. 19, 1934) (Cloyd no objection). The papers later reported that Cloyd did in fact object in a case where there was no consent.

36 TDW at 3 (July 30, 1934); WT at 95 (Claud Briggs: "yet there has been no sinews of warfare placed in the hands of the attorneys that would enable them to go out and consult or procure the services of experts . . . and when I say 'Sinews of warfare,' I mean money.").

Chapter 3: Thoroughbreds

1 Guyer, *supra* ch. 1, note 14, at 415.

2 TDW at 1 (May 11, 1934); TDW at 1 (May 12, 1934); Donald Worster, Dust Bowl: The Southern Plains in the 1930s (1979).

3 ON at 1 (May 11, 1934); PA, Vol. 753 at 110 (clipping attached).

4 *Clarence Darrow: A Great Actor*, RD at 65–67 (Sept. 1932); ON at 1 (May 11, 1934); Clarence Darrow, *The Edwardses and the Jukeses*, 6 Amerc. 147 (1925); Darrow, *The Eugenics Cult, supra* Prologue, note 2; *id.* at 131 ("gaudy little plan"); *id.* at 137 ("senseless and impudent").

5 ON at 1 (May 11, 1934); TDW at 13 (May 10, 1934).

6 Paul at 95 (Sanger and motto); Kevles at 48 (Davenport); William F. Obgurn & Meyer F. Nimkoff, Sociology 78 (1940) (college text); S. Bogardus & Robert H. Lewis, Social Life and Personality 102 (1938) (high school text); Harry H. Laughlin, *Racing Capacity in the Thoroughbred Horse, Part I*, 38 Sci. Monthly 210–22 (Mar. 1934); 2 Murray Memoir *supra* ch. 1, note 13, ch. W, §766; French Strother, *Crime and Herdity*, 48 WW at 557 (Sept. 1924); Kevles at 54 (interest of eugenic funders in breeding horses).

7 Charles Darwin, The Descent of Man 136 (1898) ("worst animals to breed"); Albert E. Wiggam, *New Styles in Ancestors*, 55 WW 142, 143

(Dec. 1927) (quoting Spencer); Paul at 32 (Galton, recently risen ape); Newman at 443–44 (quoting Leonard Darwin, "upward march").

8   Wiggam, *supra* note 7, at 142, 143–44, 149.

9   Selden, *supra* ch. 1, note 9, at 23–25 & fig. 2.2 (display); Wiggam, *supra* note 7, at 142, 145–6; Am. Phil. Soc'y Image No. 9, Eugenicsarchive .org, (crime costs $100,000).

10   David Starr Jordan, The Heredity of Richard Roe 106 (1911) ("never been born"); Larson at 38 ("it is better not to be born").

11   Parnell, *supra* ch. 2, note 25, at 30 ("old timers spot the young kids" and bid on them); *id.* at 44 (separate water barrels); *id.* at 32 (having a "punk" as a "status symbol"); Walter Biscup, TDW, sec. 4, at 9 (Oct. 14, 1934). This account is confirmed by official sources, *In re the Matter of Oklahoma State Reformatory at Granite, Oklahoma*, and *Investigation by the Board of Affairs of Said Institution* at 3A (Feb. 1935 investigation, concluding in its findings that "sodomy is constantly practiced in the institution"); *id.* at 15, 35, 40, 59, 282–85 (investigating claims of a gang rape of a young prisoner at Granite), DOLA, RG 1; for other contemporaneous accounts inside prisons in the 1930s, Friedman, *supra* ch. 1, note 42, at 216–17.

12   Biscup, *supra* note 11 ("the new and the young inmates" "fights and stabbings"). On segregation by color, Parnell, *supra* ch. 2, note 25, at 75. 1934 Warden's Report, *supra* ch. 2, note 27, Ex. A (approx. 30 percent of prisoners black).

13   Biscup, *supra* note 11 (Barrow "punked"); Gerstle, *supra* ch. 1, note 55, at 54 (effeminacy as treason); on the history of manliness, Gail Bederman, Manliness and Civilization (1995); Peter Gay, The Cultivation of Hatred 94–116 (1993). TDW at 10 (June 20, 1937) (convicts in dresses); HW at 2 (May 1, 1937) (pink panties); David E. Ruth, Inventing the Public Enemy 89–92 (1996) (feminization of gangster). The picture in the text appears in Okla. Dep't of Corrections, Oklahoma Department of Corrections History: Twentieth Century 115 (2002). The latter item indicates that the practice dates from the 1920s, but such practices continued in the 1930s. HW at 2 (May 1, 1937); TDW at 10 (June 20, 1937).

14   *See, e.g.*, Washington Laws ch. 53 (1921) (sterilization of "habitual criminals, moral degenerates and sexual perverts"); Iowa Laws ch. 187 (1913) ("criminals, idiots, etc.," "if such inmate . . . is a moral or sexual pervert . . ."); California Laws ch. 363 (1913) (recidivists who have been convicted "at least two times for rape," and three times of other crimes and shall have given evidence that while an inmate "is a moral or sexual degenerate or pervert"); Nevada Laws sec. 28 (1911) ("carnal abuse" of a child or "rape"); Oregon Laws ch. 279 (1917) (all "feeble-

minded, insane, epileptic, habitual criminals, moral degenerates and sexual perverts"), *reprinted in* Laughlin at 15–16 (Washington); *id.* at 22 (Iowa); *id.* at 18 (California); *id.* at 21 (Nevada); *id.* at 33 (Oregon). For later laws in other states covering perversion, *see* Landman at 67, 71–72, 75, 87.

15 *Davis v. Walton*, 276 P. 921, 924 (Utah 1929) (Walton, described in the case as a "negro," had "acted lovingly toward other boys").

16 Jeffrey Weeks, Making Sexual History 136 (2000) (myths of sexuality and race); Ronald T. Takaki, A Different Mirror 149 (1993) (Irish the "slaves" of "passion," lacking in self-control); *id.* at 205 (Chinese lustful and depraved); Jacobson, *supra* ch. 1, note 55, at 65 (E. A. Ross); *id.* at 65–66 (lechery, libertine Jew, Leo Frank). On the use of sexualization to mark race: Linda Gordon, The Great Arizona Orphan Abduction 76 (1999) (use of pornography to mark the distance between the savage and the white, Anglo/Mexican-American context); Thomas Gossett, Race: The History of an Idea in America 273, 291 (1992) (sexualization of African-Americans and Chinese); George Mosse, Nationalism and Sexuality: Middle-Class Morality and Sexual Norms in Modern Europe 144–45 (1985) (Jews). On sterilization called "legal lynching," NYT at 2 (May 29, 1935). On castration and lynching, Philip Dray, At the Hands of Persons Unknown: The Lynching of Black America 30, 81, 94, 144–45, 268–69, 349 (2002); Jacob Aronoff, 1 St. John's L. Rev. 146, 147 (1926) ("the general public knows").

17 One surely cannot say that eugenicists hated women; they often idealized women and their procreative capacities. Women were often enthusiastic supporters of eugenics. They had been raised on advice manuals extolling woman's place in the moral and social order, as the protector of the race. See W. Grant Hague, The Eugenic Mother and Baby: A Young Wife's Complete Guide preface (1913). Eugenics, made scientific, gave an aura of legitimacy to what seemed radical and was still declared obscene in many states—birth control. It is likely that many sterilization laws could never have been passed without the activism or at least the support of women's groups. If gender is expressed less in terms of individuals and more in terms of an ideology, however, gender played an important part in eugenics: transgressing gender roles was a sign of the "unfit." Visibly sexualized women were considered for that reason "unfit" (witness Carrie Buck). Feebleminded men were also gender failures: they were often termed not sufficiently sexual. Other purported deviations from traditional gender roles, such as homosexuality, suffered the same fate. As one eugenicist explained, the feebleminded man was undersexed and lack-

ing in aggressiveness and unable to compete with normal males. E. S. Gosney & Paul Popenoe, Sterilization for Human Betterment 39–40 (1929, 1980 reprint).

18 S. J. Holmes, Human Genetics and Its Social Import 372 (1936); Gosney & Popenoe, *supra* note 17, at 39 ("three-fourths of the sterilized feeble-minded girls of our study had been sexually delinquent prior to commitment"). This was not idiosyncratic. *See, e.g.,* Kevles at 53 (reporting, in a study of "wayward" girls, that Charles Davenport concluded that the cause of prostitution was an "innate eroticism"). By contrast, the feebleminded man was not given to sex offenses. *See* Holmes at 372.

19 1931 Okla. Statutes, art. 3, §665 (impotency and conviction grounds for divorce); Vinita Memoir, *supra* ch. 1, note 2, at 130 ("the divorce laws of practically every state recognize this when they make sterility of one of the contracting parties a good and sufficient ground for divorce"); Orlando Patterson, Slavery and Social Death: A Comparative Study 5–10 (1982) (natal alienation and social death).

20 ACLU Clipping of New York Telegram, undated, UP byline May 12, 1934 (Winkler printer and "law student"); Lucille B. Milner to George Winkler (May 16, 1934) ("following the case"); George Winkler to Lucille B. Milner, ACLU (May 24, 1934) ("hearty and sincere thanks," $150, "monetary requirements"), PA, Vol. 753 at 110–13.

21 Vinita Memoir, *supra* ch. 1, note 2, at 125 ("editors are afraid of offending some narrow or prudish reader, so such vital facts are largely avoided").

22 Edith Johnson, DO at 8 (May 19, 1934); WT at 90 (July 30, 1934); Okla. AAG Jesse Ballard, DOLA, RG1 (poem).

Chapter 4: Heat and Love

1 Okla. AAG Jesse Ballard, DOLA, RG1.

2 DO at 1 (Aug. 7, 1934) (twenty-four states and 26 million people); DO at 8 (Aug. 14, 1934); DO at 1 (Aug. 6, 1934) (praying for rain); DO at 3 (Aug. 4, 1934) (bombing clouds); DO at 18 (Aug. 3, 1934); DO at 8 (Aug. 2, 1934) (letter to the editor re: hoisting hose); Editorial, DO at 8 (Aug. 1, 1934) ("fiery furnace[s]", "hadean days"); DO at 6 (July 22, 1934) ("blazing rainless[ness]").

3 On the heat, DO at 1 (July 31, 1934); MDP at 1 (July 30, 1934) ("big house," "fretful"); *id.* at 1 (July 31, 1934) ("grapevine," "stealthy news," "grim[ly]"); ON at 1 (July 30, 1934) ("the chief topic of conversation"); Walter Biscup, TDW at 3 (July 30, 1934) ("surgeon hovering," warden

apprehensive). The Muskogee papers put the number at 582 third-termers, although the reported numbers varied quite a bit, MDP at 1 (July 31, 1934).

4   ON at 1 (July 30, 1934) (twenty men in warden's office, committee at counsel table, Winkler smoking); *id.* at 10 (picture of Winkler); DO at 1 (July 31, 1934) (Winkler printer); DO at 10 (Nov. 7, 1934) (son of carpenter); *Oklahoma Puts Sterilization Law into Effect*, LD at 17 (May 12, 1934) (Board of Affairs). Briggs received a $1,000 retainer in May, 1936—two years later. In 1934, the lawyers had "received practically no money at all—barely enough to pay the transportation expense back and forth" and none to hire experts. WT at 91.

5   *In re Main*, 19 P.2d 153 (Okla. 1933).

6   WT at 6 ("a class of citizens"); Landman at 117 (class legislation objection); Whitney, *supra* ch. 1, note 14, at 212–13; *Davis v. Walton*, 276 P. 921, 923 (Utah 1929) ("the act is class legislation").

7   *See, e.g., Packer Corp v. Utah*, 285 U.S. 105, 108–10 (1932); *Sproles v. Binford*, 286 U.S. 374, 391–92 (1932); *State Board of Tax Commissioners v. Jackson*, 283 U.S. 527, 537–39 (1931).

8   *State v. Schaffer*, 270 P. 604, 605 (Kan. 1928) ("patently disadvantages"); *In re Main*, 19 P.2d 153, 156 (Okla. 1933) ("cannot be extended"); *State v. Troutman*, 299 P. 668 (Ida. 1931) (upholding constitutionality); *In re Clayton*, 234 N.W. 630 (Neb. 1931) (same); *Davis v. Walton*, 276 P. 921, 924 (Utah 1929) (upholding constitutionality—"the rule announced by . . . the case of *Buck v. Bell* . . . is a complete answer" to the Fourteenth Amendment claims—but finding insufficient evidence); *Brewer v. Valk*, 167 S.E. 638 (N.C. 1933) (insufficient hearing); *In re Opinion of the Justices*, 162 So. 123, 128 (Ala. 1935) (sterilization was within the police power but required a hearing). Pre-*Buck* cases, see *supra* ch. 1, note 35.

9   Ronald Steel, Walter Lippmann and the American Century 310 (1980) (Liberty League); *A Peep Inside the Legal Mind*, CC at 1181 (Sept. 9, 1936) (ABA extols liberty and opposes child labor amendment. On liberty and Scottsboro, Felix Frankfurter, *The Supreme Court Writes a Chapter on Man's Rights*, in Law and Politics: Occasional Papers of Felix Frankfurter 1913–1938 at 189–94 (E. F. Prichard, Jr. & Archibald MacLeish eds., 1939, 1962 edition).

10   Lawrence M. Friedman, Crime and Punishment in American History 208 (1993).

11   WT at 18 ("canned goods"); *id.* at 20–21 (Bertillon man); *id.* at 27 (Winkler's last sentence).

12   *Id.* at 42, 44 (Griffin); *id.* at 60 (Steen); *id.* at 67–68 (Munn); *id.* at 47 ("One of the members").

13 *Id.* at 75; *id.* at 76–77; *id.* at 80 ("the mere fact"); *id.* at 81 ("partially paralyzed").

14 *Id.* at 78 (Board ruling); *id.* at 79 (Briggs objection); *id.* at 82 (Hulsey objection); *id.* at 83 (Board's position).

15 *Id.* at 85 (" law education here"); *id.* at 88, 89.

16 TDW at 1, 14 (July 31, 1934); MDP at 1 (July 31, 1934) (headline).

17 TDW at 1, 14 (July 31, 1934); MDP at 1–2 (Aug. 1, 1934) (gunfight); DO at 6 (July 22, 1934) (deaths due to heat); MDP at 1–2 (July 31, 1934) (taxi).

18 MDP at 1 (Aug. 1, 1934) (indictments); Editorial, *Outrage*, TDW at 4 (Aug. 1, 1934) ("How many murders"); MDP at 1 (Aug. 2, 1934) (Hensley funeral); on the Robin Hood image, MDP at 15 (May 12, 1934).

19 MDP at 2 (Aug. 1, 1934) ("Martin was worried about the eugenics program at the penitentiary and escaped at the hour that the first sterilization was ordered. A third-termer, serving 30 years for robbery, he would have been subject to sterilization."); MDP at 2 (July 31, 1934) ("I did it for her").

20 Claud Briggs to ACLU (Aug. 8, 1934), PA, Vol. 753 at 128; Herbert Jacobi to ACLU (June 1, 1934), PA, Vol. 753 at 115–19; Memorandum, *Sterilization Laws Affecting Criminals* (June 1935) PA, Vol. 787 at 288–89 (cruel and unusual punishment); *id.* at 291 (stating that in Germany "[a]n habitual criminal . . . may be an opponent convicted of political offenses . . . The Hitler Government is committed to gross discriminations against 'non-Aryans.' It should surprise no one to learn that Jews may be put on the list of 'socially inadequate' and sterilized"); *id.* at 291-92 (noting that convictions for felonies were "fairly common" in labor strikes); *id.* at 296 (sterilization a "means of class or racial control").

21 Kevin Boyle, Arc of Justice 236, 285 (2004) (Hays as "the logician, relentless, keen, incontrovertible," Darrow on "Nordic" mob); Arthur Garfield Hays to ACLU (July 17, 1934), PA, Vol. 753 at 127 ("inheritable," "alien field").

22 ALW to Claud Briggs (Aug. 14, 1934), PA, Vol. 753 at 129.

Chapter 5: White Trash

1 Guyer, *supra* ch. 1, note 14, at 425.

2 TDW at 9 (Sept. 23, 1934).

3 *Id.*

4 *Id.*

5 *Id.*

6 *Id.*

7 *Id.* ("as well versed"); TDW at 11 (May 13, 1927) (mustache); DOC No. 18051; TDW at 1, 6 (July 31, 1934) (King as a psychologist; "[s]everal physicians who were in attendance [at Winkler's hearing] admitted they considered King the leading Oklahoma authority on sterilization despite his lack of technical training").

8 TDW at 9 (Sept. 23, 1934).

9 NYT at 21 (July 8, 1934); TDW at 1 (Feb. 3, 1935).

10 NYT at 21 (July 8, 1934) ("insist upon proper treatment"); Lynn Musslewhite & Suzanne Jones Crawford, One Woman's Political Journey: Kate Barnard and Social Reform 1875–1930 84, 91–92 (2003); Harvey R. Hougen, *Kate Barnard and the Kansas Penitentiary Scandal, 1908–1909,* J. of the West 9, 10 (Jan. 1978).

11 TDW at 2 (Sept. 26, 1934) (Mrs. Bassett's criticisms); OCT at 10 (Nov. 13, 1934) (same); ON at 3 (Sept. 27, 1934) (Board of Affairs forecasts change in law); ON at 5 (Dec. 2, 1934) (attorney general drafting changes in law). The Board of Affairs was a patronage plum yielding a paycheck at the time of $320 per month for the vice-chairman. See ON at 1 (Dec. 17, 1934).

12 NYT at 5 (Jan. 15, 1935); HW at 13 (June 9, 1934); Bryant, Alfalfa Bill Murray, *supra* ch. 1, note 5, at 253–54.

13 ON at 1 (Jan. 8, 1935); OCT at 1 (Jan. 29, 1935); NYT at 3 (Jan. 9, 1935).

14 LAT at 3 (Apr. 23, 1931) (sterilization will stop crime); TDW at 1 (June 24, 1934) (parole scandal, Murray cartoon); TDW at 8 (Jan. 6, 1935) (100 felons "went free" each day).

15 3 Murray, *supra* ch. 1, note 13, App. W at 637 ("escaped convict"); *id.* at 639–40 (drones, ease); *id.* at 640 ("pure blood and strong"); *id.* at 639 ("let the ignorant rave"); ON at 1 (Jan. 8, 1935); TDW at 20 (Aug. 10, 1934) (actual convict story).

16 3 Murray, *supra* ch.1, note 13, at 638 ("Jutes" and "Killikuks"); Goddard, *supra* ch. 1, note 28 (the Kallikak study); Richard Dugdale, The Jukes: A Study in Crime, Pauperism, Disease, and Heredity (1877). Despite their age, the stories remained alive in the 1930s, and were defended against attack by some experts. Whitney, *supra* ch. 1, note 14, at 105; John Lewis Gillin, Clarence G. Dittmer & Roy J. Colbert, Social Problems 225–26 (1932); East at 226–34.

17 Paul at 52 (Martin Kallikak's story, "dallied with a feebleminded girl," "Old Horror"); 3 Murray, *supra* ch. 1, note 13, at 638 ("What a pity"). On the parable quality, Paul at 60–61 (referencing Zenderland). East at 234 ("multitude of descendants"). The data produced in the Kallikak study purported to show that of the 496 legitimate descendants,

only one was not "definitely normal," while only forty-six of 480 illegitimate descendants were "definitely normal." Gillin, Dittmer & Colbert, *supra* note 16, at 226, Table 16.

18 Dugdale, *supra* note 16; Nicole Hahn Rafter, White Trash: The Eugenic Family Studies 4 (1988); I. S. Caldwell, 3 Eugenics 203 (June 1930) (Bunglers); Kevles at 71 ("no single work" better known than Jukes study); Paul at 50 (twelve editions and Broadway play, references everywhere); *id.* at 49 (1915 Estabrook replication of Jukes study); East at 226–34 (repeating studies).

19 Rafter, *supra* note 18, at 170 (the Pineys); *id.* at 72 (the Zeros); *id.* at 185, 189 (Sam Sixty); I. S. Caldwell, *The Bunglers, supra* note 18.

20 DO at 1 (Nov. 12, 1934); OCT at 1 (Jan. 29, 1935); ON at 1 (Nov. 11, 1934); The WPA Guide to 1930s Oklahoma 119, 121, 298 (1986).

21 Lombardo, *supra* ch. 1, note 29, at 9–10 (testimony of Dr. Albert Priddy on white trash); Holmes, *supra* ch. 1, note 56, at 382 (race suicide); *id.* at 94 (pauperism as inherited defect); Stoddard, Rising Tide, *supra* ch. 1, note 57, at 9 ("surplus"); Albert E. Wiggam, *The Rising Tide of Degeneracy*, 53 WW 25, 26 (Nov. 1926) ("social wreckage"); Guyer, *supra* ch. 1, note 14, at 412 (1927) ("social wastage"); Grant, *supra* ch. 1, note 12, at 54 ("human residuum"); *id.* at 89 ("sweepings").

22 Briggs WPA Questionnaire, OHS at 284–85; Stoddard, Revolt, *supra* ch. 1, note 57, at 30 ("iron law of inequality"); Charles Benedict Davenport, Heredity in Relation to Eugenics iv (1911) ("*bound* by their protoplasmic makeup," emphasis in original); East at 16 ("cult of *égalité*"); Kevles at 76 (quoting Osborn, "political sophistry"); Albert E. Wiggam, The Fruit of the Family Tree 80 (1925) ("irremediably and ineradicably," emphasis in original); S. J. Holmes, *Eugenics Vital to the Human Race*, CH Vol. 25 at 348, 349 (Dec. 1926) ("thrown absolutely out of court").

23 Albert E. Wiggam, The Next Age of Man 96 (1927) (equality "grotesque"); *id.* at 287 (quoting a letter stating democracy a dream); *id.* at 92 (masses cannot rule themselves); Albert E. Wiggam, *When a Woman Is Asked to Marry*, 25 PR 2 (Mar. 1924); Albert E. Wiggam, *Bringing Up Grandfather*, 25 PR 2 (Apr. 1924); French Strother, *What Eugenics Is and Isn't*, 49 WW 442 (Feb. 1925); French Strother, *Crime and Eugenics*, 49 WW 168 (Dec. 1924).

24 To be sure, there were those more willing to distinguish between the natural and the political: H. S. Jennings, The Biological Basis of Human Nature 220 (1930); J. B. S. Haldane, The Inequality of Man And Other Essays (1932). But this does not describe the average eugenic popularizer's conflation of natural and political inequality.

Historians of eugenics have recently emphasized its diversity across cultures, which is both commendable and true. *See, e.g.*, Nancy Leys Stepan, "The Hour of Eugenics": Race, Gender and Nation in Latin America (1991). Nevertheless, in the Anglo-American world, eugenicists did share a set of basic premises or ideas about the "naturally unfit"—ideas in open tension with democracy and political equality. As Diane Paul writes, none of the left-leaning supporters of eugenics doubted the possibility of the genetically unfit. Paul at 113–14. The oft-noted communistic persuasions of the geneticist Muller did not prevent him from adopting strong notions of "genetic merit" and superior heredity. H. J. Muller, Out of the Night: A Biologist's View of the Future 80–81, 85, 112–13, 120 (1935, reprinted 1984).

25 Popenoe & Johnson, *supra* ch. 1, note 16, at 361 (democracy dangerous); Landman at 6 (quoting Pitkin, Platonic aristocracy).

26 TDW at 2 (Dec. 15, 1934).

27 1935 Okla. Sess. Laws, ch. 26 at 94–99.

28 Okla. Senate Journal, 15th Legis. at 246 (Jan. 30, 1935); *id.* at 270–71 (Jan. 31, 1935); *id.* at 283 (Feb. 1, 1935); *id.* at 307 (Feb. 5, 1935).

29 TDW at 1 (Feb. 18, 1935) (Granite); Okla. Senate Journal, 15th Legis. at 489 (Feb. 18, 1935) (reconsider vote to add punishment language, tabled); *id.* (felony involving moral turpitude amendment); on crime of moral turpitude and its difficulties at the time, *Nagle v. Lim Foon*, 48 F.2d 51 (9th Cir. 1931); U.S. v. Day, 34 F.2d 920 (2d Cir. 1929).

30 *Norris v. Alabama*, 294 U.S. 587 (argued Feb. 15 and 18, 1935); *id.* at 598–99 ("The general attitude of the jury commissioner is shown by the following extract from his testimony: 'I do not know of any negro in Morgan County over twenty-one and under sixty-five who. . . has never been convicted of a crime involving moral turpitude.' "); Thomas Reed Powell, *Compulsory Vaccination and Sterilization: Constitutional Aspects*, 21 N.C. L. Rev. 253, 261 (1942–43) (noting the association, in the South, between habitual criminality and race). See *Hunter v. Underwood*, 471 U.S. 222 (1985) (striking down provision of one southern state constitution that denied voting based on commission of a crime of moral turpitude).

31 Okla. Senate Journal, 15th Legis. at 489–90 (Feb. 18, 1935); *id.* at 492 (amendment exempting political, tax, and liquor offenses).

32 Lucille B. Milner to Claud Briggs (Apr. 8, 1935), PA, Vol. 854 at 4; Claud Briggs to Lucille B. Milner, ACLU (May 3, 1935), PA, Vol. 854 at 6 ("before final adjournment"); see Okla. Senate Journal 15th Legis.; at 2276, 2302 (Apr. 30, 1935); Telegraph, ACLU to Gov. Marland (May 7, 1935), PA, Vol. 854 at 7–8. The ACLU told Briggs during this exchange that it was preparing a memorandum against sterilization;

Briggs requested this memo in June 1935. PA, Vol. 854 at 14 (June 3, 1935). Mrs. Milner also wrote to the eugenicist Harry Laughlin who assured her that "all punitive elements" had been eliminated from sterilization statutes. *Id.*, Vol. 787 at 315 (June 10, 1935). A memo was prepared dated June 1935 opposing sterilization on grounds of "cruel and unusual punishment." *Id.* at 284–96. Archives indicate that there was work done by the ACLU in 1936 on sterilization, but that the ACLU wanted to limit its opposition to the sterilization of criminals. PA, Vol. 890 at 334–36.

33 DO at 1 (Dec. 14, 1934) (Marland's "war on crime"); DO at 12 (May 16, 1935) (Marland signs bill); Mary Gawthorpe to Mrs. Milner, ACLU, PA, Vol. 854, at 9 (May 17, 1935) (attached clipping from *Herald Tribune* on Marland's statements on "dodging" and "enormous social importance"); ON at 5 (Dec. 31, 1934) ("a lot of criminals").

Chapter 6: Skinner's Trial

1 ST at 127.

2 *Oklahoma v. Moore*, Okla. Pitts. Co. Dist Ct. No. 15666 (May 12, 1936); MNC at 1 (May 13, 1936) ("lowest class convicts"); NYT at 3 (May 14, 1936) (ten wounded); MDP at 1 (May 16, 1936) (men hanging on car); ON at 8 (May 14, 1936) (same). The Moore petition was filed at 4 p.m. on Tuesday, the 12th. The break was on Wednesday, the 13th. NYT at 3 (May 14, 1936); ON at 8 (May 15, 1936) ("sensational brickyard riot at McAlester penitentiary Wednesday").

3 MNC at 1 (May 14, 1936) (troops to stand by); MNC at 1 (May 15, 1936) (shoot-to-kill); ON at 1 (May 14, 1936) (200 posse men); NYT at 3 (May 15, 1936); ON at 1, 8 (May 15, 1936) (Rattlesnake Mountain); MDP at 1 (May 16, 1936) (Kenny and bloodhounds); MDP at 1 (May 17, 1936).

4 MNC at 1 (May 14, 1936); NYT at 3 (May 16, 1936); NYT at 3 (May 15, 1936); NYT at 38 (May 17, 1936); MDP at 1 (May 21, 1936) (capture of Beavers); DO at 3 (Aug. 11, 1941) (history of 1936 break).

5 *Oklahoma v. Moore*, *supra* note 2 (Moore to be sterilized); MNC at 1 (May 13, 1936); ON at 1, 5 (May 13, 1936); ON at 1 (May 14, 1936) ("Chairman L. M. Nichols says new sterilization law one of factors in causes for the break").

6 ON at 1, 5 (May 13, 1936) (warden's denial); ON at 10 (Nov. 21, 1936) (Kenny biography); DO at 2 (May 20, 1936) ("Retained by penitentiary prisoners for a $1,000 fee, Claud Briggs . . . said he would attack the state's sterilization law"); DO at 4 (June 8, 1942) ("Convicts at

McAlester penitentiary had financed the fight against the law"); Owen J. Watts to Judge R. W. Higgins (July 23, 1937) ("the attorney fees in this case were paid out of the canteen fund maintained by the prisoners").

7 Briggs to Court Clerk re: Moore (Aug. 13, 1936), DOLA; Notice of Withdrawal as Attorney, Okla. Pitts. Co. Dist. Ct. No. 15666 (Aug. 15, 1936); Petition, *Oklahoma v. Skinner*, Okla. Pitts. Co. Dist. Ct. No. 15734 (June 12, 1936).

8 DOC No. 30504; Jack Skinner, Soc. Security Appl'n (June 14, 1940) (naming Andrew Skinner as Skinner's father); ST at 102 (father died while infant and Skinner lost foot as teenager); MNC at 1 (Feb. 18, 1941) ("cripple"). The prison slang term may be a reversal of the older slang meaning of "skinner" as one who disrobed children to eye them lustily. Eric Partridge, A Dictionary of Slang and Unconventional English (1984).

9 ST at 123–25; *State v. Jack T. Skinner*, Prelim. Information, Okla. Okla. Co. Dist. Ct. No. 9743 (offense, July 1934).

10 ST at 125–27.

11 DO at 3 (Oct. 21, 1936); ON at 1, 2 (Oct. 19, 1936).

12 ON at 1 (May 11, 1936).

13 ST at 28–29.

14 *Id.* at 31, 34–35.

15 *Id.* at 37, 38–41.

16 *Id.* at 41–44.

17 *Id.* at 44–45 (qualifications); *id.* at 46–49 (operation).

18 *Id.* at 50–51.

19 *Id.* at 53.

20 *Id.* at 54–55.

21 *Id.* at 55–56.

22 *Id.* at 56–58.

23 ST at 58–59; Eugenical Sterilization: The Committee of the American Neurological Association for the Investigation of Eugenical Sterilization (Abraham Myerson et al. eds., reprint 1980) [Myerson report]. The Myerson report was in fact rather ambivalent, authorizing sterilization for a variety of illnesses, including "familial feeble-mindedness," *id.* at 179. However, "historians generally credit" the report with "helping to turn the tide of scientific and medical opinion against eugenic sterilization in the United States." Larson at 148; Editorial, NYT at E8 (Jan. 26, 1936).

24 ST at 60.

25 *Id.* at 61.

26 *Id.* at 61, 162 ("fallacious attorney").

27 *Id.* at 62, 63.

28 *Id.* at 67–68.

29 *Id.* at 68–69.

30 *Id.* at 70–73.

31 *Id.* at 75–76.

32 *Id.* at 77–78.

33 *Id.* at 79–80.

34 *Id.* at 89–92.

35 *Id.* at 99–100. The reference to six chickens may indicate that Skinner only stole six and the others were stolen by the named confederate (the information noted twenty-three chickens stolen).

36 *Id.* at 100–02.

37 *Id.* at 102–03, 105–07.

38 *Id.* at 109–10; *id.* 112–13; *id.* at 115–16.

39 *Id.* at 124.

40 *Id.* at 125.

41 *Id.* at 125–27; *id.* at 128.

42 *Id.* at 157–59.

43 *Id.* at 160.

44 *Id.* at 161, 165–68.

45 *Id.* at 166–67.

46 *Id.* at 169–72.

47 MNC at 1 (Oct. 20, 1936); TDW at 1 (Oct. 21, 1936); DO at 64 (Nov. 1, 1936).

Chapter 7: The Supreme Court in 1937

1 *The New Deal Versus the Old Courts*, LD at 5 (Feb. 13, 1937).

2 TDW at §4, p. 12 (Nov. 22, 1936).

3 David M. Kennedy, Freedom From Fear 238–39 (1999) (Huey Long); *id.* at 232 (Coughlin), *id.* at 224–25, 239 (Townsend). As of July 1936, the U.S. population was approximately 128 million and Kennedy reports that 25 million "had signed Townsend's petitions." *Id.* at 225. *Id.* at 242 (FDR: "I am fighting Communism").

4 *Id.* at 384, 397–98 (Rhineland, Ethiopia, Franco); *see, e.g.,* WP at 1 (June 11, 1937) (wage and hour bill as "fascism, Bolshevism and Naziism").

5 MDP at 1 (Oct. 21, 1936) (Landon, "form of government"); ON at 1 (Oct. 21, 1936) ("gone undemocratic"); NYT at 1 (Oct. 22, 1936) ("selfish minorities"); Kennedy, *supra* note 3, at 286 (unprecedented nature of victory); CDT at 16 (Nov. 4, 1936) ("new chapter"); Atl. J. at 6 (Nov. 4, 1936) ("unparalleled since Washington"); William Allen

White, *Reflections of a Landon Warwick*, St. L. Dis. at 2-I (Nov. 8, 1936) ("grand and awful time," "revelation").

6   William Allen White, *supra* note 5, at 2 ("cunning greed"); HW at 6 (Nov. 28, 1936) ("Humanity now rules"); *Facing the Future with Roosevelt*, SFE at 1B (Nov. 4, 1936) (Hearst papers worrying about "constitutional government"); W. R. Hearst, *W. R. Hearst's Views on Democratic Principles and American Ideals*, SFE at 2 (Nov. 8, 1936) ("new birth of freedom").

7   Arthur Sears Henning, *Court's Crisis Held Greatest Since Slavery*, CDT at 1 (Feb. 7, 1937) ("greatest constitutional crisis"); Richard L. Neuberger, *America Talks Court*, CH at 33–38 (June 1937); William E. Leuchtenburg, The Supreme Court Reborn 134 (1995) ("unmatched by any legislative controversy").

8   NW at 2 (June 1, 1935) ("Nine out of every ten wage-earners"); *Topics of the Day*, LD at 1 (June 8, 1935); Heywood Broun, *Nine Against Labor* 140 The Nation at 3650 (June 12, 1935); BW at 7 (June 8, 1935). Long before 1937, *e.g. The Next National Crisis*, CC at 807 (June 25, 1933); BW at 5 (Jan. 11, 1936) ("whole New Deal"); Marian C. McKenna, Franklin Roosevelt and the Great Constitutional War 73 (2002) ("a dozen New Deal laws"); *United States v. Butler*, 297 U.S. 1 (decided Jan. 6, 1936); Leuchtenburg, *supra* note 7, at 98 ("two billion dollars").

9   *Morehead v. New York ex rel. Tipaldo*, 298 U.S. 587 (June 1, 1936); Leuchtenburg, *supra* note 7, at 105 ("national outcry"); *31c. an Hour*, LD at 6 (June 13, 1936) (quoting Dorothy Thompson, "one-third of the States"); *id.* (quoting FDR, "[n]o man's land").

10 Neuberger, *supra* note 7, at 33 (June 1937) ("on a good many trains"); *Court Plea to Public*, LD at 4 (Mar. 20, 1937) (Great Issue of 1937). On child labor, NYT at 5 (Jan. 9, 1937); *id.* at 65 (Jan. 17, 1937); *id.* at 12 (Feb. 5, 1937); *id.* at 54 (Feb. 21, 1937); Arthur M. Schlesinger, Jr., 3 The Age of Roosevelt 489 (1960) (after *Tipaldo*, nearly "sixty papers" called for constitutional amendments); Time at 81–82 (June 7, 1937) (other presidents' court-packing attempts); Schlesinger at 493 (Roosevelt "stop a constitutional amendment cold").

11 *The New Deal Versus the Old Courts*, *supra* note 1 ("personal control of the entire Government"); *id.* ("abandon Constitutional Government"); *id.* at 6 ("*L'Etat ç'est moi*"); *Court Plan Dead, But Not Buried*, LD at 3 (May 29, 1937) ("masters of the courts"); Sheboygan Press at 12 (Mar. 30, 1937) ("rape," "subalterns," "wet nurses," "marionettes"); CDT at 9 (Mar. 14, 1937) ("I would rather put my back to a blank wall").

12 *The New Deal Versus the Old Courts*, *supra* note 1 (quoting William

Allen White, italics in original, "In a world-challenging democracy"). As early as 1935, comparisons were made to Germany and Fascism in relation to the Court and the president. *See, e.g.*, CC at 38 (Jan. 9, 1935) (claiming Hearst papers frantic about the Supreme Court being packed); *The Supreme Court Disposes*, BW at 48 (June 1, 1935) (NRA as economic Fascism); Oswald G. Villard, *Issues and Men: The Supreme Court Bombshell*, 140 Nation 675 (June 12, 1935) (it would be Fascism to pack the Court to achieve the New Deal). For comparisons after the plan was introduced, *see, e.g.*, *FDR Cracks Whip for Court Plan*, BW at 15 (Feb. 27, 1937); LAT at 1 (Apr. 1, 1937); CDT at 4 (Feb. 23, 1937). Journalists wrote that the justices believed they were saving America "from centralization, perhaps with an eye on Hitler, Mussolini, and Stalin," 140 Nation 672 (June 12, 1935); and that the court's decisions would "bring us five years closer to fascism," *id.*

13 *Job Insurance*, LD at 4 (Dec. 5, 1936); Neuberger, *supra* note 7, at 36 (June 1937) ("which side" Roberts will flop, "help the little fellow").

14 Neuberger, *supra* note 7, at 36 (June 1937) ("Who elected [Roberts] to be our dictator?"); LAT at 1 (Apr. 1, 1937) (Roberts held the power of Mussolini); *id.* at 5 (Apr. 27, 1937) (how a single justice could "paralyze" the nation).

15 *Nebbia v. New York*, 291 U.S. 502 (1934); Barry Cushman, Rethinking the New Deal Court: The Structure of a Constitutional Revolution (1998).

16 Law and Politics, *supra* ch. 4, note 9, at 189 ("The evolution of our constitutional law"); Neuberger, *supra* note 7, at 38 (June 1937) ("dirt farm," drive a truck); HSP, Corr. on *Butler* (Jan. 20, 1936), ("favoring a few").

17 NYT at 39 (Jan. 29, 1936) ("liberty to starve"); Schlesinger, *supra* note 10, at 489 (recounting Cardozo to Stone letter explaining that both political parties agreed that legislation was necessary which the Supreme Court had held was a denial of "liberty").

18 *West Coast Hotel v. Parrish*, 300 U.S. 379 (decided Mar. 29, 1937). Because *Parrish* was decided *before* the president's plan was announced on February 5, but issued after it, some have argued that FDR's plan could have done little to influence the Supreme Court. Cushman, *supra* note 15, ch. 1. But the Court's status, not to mention court-packing, had been debated for years by the time of FDR's plan. As early as 1935, after the NRA decision, there were insistent comparisons made to dictatorship and fascism as well as fears of court-packing in the press. *See, e.g.*, Villard, *supra* note 12, at 675 (it would be Fascism to pack the Court as had been rumored). Given widespread popular knowledge and public attention to the institutional clash years before

1937, it strikes one as implausible that the members of the Supreme Court were not aware of the larger, structural implications of their decisions long before Parrish.

19 See NLRB v. Jones & Laughlin Steel Corp., 301 U.S. 1 (decided April 12, 1937) (labor); Steward Machine Co. v. Davis, 301 U.S. 548 (decided May 24, 1937) (social security); What the Court Did to Business, BW at 17 (June 5, 1937) ("amended . . . by legal interpretation"); CC at 768 (June 16, 1937); Santa Clauses, LD at 5 (June 5, 1937).

20 The "choice" was a pincer movement, as both Congress and the president were seeking major changes in the Court's power. Senator Burton Wheeler, who led the opposition to FDR, proposed a "compromise" amendment that gave Congress the power to overturn Supreme Court decisions. Bruce Ackerman, 2 We the People 320–24 (1998). Even if the president failed, there remained the risk of serious structural change from Congress.

21 One of the arguments used against the Court plan was that it would limit the Court's ability to protect individual rights, opponents noting practices, like Hitler's power over religion, that might not be subject to attack if the court were packed. CDT at 4 (Feb. 23, 1937).

22 The Court was quite hostile to presidential power at this time. The decision striking down the NRA was not a labor decision but a ruling that the law gave the president too much power. United States v. Schechter Poultry, 295 U.S. 495 (1935); see also Humphrey's Executor v. United States, 295 U.S. 602 (1935).

23 This account differs from both internalist and externalist accounts. Leuchtenburg's externalist Reborn, supra note 7, does not emphasize the shadow of dictatorship from abroad; Cushman's internalist Rethinking, supra note 15, fails to examine the larger structural questions that were so obvious at the time. Cushman is right to emphasize the noticeable shift in Nebbia, yet must remember that the Supreme Court treated "price regulation" differently from "labor laws." See Howard Gillman, The Constitution Besieged (1995); William E. Forbath, Law and the Shaping of the American Labor Movement (1991).

24 274 U.S. 200, 208 (1927).

Chapter 8: Science in a Foreign Mirror: 1937–1941

1 S. J. Holmes, The Opposition to Eugenics, Science 353 (Apr. 21, 1939).

2 DO at 48 (July 11, 1937); Order, Okla. Pitts. Co. Dist. Ct. No. 15734 (July 12, 1937).

3 ON at 11 (Oct. 28, 1937); Petition, Okla. Sup. Ct. No. 28229 (filed Oct. 27, 1937).

4   Public Opinion Poll, WP at B1 (May 23, 1937); Kevles at 114 (*Fortune* poll); GP 19.3 (undated press release re: Northwestern Mutual Life survey).

5   WP at 1 (Jan. 7, 1936); *id.* at 3 (Jan. 8, 1936); LAT at 3 (Jan. 8, 1936); WP at X26 (Aug. 18, 1936); CDT at 9 (Aug. 18, 1936); Modesto Bee (Jan. 27, 1936) in GP, 11.9. Mrs. Hewitt claimed "that the girl was oversexed, that she had an affair with a chauffeur some years ago . . . to whom she sent numerous letters, among which was particularly one . . . which enclosed a lock of hair from her head and also hair from her pubic regions . . . and that she was . . . familiar with a negro porter on [a] train." I. M. Golden to Paul Popenoe at 2 (May 23, 1936), GP 11.9; WP at X3 (Aug 20, 1936); LAT, *"Judge Given Child Rating"* (Feb. 19, 1936), GP 11.9; Life at 67 (Feb. 26, 1940) (Hewitt one of top stories of 1930s).

6   Sex crime panic, Estelle B. Freedman, *"Uncontrolled Desires": The Response to the Sexual Psychopath, 1920–1960,* 74 J. of Am. Hist. 83 (1987); Marjorie Van De Water, *Sex Crimes,* ON at B2 (Oct. 10, 1937) (sex crimes feature); CDT at 10 (Feb. 27, 1938) (same); NYT at 19 (Feb. 20, 1937) (Georgia); NYT at 25 (Mar. 9, 1937) (Indiana); NYT at 6 (Feb. 10, 1937) (Puerto Rico); NYT at 7 (Apr. 8, 1937) (same); NYT at 2 (May 15, 1937) (same); NYT at 2 (May 29, 1935) (Bermuda—"legal lynching") GP 15.5 (copies of laws from Georgia, Indiana, proposals in California, Puerto Rico, and Alberta); Reilly, *supra* ch. 1, note 20, at 97 (yearly operations reached a high in 1935 with 3,103; in 1936 there were 2,237; in 1937, 2,466; and in 1938, 2,821). On the HBF, GP Corr. 10 & 11; Joe G. Crick, *Report of the Secretary,* GP 1.3 (in 1940, 107,547 pamphlets mailed). On the 150 million figure, E. S. Gosney, *Eugenics in California,* NYT at E5 (Jan. 14, 1934). By the mid-1930s, the Carnegie Institute had begun an investigation of the major eugenic research institution in the United States—the Cold Spring Harbor laboratory—and by 1940 the laboratory shut its doors. Kevles at 199; WP at B5 (Aug. 4, 1935) (critics); *but see* Fred Hogue, *Social Eugenics,* LAT at I23 (Apr. 2, 1939) ("In Germany, where the [sterilization] law has been operative for about three years, the effect has been so salutary" that other countries have followed suit); *id.* at I19 (June 4, 1939) ("How long will the governments of our own country permit the hereditary poisoning of our human blood stream to continue?").

7   DO at 10 (Jan. 15, 1937) ("sissy about," "criminals and morons and the mentally sick"); *see, e.g.,* DO at 27 (Jan. 9, 1938) (sterilization continues in asylums).

8   *Skinner v. Oklahoma,* Brief of Plaintiff, Okla. Sup. Ct. No. 28229, at 15–23 (filed Feb. 25, 1938).

9   *Id.* at 15. Perhaps Briggs was simply following the ACLU. PA, Vol. 787 at 284–96. The 1935 ACLU memorandum claims laws aimed at criminals violated "cruel and unusual punishment." In retrospect, it seems an extraordinarily weak argument. As the Supreme Court noted in *Weems v. United States*, even the "whipping post" was not necessarily "cruel and unusual punishment" at the time. 217 U.S. 349, 377 (1910).

10 *See* ch. 9 & note 45; epilogue, note 11.

11 Harry H. Laughlin, Further Studies on the Historical and Legal Development of Eugenical Sterilization in the United States 96 (1936) ("inherent right"); Guyer, *supra* ch. 1, note 14, at 437 (how much "liberty" was to be experienced by the "ill-fated descendants of the epileptic, the habitual drunkard or criminal").

12 Brief of Defendant, Okla. Sup. Ct. No. 28229, at 11 (filed Aug. 11, 1938) (quoting treatise, "Courts are not at liberty"); *id.* at 10 (quoting *Smith v. Command*, 204 N.W. 140, 142, "the state, in the exercise of its police powers").

13 Reply Brief of Plaintiff, Okla. Sup. Ct. No. 28229, at 2 (filed Aug. 30, 1938) ("brutal, disgusting and revolting"); *id.* at 3 (Ritzhaupt's crime deterrent testimony); *id.* at 5 ("vicious"); *id.* at 8 ("swept aside all caution," "ardent desire," "*en masse*," italics in original).

14 *Id.* at 8.

15 NYT at 2 (Aug. 19, 1938) (Roosevelt); Kennedy, *supra* ch. 7, note 3, at 418 (digging air raid shelters, France reservists); *id.* at 415 (Kristallnacht); *id.* at 421–22 (Hitler motors through Prague on Mar. 15, 1939); *id.* at 409–10 (Austria in March 1938); on American reaction to Kristallnacht, *see, e.g.*, NYT at 6 (Nov. 12, 1938).

16 Anne O'Hare McCormick, *For State or—Church?*, NYT at SM4–5, 15 (Mar. 1, 1936) ("What strange impulse"); on persecution of Protestants, NYT at 69 (Nov. 14, 1937); on Catholics, CDT at 1 (Mar. 22, 1937), NYT at 7 (June 22, 1936); on paganism, CDT at 1 (Apr. 2, 1937); NYT at 10 (Jan. 2, 1937).

17 NYT at 5 (Mar. 25, 1935) ("Miracles of Life"). On May 24, 1935, the Germans reported that there were 56,244 in the year 1934, NYT at 1 (May 25, 1935) ("eugenic purity"); WP at B10 (July 21, 1935) (1,000 per week); NYT at 1 (July 18, 1935) ("The mixture of races," "heavy penalties"); on the Italian manifesto, *see* NYT at 6 (July 15, 1938) (Italian race declared "Aryan, Nordic and heroic"); Waldemar Kaempffert, *"Aryans" Viewed as a Myth*, NYT at 52 (July 24, 1938) ("Italy has gone 'Aryan' ").

18 NYT at 35 (Nov. 22, 1936) (wars on "Jewish" science), Editorial, *Ger-

man Science Goose-Steps, NYT at 20 (Mar. 12, 1936) (quoting Lenard's *Deutsche Physik*, "Science . . . is racial"); NYT at 14 (June 30, 1936) ("objectivity," "old idea . . . gone," "Nazi concepts of race, blood and the like"); on the Jewish physics controversy, Alan D. Beyerchen, Scientists under Hitler: Politics and the Physics Community in the Third Reich (1977).

19 Emil Lengyel, *Hitler's Reich Outstrips Kaiser's*, NYT at 66 (Sept. 25, 1938) (*Mein Kampf*); Sen. Lewis B. Schwellenbach, *Freedom of Science* in 5 Vital Speeches at 310 (Mar. 1, 1939); Editorial, *Science Strikes Back*, NYT at 92 (Dec. 11, 1938) (American scientists and manifesto); *The Nazi Primer*, 177 Harper's 240 (Aug. 1938).

20 NYT at 34 (Feb. 12, 1939); Henry A. Wallace, *Racial Theories and the Genetic Basis for Democracy*, Science at 140–43 (Feb. 17, 1939)—this was broadcast over NBC radio; *id.* at 140 ("never before in the world's history," "Western Race . . . passionate"); *see also* NYT at 48 (Oct. 15, 1939) (Wallace assails race prejudice).

21 Editorial, *Minute Men of Science*, NYT at 80 (Feb. 12, 1939).

22 *See, e.g.*, NYT at 16 (Sept. 17, 1936); NYT at 20 (Dec. 29, 1936); NYT at 43 (Mar. 21, 1937) (Boas); Editorial, *Science Aroused*, NYT at 18 (Jan. 1, 1938); Jacques Barzun, Race: A Study in Modern Superstition (1937); Otto Klineberg, Race Differences (1935); NYT at BR12 (Sept. 15, 1935); *see also* Ruth Benedict, Race: Science and Politics (1940); *see generally*, Edward A. Purcell, Jr., The Crisis of Democratic Theory 133–38 (1973).

23 Jonas Robitscher, Eugenic Sterilization, App. 2 at 122 (1973). As of the beginning of 1935, the cumulative number of operations performed since 1907, a twenty-eight-year period, was 20,000; in the next five years, there would be approximately 16,000 more. The average annual number of operations from 1921 until 1930 was 849; from 1930 to 1941 it was 2,273.

24 Editorial, *Science and Freedom*, NYT at 20 (Dec. 29, 1936) ("when we study"); Waldemar Kaempffert, *The Week in Science: Theories of the Eugenists*, NYT at 159 (June 7, 1936) ("curb the 100-percenters"); Wallace, *supra* note 20; NYT at 48 (Oct. 15, 1939) (quoting Wallace, no "such thing," "mentally superior or inferior").

25 Holmes, *supra* note 1; *id.* at 352 ("natural inequality of man"); *id.* at 353 ("influence of emotional bias," "sentiment in favor of race egalitarianism").

26 Myerson Report, *supra* ch. 6, note 23, at 178–80; *id.* at 180 ("There need be no hesitation in recommending sterilization in the case of feeblemindedness"). This explains why eugenic enthusiasts found

little in the Myerson report to deter their progress. Frank C. Reid, Comment on Myerson report, GP 1.6 ("the final conclusions are surprisingly favorable, and such as, for the most part, are in agreement with our own conclusions); *id.* 10.3, Frank C. Reid to Irving Goldberg (Myerson concedes the HBF [Human Betterment Foundation] position in its conclusions"); Kaempffert, *supra* note 24 ("genetic research must teach us"); NYT at 43 (Mar. 21, 1937) (Boas: sterilization is "justifiable" where "hereditary unfitness has been established"); *Plan for Improving Population Drawn by Famed Geneticists*, Science News Letter 131, 132 (Aug. 26, 1939) ("unscientific doctrine"); NYT at 6 (Aug. 28, 1939); *id.* at 4 (Aug. 26, 1939).

27 NYT at 5 (Dec. 27, 1940) (enslave Europe); E. S. Gosney to Frank C. Reid, GP 1.1 (Sept. 9, 1940) ("steer clear of [German emphasis on racial integrity] lest we should be misunderstood"); Time at 34 (Sept. 9, 1940) ("new, environmental eugenics," "presented the scientific evidence to demolish"); Frederick Osborn, Preface to Eugenics (1940).

28 East at 16 (equality a "cult"); S. J. Holmes, The Eugenic Predicament 165 (1933) ("fetish of democracy"); Michael F. Guyer, Speaking of Man: A Biologist Looks at Man 224 (1942) ("misleading," "beautiful"); Guyer, *supra* ch. 1, note 14, at 425 (sentiment of "eugenic aristocracy"); Popenoe & Johnson, *supra* ch. 1, note 16, at 305; S. J. Holmes, *supra* note 1 ("natural inequality of man"); *see also* Grant, *supra* ch. 1, note 12, at 79 ("rule of the worst," a "cacocracy"); Wiggam, *supra* ch. 3, note 7, at 268 (democracy a "political sham").

29 Frederick Osborn, *Eugenics Today*, Sci. Dig. 60, 67 (Jan. 1941) ("Sterilization on leaving institutional care, or the absolute prevention of marriage, would be a substantial forward step"—referring to defectives).

30 *See* DO at 12 (Dec. 2, 1937); DO at 34 (Mar. 6, 1938); Ada Evening News at 11 (Dec. 31, 1939); DO at 2 (July 26, 1940) (Lester).

31 *Skinner v. State*, 115 P.2d 123, 127 (Okla. 1941); see *id.* at 127–28 (the legislature may assume facts as a basis for the assertion of the police power).

32 *Id.* at 129 (Osborn, J., dissenting); HW at 14 (Dec. 4, 1937).

Chapter 9: Deciding *Skinner*

1 Albert Wiggam, The New Decalogue of Science 286 (1925).

2 DO at 1, 2 (Aug. 11, 1941); DO at 1 (Nov. 21, 1936); Jess Dunn to C. W. Butler at 2 (Jan. 21 & Feb. 5, 1941), DOLA.

3 DO at 1 (Aug. 11, 1941) ("get that . . . kid"); TDW at 1 (Aug. 11, 1941) ("My God Ben"); NYT at 1 (Aug. 11, 1941).

4 TDW at 1, 2 (Aug. 11, 1941) ("kept on shooting," "blood running"); DO at 1 (Aug. 11, 1941) ("Let us pass"); MNC at 1, 2 (Oct. 7, 1941).

5 Chuck Ervin, *Black Sunday at McAlester*, Oklahoma's Orbit at 6 (Aug. 20, 1961), OHS Crime file ("bloodiest"); TDW at 1 (Aug. 11, 1941); NYT at 1 (Aug. 11, 1941); TDW at 2 (Aug. 13, 1941) ("hope of self-redemption"); MNC at 1 (Aug. 14, 1941) (CBS); MNC at 1 (Aug. 12, 1941) (Hunt); MNC at 1 (Sept. 22, 1941) (rodeo brings 32,000).

6 TDW at 1, 2 (Aug. 11, 1941); DO at 3 (Aug. 11, 1941). Earlier breaks, chs. 4 & 6.

7 DOC No. 30504 (Skinner); DOC No. 10072 (Kelly); MNC at 7 (May 1, 1940) (Hyde parole); *Exec. Parole: Ralph Bainum*, Records of Sect'y of State, DOLA (Apr. 3, 1937); Briggs's stalling, Application for Extension of Time, Okla. Sup. Ct. No. 28229 at 2 (May 31, 1941); Motion for Extension of Time, Okla. Sup. Ct. No. 28229 (Feb. 27, 1941); *id.* (Apr. 14, 1941); *id.* (May 31, 1941); Rehearing Brief (June 12, 1941); Mandate, Okla. Sup. Ct. No. 28229 (July 17, 1941).

8 DO at 24 (June 5, 1941) ("I won't let the boys down"); Claud Briggs to Jess Dunn, return Dunn to Briggs (Mar. 18 & 19, 1941), DOLA. Briggs asked Dunn to meet with him on the sterilization matter and Dunn replied politely that he would, suggesting that it was not Dunn who objected to the appeal.

9 MNC at 1 (Oct. 8, 1941); DO at 15 (Oct. 8, 1941) ("left... by airplane"); Motion, *Skinner v. Oklahoma*, NA at 3 [US Ext. Motion] ("Thereafter a motion was duly filed asking stay of execution and notice of intention to appeal was given and execution was on August 5, 1941 by such Court ordered stayed until the 8th of October, 1941").

10 3 Canadian at 1431–32; 3 Thoburn at 1060 (1929); Harlow at 673–74; *New State Ice Co. v. Liebmann*, 285 U.S. 262, 311 (1932) (Brandeis, J., dissenting).

11 TDW at 1 (Aug. 12 & 13, 1941); MNC at 1 (Aug. 28 & 29, 1941).

12 The 1936 break occurred on May 13, 1936; the retainer was released on May 19, 1936. DO at 1 (May 19, 1936) ("Claud Briggs . . . has been paid a fee of $1,000 by McAlester state penitentiary inmates to fight the sterilization act, a voucher received at the state treasury disclosed Monday"). For the release of funds on the 6th, US Ext. Motion, *supra* note 9, at 4; MNC at 1 (Oct. 7, 1941) (Warden confirmed on 6th). In theory, Briggs might have filed in the Supreme Court himself, paying for the court costs, which ultimately amounted to over $200; he also might have filed for a motion that the attorney general pay the costs, but his requests for that had been denied in the Oklahoma courts. H. I. Aston later wrote the U.S. Supreme Court Clerk that McAl-

ester's warden (presumably Hunt) "with consent of the State Board of Affairs" had "directed" him "to proceed" with the petition for a writ of certiorari. H. I. Aston to E. P. Cullinan, Clerk, LSCT No. 782 (Jan. 19, 1942).

13 US Ext. Motion, *supra* note 9, at 4.

14 William Wiecek, The Birth of the Modern Constitution: The United States Supreme Court 1941–1953 76–77 (2006) (Black); *id.* at 82–83 (Reed); *id.* at 83, 88 (Frankfurter); *id.* at 93 (Douglas); *id.* at 99, 102–03 (Murphy); *id.* at 105–06 (Byrnes); *id.* at 106–07 (Jackson).

15 WDP No. 782, Box 76 ("cert.: grant-full court" and listing all members, attached to the clerk's cert. memo on *Skinner*). The classic studies of the Supreme Court of this period are William Wiecek's Holmes Devise history, Wiecek, *supra* note 14, and Melvin I. Urofsky, Division and Discord (1997). One of the best studies is David M. Bixby, *The Roosevelt Court, Democratic Ideology, and Minority Rights*, 90 Yale L. J. 741 (1981). None of these studies has any sustained treatment of *Skinner.*

16 The petitioner's principal brief included other arguments such as bill of attainder and double jeopardy, but these were included in a short section at the back of the principal brief. Brief of Petitioner, *Skinner v. Oklahoma*, LSCT No. 782, at 27–31 (Mar. 16, 1942) [USBP]. The principal argument, listed first, was based on the "Fourteenth Amendment" due process and equal protection; included was an argument that the statute made an arbitrary presumption of unfitness which violated due process. See *id.* at 11–26. Rights were mentioned at the end of the brief but in the context of the day, which required a showing that the "liberty interfered with" would only fall outside the police power if it was arbitrary. *See id.* at 25–26 (citing and quoting *Meyer v. Nebraska* for this principle).

17 *Id.* at 9–11, 19 ("unreasonable standard").

18 *Skinner v. Oklahoma*, Petition for Writ of Certiorari, LSCT No. 782, at 23 (Dec. 4, 1941).

19 USBP, *supra* note 16, at 9, 10–11 ("aristocracy of crime").

20 Rex Fletcher, *The Absurdity of Sterilization*, McAlester Prison Newspaper, DOLA (undated) ("pro-sterilization gentry"); Guy Andrews to Charles Cropley, clerk, LSCT No. 782 (Apr. 1, 1942) (both parties agree to waive argument); Mac Williamson to Charles Cropley, clerk (Apr. 27, 1942), LSCT No. 782 (case had been submitted on the briefs on April 9).

21 This account is based on the original notes of Justice Douglas and Justice Murphy. WDP, Box 76, No. 782 ("presumption of consti-

tutionality"); FMP, Reel 125 [FM Notes] ("There is a Harvard law review article"). Justice Murphy's notes are not dated but have a close content correspondence to Douglas's notes from the April 11 conference. There are two sets of Douglas notes, one dated April 11, 1942 [WD Apr. notes] and one dated May 7, 1942 [WD May notes]. The Thayer article is *The Origin and Scope of the American Doctrine of Constitutional Law*, 7 Harv. L. Rev. 129 (1893). A version of the Murphy and Douglas notes appears in The Supreme Court in Conference 794 (1940–1985) (Del Dickson ed., 2001) [Discussions].

22 *Carolene Products v. U.S.*, 304 U.S. 144, 152 n.4 (1938); Alpheus T. Mason, Harlan Fiske Stone: Pillar of the Law 515 (1956) (Stone to Judge Irving Lehman, the day after *Carolene Products* was decided, "I have been deeply concerned"); Louis Lusky, *Footnote Redux: A Carolene Products Reminiscence*, 82 Colum. L. Rev. 1093 (1982).

23 Footnote four inspired the single most influential book on constitutional law in the twentieth century. John Hart Ely, Democracy and Distrust (1980). *See Pierce v. Society of Sisters*, 268 U.S. 510, 535–36 (1925); *Meyer v. Nebraska*, 262 U.S. 390 (1923).

24 Derrick A. Bell, Jr., *Brown v. Board of Education and the Interest-Convergence Dilemma*, 93 Harv. L. Rev. 518 (1980); NYT at 5 (Oct. 26, 1940); NYT at 3 (Jan. 17, 1941); NYT at C20 (June 10, 1942) ("small . . . obnoxious sect"); *see* NYT at 17 (June 17, 1940); *id.* at 13 (May 24, 1940); *id.* at 26 (Sept. 17, 1939); *Lovell v. City of Griffin*, 303 U.S. 444 (1938); *Schneider v. State*, 308 U.S. 147 (1939); *Cantwell v. Connecticut*, 310 U.S. 296 (1940); *Minersville School Dist. v. Gobitis*, 310 U.S. 586 (1940); *Jones v. Opelika*, 316 U.S. 584 (1942); *Murdock v. Pennsylvania*, 319 U.S. 105 (1943) (overruling *Opelika*) and *West Virginia State Bd. of Educ. v. Barnette*, 319 U.S. 624 (1943) (overruling *Gobitis*); *Chaplinsky v. New Hampshire*, 315 U.S. 568 (1942). Today, these cases tend to be characterized by lawyers as ones of free exercise of religion or speech; at the time, they were linked to minority protection, *see, e.g., Jones v. Opelika*, 316 U.S. 584, 612, 621 (Murphy, J., dissenting) (characterizing Witnesses as "unpopular" and a "dissident minority"); *id.* at 623 (separate opinion of Black, Douglas, Murphy, JJ.) (suppression of religion "by a minority group"); Louis Lusky, *Minority Rights and the Public Interest*, 52 Yale L. J. 1, 30 n. 83 (1942) ("*Skinner* . . . is another reflection of the Court's interest in the minorities problem"); Bixby, *supra* note 15, at 741.

25 *See, e.g., Hill v. Texas*, 316 U.S. 400 (1942); *Smith v. Texas*, 311 U.S. 128 (1940); *Pierre v. Louisiana*, 306 U.S. 354 (1939); *Hale v. Kentucky*, 303 U.S. 613 (1938); *Ward v. Texas*, 316 U.S. 547 (1942); *United States*

v. *Classic*, 313 U.S. 299 (1941); *Lane v. Wilson*, 307 U.S. 268 (1939); *Chambers v. Florida*, 309 U.S. 227 (1940); *New Negro Alliance v. Sanitary Grocery*, 303 U.S. 552 (1938); *Mitchell v. United States*, 313 U.S. 80 (1941); *Missouri ex rel. Gaines v. Canada*, 305 U.S. 337 (1938).

26 MNC at 4 (Jan. 15, 1942) ("breed mistrust and suspicion"); MNC at 4 (Jan. 16, 1942) (Ford); LAT at 22 ("hate-mongering," "any racial group"). War cases: *Ex Parte Quirin*, 317 U.S. 1 (argued and decided per curiam, July 31, 1942); *Hirabayashi v. United States*, 320 U.S. 81 (1943).

27 FM Notes, *supra* note 21 ("[t]he technical difficulty with this case"); WD Apr. Notes, *supra* note 21 ("presumption of constitutionality—if we indulge in that we have nothing to upset this—").

28 William O. Douglas, The Court Years 1939–1975 44 (1980) (Frankfurter "was our hero"); FM Notes, *supra* note 21; Discussions, *supra* note 21, at 794. Frankfurter referred to §24, whereas in the final opinion, the same section is referred to as §195, 316 U.S. at 537, as this was the section number when the bill was codified. Frankfurter, the only justice to add anything to the draft, added the words "clearly condemns" to a line referring to "equal protection." WDP, Box 76, No. 782.

29 FM Notes, *supra* note 21; Discussions, *supra* note 21, at 794 (Roberts and Stone, April 11, 1941); *see* Mac Williamson to Charles Cropley, clerk, LSCT No. 782 (stating that the Court ordered the case restored to the docket on April 13, and informed Williamson of this by letter of April 14, 1942); *see also* Western Union Telegram, Charles Cropley, clerk, to Mac Williamson (Apr. 28, 1942), LSCT No. 782.

30 There is no official record of the oral argument, as the Supreme Court did not begin recording arguments until later. This account is based on the report of the argument in DO at 15 (May 7, 1942) ("eugenic measure"); TDW at 5 (May 7, 1942) ("maintain the purity"), and a communication from Mac Williamson in 1942 to the Yale Law Journal, Note, 51 Yale L. J. 1380, 1385 n.34 (1942); Life at 50 (Feb. 12, 1940) ("marble palace").

31 DO at 15 (May 7, 1942) (all quotes).

32 TDW at 5 (May 7, 1942) (quoting Justice Byrnes); DO at 15 (May 7, 1942) ("Several justices" asked "why stealing chickens was included"); TDW at 5 (May 7, 1942) ("elements of violence") (quoting Williamson); DO at 15 (May 7, 1942) ("Not if done surreptitiously") (quoting Stone, C.J.); *id.* ("very difficult to reconcile") (quoting Williamson); see Note, 51 Yale L. J. 1385 n. 34 (Williamson argued that the law distinguished between claims of artfulness and violence); TDW at 5 (May 7, 1942) (AG "conceded . . . serious doubts").

33 Discussions at 794 ("moronic minds"); WD Apr. Notes, *supra* note 21 (same); WD May Notes, *supra* note 21 ("CJ . . . does not like equal protection point tho he will go along with it"); O. W. Holmes to H. Stone (Aug. 11, 1925), HSP, Box 75, Holmes Corr. (no "stock in a priori human rights or in the passion for equality"); *Buck v. Bell*, 274 U.S. 200 (1927).

34 As the zoologist S. J. Holmes explained the racial stereotypes of the day: "As a rule . . . the Jews are hostile to any kind of racial discrimination, and they are often antagonistic to eugenics for the same reason. Doubtless one cause of this attitude is the fact that the Jews have long been victims of oppression and ostracism on account of their race." S. J. Holmes, The Eugenic Predicament 122 (1933); Franz Boas to Felix Frankfurter (Feb. 14, 1934), Glueck files, HLL, Reel 52, No. 334–36; *id.* at 333, 336; on Frankfurter's approach to anti-Semitism, *see* Liva Baker, Felix Frankfurter 198–200 (1969). On Frankfurter's idolization of Holmes, see Frankfurter, *Justice Holmes Defines the Constitution*, *supra* Epigraphs note 1; on Frankfurter's background, see Matthew Josephson, *Profiles: Jurist–II*, New Yorker 34 (Dec. 7, 1940); Editorial, *Democracy and Eugenics*, NYT at 66 (May 16, 1937) ("cloak for class snobbery"); Felix Frankfurter: A Tribute 170 (Wallace Mendelson ed., 1964) (Alexander Bickel quoting Frankfurter on "gather[ing] meaning" from "reading life"); Felix Frankfurter to E. M. Morgan (Feb. 11, 1941), HSP Box 74 ("live but groping attempts").

35 *Minersville School Dist. v. Gobitis*, 310 U.S. 586 (decided June 3, 1940, Frankfurter, J.); NYT at 6 (June 9, 1940) (Witnesses and violence); NYT at 27 (June 11, 1940) (same); NYT at 8 (July 26, 1940).

36 *Jones v. Opelika*, 316 U.S. 584 (June 8, 1942); *id.* at 623–24 (dissenting opinion of Douglas, Murphy, and Black, JJ.); *id.* at 624 (*Gobitis* was "wrongly decided"); WD May Notes, *supra* note 21. The Discussions (*supra* note 21) version of the May 7 conference implies that Justice Roberts was a strong supporter of equal protection. It reads for Roberts: "I would go on the equal protection clause," but Douglas's notes actually are far more equivocal, saying merely "Roberts—equal protection clause—." Justice Roberts seems most likely to have simply gone along, like the Chief: see his comment on the Douglas draft, suggesting doubts about equal protection ("I guess I agree. I shall probably not burst forth in print if the rest keep quiet.") WDP Box 76, No. 782.

37 Washington & Jefferson College Address, May 23, 1942, WDP, Box 690. WDP, Box 76, Draft Opinion, *Skinner v. Oklahoma*, No. 782; 316 U.S. 535, 537 (1942); *id.* at 539 ("enters a chicken coop"); *id.* at 538 ("appropriates over $20"); *id.* at 539.

38 Today's experts in equal protection law may find this odd for two rea-
    sons: one, the assumption that Holmes was right that equal protection law
    had died by 1927, *see Buck v. Bell*, 274 U.S. at 208; and two, the assump-
    tion that class legislation was only a doctrine of substantive due process,
    rather than equal protection. Both claims are wrong as a historical matter.
    Even if the equal protection clause did not protect those we would protect
    today, it did not die but appeared in different guise, known as "class leg-
    islation." For a review of equality cases prior to *Buck, see* Siegel, *supra* ch.
    1, note 36. For a history of class legislation in substantive due process, see
    Howard Gillman, The Constitution Besieged (1995); for its earlier his-
    tory, William E. Nelson, The Fourteenth Amendment (1988); Melissa L.
    Saunders, *Equal Protection, Class Legislation, and Color Blindness*, 96 Mich.
    L. Rev. 245 (1997); Mark G. Yudof, *Equal Protection Class Legislation, and
    Sex Discrimination: One Small Cheer for Mr. Herbert Spencer's Social Statics*,
    88 Mich. L. Rev. 1366 (1989) (reviewing Nelson). Class legislation was as
    much a popular political term as a legal concept. *See, e.g.*, NYT at 18 (Dec.
    1, 1939) (law denying employment to aliens was "class legislation"); NYT
    at 12 (Jan. 7, 1936) (business charges AAA as being "class legislation").
    For the classic post-1900 cases striking down laws under this theory, *see
    Cotting v. Kansas City*, 183 U.S. 79 (1901); *Connolly v. Union Sewer Pipe Co.*,
    184 U.S. 540 (1902); *Truax v. Raich*, 239 U.S. 33 (1915); *Truax v. Corrigan*,
    257 U.S. 312 (1921); *Yu Cong Eng v. Trinidad*, 271 U.S. 500 (1926). *See* Oral
    Interview of Justice Douglas, Princeton Univ. Mudd Lib. Cassette 7B
    (Jan. 18, 1962) (confirming *Skinner* as equal protection case).
39 USBP, *supra* note 16, at 10 ("aristocracy of crime"); Thomas M. Cooley,
    A Treatise on the Constitutional Limitations 483 (1890) ("governed
    by general rules," "one rule for rich and poor").
40 *Skinner*, 316 U.S. at 541 ("inheritable traits"); *id.* at 542 ("neat legal
    distinctions"); Walter Wheeler Cook, *Eugenics or Euthenics*, 37 Ill. L.
    Rev. 287, 324 (1943) ("Fascist Italy").
41 *Skinner*, 316 U.S. at 542 ("a rule of human genetics"); *id.* at 541 ("selected a
    particular race"); for usage, *Hill v. Texas*, 316 U.S. 400, 402 (1942) ("white
    race," "colored race"); *Mitchell v. United States*, 313 U.S. 80, 95 n. 2 (1941)
    ("white race"); *Morrison v. California*, 291 U.S. 82, 85 (1934) ("Japanese
    race"); *Near v. Minnesota*, 283 U.S. 697, 703, 724, 729 (1931) ("Jewish
    race"); *Nagle v. Loi Hoa*, 275 U.S. 475, 477–78 (1928) ("Chinese race");
    Gong Lum v. Rice, 275 U.S. 78, 80–82, 84 (1927) ("Caucasian race"); *Ohio
    ex rel. Clarke v. Deckebach*, 274 U.S. 392, 396 (1927) ("alien race"). *See, e.g.*,
    Audrey Smedley, Race in North America 28 (1999) (race was inherited,
    "fixed and unalterable . . . never bridged or transcended"); Patterson,
    supra ch. 3, note 19, at 9 ("the relation was perpetual and inheritable").

42 Douglas's reference to the "Nordic race" appears in his original draft. WDP, Box 76, No. 782, yellow-lined draft at page 15. It is later changed to refer to a "rule of human genetics," before the draft is circulated to the other justices. *Id.* (Rider 6 to p. 6 draft of May 18, 1942).

43 316 U.S. at 541 ("When the law lays an unequal hand on those who have committed intrinsically the same quality of offense and sterilizes one and not the other, it has made as invidious a discrimination as if it had selected a particular race or nationality for oppressive treatment," citing two prominent race cases: *Yick Wo v. Hopkins*, 118 U.S. 356 [1886], and *Missouri ex rel. Gaines v. Canada*, 305 U.S. 337 [1938]); Thomas Reed Powell, *supra* ch. 5, note 30, at 261 (emphasis added); *id.* at 262 (habitual criminals).

44 *Skinner*, 316 U.S. at 536; WDP, Draft Opinion, Box 76, No. 782.

45 Only by focusing on the now-questioned anti-labor cases of the period does one come to the selective (and false) conclusion that rights triggered something akin to strict scrutiny in the period 1880–1930. The vast majority of cases, even cases regulating what we would today call rights, proceeded along the line that a right could be defeated by claims of the common welfare. *See, e.g., Williams v. Arkansas*, 217 U.S. 79 (1910) ("It is a principle which underlies every reasonable exercise of the police power that private rights must yield to the common welfare) (opinion by Fuller, C.J.). *Lochner, Adair,* and *Coppage* were controversial for this reason. *Coppage v. Kansas*, 236 U.S. 1, 28 (1915) (Day, J., dissenting) ("nothing is better settled by the repeated decisions of this court than that the right of contract is not absolute and unyielding, but is subject to limitation and restraint in the interest of the public health, safety and welfare"). Even cases that rejected state laws as inconsistent with due process did not disavow the principle, they simply found the law arbitrary, *see Adair v. U.S.*, 208 U.S. 161, 174 (1908) ("the rights of liberty and property guaranteed by the Constitution against deprivation without due process of law, is subject to such reasonable restraints as the common good or the general welfare may require"). For a lengthier defense of this position, *see* Victoria F. Nourse, *A Tale of Two Lochners* (forthcoming).

46 Prior to 1937, "in simple quantitative terms, the Supreme Court upheld most federal and state regulatory legislation coming before it." William Wiecek, The Lost World of Classical Legal Thought 158 (1998) (citing Charles Warren's study, 13 Colum. L. Rev. 294 [1913]); David E. Bernstein, *Lochner's Legacy's Legacy*, 82 Tex. L. Rev. 1 (2003) *but see* Barry Friedman, *The History of the Countermajoritarian Diffi-*

culty, Part Three: The Lesson of Lochner, 76 N.Y.U. L. Rev. 1383 (2001). The most balanced view of this period appears in Friedman, *supra* ch. 1, note 42, ch. 1 (2002). On *Skinner* and rights today, *see Washington v. Glucksberg,* 521 U.S. 702, 727 n. 19 (1997); *City of Cleburne v. Cleburne Living Center,* 473 U.S. 432, 463 (1985); *Roe v. Wade,* 410 U.S. 113, 152 (1973); *Griswold v. Connecticut,* 381 U.S. 479, 484–85 (1965).

47   WDP, Box 76, No. 782 (notes of other Justices on galley copies of draft opinion).

48   WD May Notes ("leg. knows nothing"); Discussions, *supra* note 21, at 794.

49   316 U.S. at 543 ("If Oklahoma may resort") (Stone, C.J., concurring). Holmes was right to question the logic of the argument if equal protection is a matter of textual classification; if equal protection means something else, such as a means to discipline legislative self-dealing or combat certain forms of social aristocracy, then the classification argument is nonresponsive. If the idea that legislatures must classify is enough to eliminate all arguments of equality, there is nothing left of equality arguments.

50   316 U.S. at 546 (Jackson, J., concurring) ("There are limits").

51   316 U.S. at 541 ("reckless hands"). Today, the reference here appears to be Hitler; at the time, it was interpreted as giving the potential to the government to sterilize "subversives," referring either to Communists or—more likely at the time—to alien enemies (the fifth column fear of those within the United States seeking to plot with her enemies, which had happened in Norway). 51 Yale L. J. 1380, 1387 (1942).

52   NYT at 1 (June 2, 1942) (Cologne); NYT at 15 (June 2, 1942); *Hill v. Texas,* 316 U.S. 400 (1942); *Ward v. Texas,* 316 U.S. 547 (1942); William R. Spear, WP at 8 (June 2, 1942) ("singled out," "discrimination"); Chr. Sci. Monitor at 8 (June 1, 1942) ("equal protection"); CDT at 15 (June 2, 1942) ("Upset Because of Clause Exempting Embezzlers"); DO at 1 (June 2, 1942) ("Holds Law Is Discriminatory"); DO at 10 (June 3, 1942) ("good politics," "open violence"); TDW at 1 (June 2, 1942) ("declaring it discriminatory because it applies to chicken thieves but not embezzlers"); TDW at 6 (June 3, 1942) ("discrimination of the act").

53   John Elliott, NYHT at 13 (June 2, 1942) ("most important sociological decisions," departure from *Buck* "human rights"); NYDN at 3 (June 2, 1942) (law was discriminatory and violated a fundamental right); NYT at 15 (June 2, 1942) (liberty); LAT at 9 (June 2, 1942) ("human rights").

54 (1) Cook, *supra* note 41, at 288; (2) Osmond K. Fraenkel, *Civil Liberties Decisions of the Supreme Court, 1941 Term*, 91 U. Pa. L. Rev. 1, 16–17 (1942); (3) Robert L. Howard, *Constitutional Law Cases in the United States Supreme Court: 1941–1946*, 11 Mo. L. Rev. 197, 264–65 (June 1946); (4) Powell, *supra* ch. 5, note 30, at 260; (5) Augustin Derby, *Criminal Law and Procedure*, 1942 Ann. Surv. Am. L. 757, 768 (1942); (6) Noel T. Dowling, *Constitutional Developments in Five War Years*, 32 Va. L. Rev. 461, 487 (1946); (7) John Edmond Hewitt, *Constitutional Law*, 1942 Ann. Surv. Am. L. 63, 75–76 (1942); (8) Sylvan B. Cohen, *Habitual Criminal Law Providing for Sterilization Held Invalid*, 2 Bill Rts. Rev. 296, 296 (1942). Student notes: (9) 22 B.U. L. Rev. 590, 590–91 (1942); (10) 5 La. L. Rev. 124, 127 (1942–44); (11) 27 Marq. L. Rev. 99, 99 (1943); (12) 17 St. John's L. Rev. 36, 37 (1942); (13) 6 U. Det. L. J. 41, 41 (1942); (14) 41 Mich. L. Rev. 318, 318 (1942); (15) 91 U. Pa. L. Rev. 155, 156 (1942–43); (16) 29 Va. L. Rev. 93, 97 (1942); (17) 51 Yale L. J. 1380, 1384 (1942). Mention of a fundamental right or human rights, but in passing, and not as the holding of the opinion: Note, 22 B.U. L. Rev. 590, 594 (1942); Note, 29 Va. L. Rev. 93, 101 (1942). The Yale note was the one most enthusiastic about the notion of rights. See Note, 51 Yale L. J. 1380, 1387 (1942). See note, 27 Marq. L. Rev. 99, 99 (1943) (avoided the substantive question); Note, 41 U. Mich. L. Rev. 318, 319 (1942) ("The substantive aspects of due process go unmentioned"). On the religious characterization, *see* Note, 5 La. L. Rev. 124, 130 (1942) ("much of the opposition to sterilization" is prompted by the idea that procreation is a "God-given" privilege, and suggesting this was not a proper legal argument); Note, 27 Marq. L. Rev. 99, 101 (1942) (arguing that sterilization violates bodily right to integrity, and there is no right to procreate).

55 Powell, *supra* note 43, at 260 (the court "refrained from passing any judgment"); *id.* at 261 (race).

56 AUSA Robert M. Hitchcock to Justice Robert H. Jackson (June 8, 1942), RJP, Box 124. Hitchcock mistakenly referred to the "lawyers" statement as that of Shakespeare's Richard II; it comes in *Henry VI, Part 2*, IV. ii.

57 Larson at 135 (Georgia's Governor Talmadge vetoed a sterilization bill with a "light-hearted remark" that the bill "made no provision . . . to except the governor and the adjutant general: 'Lindley, you and I might go crazy some day and we don't want them working on us.' "). Lombardo, *supra* ch. 1, note 16, at 132.

58 *Railway Express Agency, Inc. v. New York*, 336 U.S. 106, 112 (1949) (Jackson, J., concurring).

59 Exec. Parole: Ralph Bainum, DOLA, Records of the Sect'y of State
    1–3 (Apr. 3, 1937); DOC No. 18051 (parole revoked Apr. 29, 1941);
    Letter, Parole Board to Governor Turner re: Ralph Bainum (June 24,
    1947) ("another man was guilty"); DO at 1 (June 2, 1942) (jubilation);
    DOC No. 30504 (Skinner); DOC No. 10072 (Kelly); MNC at 7 (May
    1, 1940) (Hyde); Exec. Pardon: F. C. Hyde, DOLA, Records of Sect'y
    of State, (Oct. 26, 1944).

60 DO at 1 (June 2, 1942) ("eugenics standpoint," "psychiatrically unfit,"
    "experiment").

61 NT at 1 (June 1, 1942) (Jews); NYT at 7 (June 7, 1942) (gypsies);
    NYT at 7 (Aug. 6, 1942) (Jews in Paris); NYT at 3 (Aug. 17, 1942)
    (Norway and mercy killing). Only later, after the Nuremberg trials,
    was the full extent of the Nazi sterilization program publicly revealed.
    Kevles at 169 (Nuremberg revelations).

62 *Skinner*, 316 U.S. at 541 (1942); *Zablocki v. Redhail*, 434 U.S. 374, 395
    (1978) (Burger, C.J., concurring) (citing *Buck*: equality was once the
    "last resort" of lawyers); *Regents v. Bakke*, 438 U.S. 265, 326 (1978)
    (Brennan, J., concurring and dissenting) (approving *Buck's* statement
    that equal protection was moribund); *Roe v. Wade*, 410 U.S. 113, 153
    (1973) (citing *Buck* for the proposition that the court had not embraced
    an unlimited right to privacy); *Fieger v. Thomas*, 74 F.3d 740, 750 (6th
    Cir. 1996) (citing *Buck* for the proposition that equality is an argu-
    ment of last resort and that this part of *Buck* had not been repudiated).
    More recently, the Supreme Court has expressed disapproval with the
    "extreme measures" of sterilization affirmed in *Buck*, *Alabama v. Gar-
    rett*, 531 U.S. 356, 369 (2001).

63 *Relf v. Weinberger*, 372 F. Supp. 1196, 1199 (D.D.C. 1974), (100–150,000
    sterilized under federal programs), *on remand*, *Relf v. Mathews*, 403 F.
    Supp. 1235 (D.D.C. 1975), *vacated*, *Relf v. Weinberger*, 565 F.2d 722
    (D.C. Cir. 1977); see Dorothy Roberts, Killing the Black Body 93
    (1997) (half black).

64 Jim Crow's inadvertent effects, *see* Larson; contrary practice in North
    Carolina, *see* Roberts, *supra* note 63, at 90 (North Carolina sterilized
    8,000 defectives in the 1930s and 1940s, 5,000 of whom were black);
    Nancy Ordover, American Eugenics: Race, Queer Anatomy, and the
    Science of Nationalism 161–63 (2003).

65 In fact, the racism reflected the racial issues of the day. Immediately
    prior to the war, one author scandalized the country by claiming
    that America should sterilize all Germans (a claim the Nazis used to
    frighten their own citizens into continued battle). Theodore H. Kauf-
    man, Germany Must Perish! (1941); Time at 95 (Mar. 24, 1941); NYT

at 8 (Hitler: if the Allies win they will sterilize male youth). After America's entry into war, an Oklahoma congressman proposed that the Japanese should be sterilized. Decades later, it would be revealed that other racial minorities including Native Americans and Hispanics were subject to sterilization abuse in the following decades. *See* Ordover, *supra* note 64, at 160 (Japanese); *id.* at 171–72 (Native Americans); *id.* at 173–75 (Mexican-Americans).

66 Leuchtenburg, *supra* ch. 7, note 7, at 24–25 ("North Carolina jury").
67 *Korematsu v. United States*, 323 U.S. 214, 216 (1944); *Perez v. Sharp*, 198 P.2d 17, 19 (Cal. 1948) (quoting opening lines of *Skinner*); *Loving v. Virginia*, 388 U.S. 1 (1967) (federal anti-miscegenation case).
68 Jack Skinner, Soc. Security Appl'n (marriage); *Deaths*, Visalia Times–Delta (Oct. 19, 1977) (Skinner obituary: six grandchildren, ten great-grandchildren, one stepdaughter); Cal. Death Records (Skinner died Oct. 18, 1977, Tulare County); *Deaths*, Visalia Times–Delta (Apr. 2, 1991) (obituary for Laura "Jane" Skinner) (married Skinner in 1940 and moved to California that year); Report of Marquardt & Assoc. (Skinner investigation on file with author including news reports); Francis Hyde, DOC No. 28404 (paroled 1940, pardoned 1944); Soc. Security Death Index (died Apr. 1981, Juneau, Alaska); Francis Hyde, Exec. Pardon, DOLA Records of Sect'y of State (traveled to Ketchikan, Alaska, and became a commercial fisherman); Francis Hyde, Soc. Security Appl'n (Hyde remarried); Ralph Bainum DOC No. 18051 (reparoled July 1947, parole revoked March 1949, died in prison hospital 1958); Ralph Bainum, Exec. Revocation of Parole, DOLA, Records of Sect'y of State (Mar. 29, 1949).
69 DO at 18 (Feb. 9, 1965) (Briggs); DO at 5 (Sept. 19, 1964) (Ritzhaupt); DO at 35 (July 18, 1955) (Andrews).

Epilogue: Failures of Modern Memory

1 Wiggam, *supra* ch. 9, note 1, at 22.
2 Gould, *supra* ch. 1, note 28, at 60–61 ("falsely identified as lying within"); Wrestling with Behavioral Genetics: Science, Ethics, and Public Conversation 90 (Erik Parens, Audrey R. Chapman, and Nancy Press eds., 2006) ("there is no such thing as an 'aggression' or 'criminal' gene"); *see id.* at 89–93 (the MAOA gene mutation controversy); Genetics and Criminal Behavior 9–12 (David Wasserman and Robert Wachbroit eds., 2001) (MAOA and XYY studies); Randy Thornhill & Craig T. Palmer, A Natural History of Rape (2000) (arguing for evolutionary origins of rape); *see* critiques by Frans B. M. de Waal, *Survival of the Rapist*, NYT Book Rev. at 24 (Apr. 2, 2000);

Jerry A. Coyne & Andrew Berry, *Rape as an Adaptation*, 404 Nature 121 (2000) (book is advocacy, not science); Elisabeth A. Lloyd, *Science Gone Astray: Evolution and Rape*, 99 Mich. L. Rev. 1536 (2001) (same); see Arthur E. Fink, Causes of Crime: Biological Theories in the United States 1800–1945 (1962).

3 *Skinner v. Oklahoma*, 316 U.S. 540, 542 (1942) ("rule of human genetics"); Mary Douglas, Purity and Danger (1966).

4 NYT at 8 (Jan. 26, 1936) (statistical gossip). Emphasis should be placed here on the fact that these are behavioral or psychological, not physical, claims. On the failure of many behavioral genetics studies to be retracted or replicated, *see* Virginia J. Vitzthum, *A Number No Greater than the Sum of its Parts: The Use and Abuse of Heritability*, 75 Hum. Biol. 539, 550 (Aug. 1, 2003) ("of 600 reported associations between gene variants and disease, only 166 have been studied three or more times, of which just six have been consistently replicated"). On heritability statistics *see id.*; David Moore, The Dependent Gene 40–48 (2001); Richard Lewontin, It Ain't Necessarily So 37 (2000) ("Were God to appear to me in a dream telling me the heritability of, say, coronary artery disease, to the fourth decimal place, I could not use that information for any program of amelioration, prevention, or cure, because it would tell me nothing useful about the pathways of mediation"); Elliott Sober, *The Meaning of Genetic Causation* in From Chance to Choice: Genetics and Justice (Allen Buchanan et al. eds., 2000); Evelyn Fox Keller, The Century of the Gene (2000) (gene-as-determiner is the eugenic idea and is false). For example, clones are not photocopies; they are genetically less alike than identical twins because of mitochondrial DNA (cloned sheep, for example, may have very different appearances). Stephen Jay Gould in Clones and Clones: Facts and Fantasies about Human Cloning 47 (Martha Nussbaum & Cass R. Sunstein eds., 1998). The very idea of "design" for complex traits requires the kind of strong causal connection that new evidence suggests may never exist because genes can in fact be "turned on" by the environment. If, as recent studies show, claimed genetic correlations, as for shyness, can as easily be remediated by environmental means (caregiving), why endure the pain and the extraordinary expense of "redesigning" this feature in a child? This does not mean that there are not other, less impressively technological problems that accompany reproductive technologies. For example, sex selection is currently accomplished without genetic testing and this kind of individualized eugenics can pose very serious population problems, as we know from the experience of China, where there is now a surfeit of

men precisely because of cultural preference for male children. Nor does it mean that there are not likely to be other problems (mainly genetic fraud, as people end up purchasing tests that in fact do not accomplish what they are alleged to accomplish).

5 Francis Collins et al., *Heredity and Humanity; Have no fear. Genes Aren't Everything*, TNR at 27 (June 25, 2001) ("soft" eugenics); *see* Dean H. Hamer, The God Gene: How Faith Is Hardwired into our Genes (2004); Dean H. Hamer & Peter Copeland, The Science of Desire: The Search for the Gay Gene and the Biology of Behavior (1994).

6 Robert H. Bork, The Tempting of America 63–64 (1990) (criticizing *Skinner* for its fundamental rights rhetoric); *but see* Cynthia Bowman et al., Feminist Jurisprudence 470 (3d edition 2007) (brief of Prof. Kathleen Sullivan arguing that *Skinner* supports right to abortion based on right and equality).

7 One wonders whether the analogy is apt. After all, criminal laws raise serious questions of liberty not raised by tax and welfare laws. Indeed, if one reads Skinner as it should be read, as a case both of liberty and equality, then one can make the case that criminal law should have a more exacting scrutiny in cases of economic distinctions.

8 Ruth Bader Ginsburg, *Some Thoughts on Autonomy and Equality in Relation to Roe v. Wade*, 63 N.C. L. Rev. 375 (1985); *Lawrence v. Texas*, 539 U.S. 558, 584–85 (2003) (O'Connor, J., concurring). The moderation comes, in my view, not in an exclusive reliance on equality but a recognition that the more serious the liberty interest the legislature invades, the more likely it is that legislatures have an incentive to foist such burdens onto others.

9 Justice Douglas used language of "human rights" and "civil rights" that, at the time, was considered the opposite of existing "substantive due process" law, which was associated with "property and contract rights." The term "civil rights," at the time, referred to everything from free speech to mob trial; it was not a term of constitutional art but, instead, a term connoting what it was *not*: a case that was *not* about the right to property or contract—the old "due process." *See, e.g.*, Louis B. Boudin, *The Supreme Court and Civil Rights*, Science and Society 273, 276 (1937) ("when we speak of civil rights or civil liberties we have in mind minority groups and possible discrimination against them," discrimination "because of race, or color, or religious, social or political beliefs").

10 *See* ch. 9.

11 For a lengthier defense of this proposition, which appears to defy conventional wisdom among lawyers about the strength of rights dis-

course in the *Lochner* period, *see* Victoria F. Nourse, *A Tale of Two Lochners* (forthcoming). *Lochner* was the exception, not the rule, and itself was controversial precisely because the police power doctrine could so easily have yielded the opposite result. *See, e.g, Smith v. Command*, 204 N.W. 140, 142 (Mich. 1925) ("no citizen has any rights superior to the common welfare. Acting for the public good, the state, in the exercise of its police powers, may always impose reasonable restrictions upon the natural and constitutional rights of its citizens."); *Manigault v. Springs*, 199 U.S. 473, 480 (1905) ("the police power, is an exercise of the sovereign right of the Government to protect the lives, health, morals, comfort and general welfare of the people, and is *paramount* to any rights under contracts between individuals") (emphasis added); *Williams v. Arkansas*, 217 U.S. 79, 90 (1910) ("It is a principle which underlies every reasonable exercise of the police power that private rights must yield to the common welfare.") (quoting lower court); *Chicago, Burlington & Quincy R.R. Co. v. McGuire*, 219 U.S. 549, 567 (1911) ("There is no absolute freedom to do as one wills or to contract as one chooses. The guaranty of liberty does not withdraw from legislative supervision . . . the making of contracts. Liberty implies the absence of arbitrary restraint, not immunity from reasonable regulations and prohibitions imposed in the interests of the Community."); *Schmidinger v. City of Chicago*, 226 U.S. 578, 587 (1913) (The "right of state legislatures or municipalities acting under state authority to regulate trades and callings in the exercise of the police power is too well settled to require any extended discussion.").

12 *See, e.g.*, Cass R. Sunstein, *The Right to Die*, 106 Yale L. J. 1123, 1155 (1997) (it "remains to be explained why Skinner . . . [is] treated as [an] equal protection" case); *but see* Roberts, *supra* ch. 9, note 63, at 307–08.

13 Cass R. Sunstein, *The Anticaste Principle*, 92 Mich. L. Rev. 2410 (1994). Blood laws should prompt strict scrutiny whether applied in asylums or elsewhere. That no one made this challenge at the time is likely a function of the fact that the only people who had standing to make the challenge were in asylums.

14 *Railway Express Agency, Inc. v. New York*, 336 U.S. 106 (1949) (Jackson, J., concurring). Of course, as *Skinner* demonstrates, and I argue, the "avoidance" problem only avoids successfully if it is applied consistently. In the case of sterilization, for example, it would have only avoided the problem if all sterilization laws were struck down on the same theory, but, as we know, they were not.

15 For standard run-of-the-mill cases involving equal protection claims

attached to due process ones in the business context, see cases cited ch. 4, note 7; *see, e.g., Truax v. Corrigan*, 257 U.S. 312, 331–32 (1921); Ernst Freund, The Police Power 632 (1904). For the post-1900 cases, see ch. 9, note 38.

16 *See* Jeffrey Rosen, *Class Legislation, Public Choice, and the Structural Constitution*, 1 Harv. J. L. & Publ. Pol'y 181, 182 (1997).

17 U.S. Const. Art. I, § 9.

18 Cooley, *supra* ch. 9, note 39, at 483.

19 Richard A. Epstein, *Liberty, Equality and Privacy: Choosing a Legal Foundation for Gay Rights*, 2002 U. Chi. Legal F. 73, 78; Kenneth W. Simons, *Equality as a Comparative Right*, 65 B.U. L. Rev. 387 (1985); Rebecca L. Brown, *Liberty, the New Equality*, 77 N.Y.U. L. Rev. 1491 (2002); Victoria F. Nourse & Sarah Maguire, *The Lost History of Governance and Equal Protection* (forthcoming 58 Duke L. J. [Oct. 2008]). The standard liberal argument is that equality is the enemy of liberty, a claim that assumes a particular form of equality as a fixed end-state-of-affairs (the implicit fear is the kind of coerced equality of state socialism). The argument here rests on the incentives, rather than the ends, of legislatures.

20 Economic distinctions may be benign in one context (such as a tax law) but damaging in another, as, for example, where the poor are deprived of the right to work or to vote.

21 I say "little" for a reason— there is one reference to African-American participation in Skinner's case: Elaine Ellis, *Sterilization: A Menace to the Negro*, 44 The Crisis 137, 155 (May 1937) ("Mass protest on the part of Negro and white prisoners in the state penitentiary at McAlester, Oklahoma, kept a law from going into effect two years ago").

22 316 U.S. at 541.

23 See Ellis, *supra* note 21, at 155; *Sterilization*, Pittsburgh Courier at 10 (Mar. 30, 1935); W. E. B. DuBois, *Forum of Fact and Opinion*, Pittsburgh Courier, sec. 2 at 1 (June 27, 1936); Jessie Rodrique, *The Black Community and the Birth-Control Movement* in Unequal Sisters: A Multicultural Reader in U.S. History 333 (Ellen C. Dubois and Vicki Ruiz eds., 1990); Ordover, *supra* ch. 9, note 64, at 161–78.

24 On white races, *see* ch. 1. On ethnicities as races, Gerstle, *supra* ch. 1, note 55, at 161; Jacobson, *supra* ch. 1, note 55, at 65. On sexualization to mark race, *see* ch. 3, note 16 (listing references). On weakness and femininity and dependency as a sign of race, Takaki, *supra* ch. 3, note 16, at 112; Bederman, *supra* ch. 3, note 13, at 28; Gay, *supra* ch. 3, note 13, at 95; Gerstle at 36; Jacobson at 31; *id.* at 21; Thomas F. Gossett, Race: The History of an Idea in America 343, 381, 395 (1997 edition).

On animality and primitivity and race, *see id.* at 15, 286 (African-Americans); Jacobson at 19 (Irish); *id.* at 218 (Native Americans); *id.* at 118 (Filipinos); *id.* at 184 (Russian Jews); Gerstle at 30 (Spanish); Takaki at 205 (Chinese); Linda Gordon, The Great Arizona Orphan Abduction 12 (1999) (Irish). On race and inherent criminality, see E. A. Hooten, Crime and the Man (1939); Harry Laughlin, Immigration and Conquest, Report to the Chamber of Commerce of the State of New York (May 15, 1939).

25   For a historicist notion of rights, see Richard A. Primus, The American Language of Rights (1999).

26   Patterson, *supra* ch. 3, note 19.

27   Michael Walzer, Spheres of Justice: A Defense of Pluralism and Equality (1983).

28   Editorial, NYT at 80 (Feb. 12, 1939) ("minute men of science"); L. Jaroff et al., *The Gene Hunt*, Time at 62–67 (Mar. 20, 1989) (quoting Watson: "We used to think our fate was in our stars. Now we know, in large measure, our fate is in our genes."); Vitzthum, *supra* note 4, at 539.

29   I do not mean any precise analogy to the *law* of church and state. Although science can take on the attributes of religion, as it did in the case of eugenics, there are significant institutional differences.

30   Rescuing Science from Politics (Wendy Wagner & Rena Steinzor eds., 2006).

Index

Page numbers beginning with 179 refer to endnotes.